Charles Seale-Hayne Library
University of Plymouth
(01752) 588 588
LibraryandITenquiries@plymouth.ac.uk

White Collar
and
Professional Stress

WILEY SERIES ON
STUDIES IN OCCUPATIONAL STRESS

Series Editors

Professor Cary L. Cooper
Department of Management Sciences,
University of Manchester Institute
of Science and Technology

Professor S.V. Kasl
Department of Epidemiology,
School of Medicine,
Yale University

Stress at Work
Edited by Cary L. Cooper and Roy Payne

Current Concerns in Occupational Stress
Edited by Cary L. Cooper and Roy Payne

White Collar and Professional Stress
Edited by Cary L. Cooper and Judi Marshall

Stress, Work Design and Productivity
Edited by E.N. Corlett and J. Richardson

Further titles in preparation

White Collar
and
Professional Stress

Edited by

Cary L. Cooper

University of Manchester
Institute of Science & Technology

and

Judi Marshall
University of Bath

JOHN WILEY & SONS

Chichester · New York · Brisbane · Toronto

British Library Cataloguing in Publication Data:

White collar and professional stress. —
  (Wiley series on studies in occupational stress).
  1. Job stress
  2. White collar workers — Psychology
  I. Cooper, Cary Lynn
  II. Marshall, Judi
  158.7   HF5548.85   79-41779

ISBN 0 471 27760 6

Photoset by Photo-Graphics, Stockland, Honiton, Devon.
Printed in the United States of America

Contributors

CARY L. COOPER *Editor*	*Professor of Management Educational Methods, Department of Management Sciences, University of Manchester Institute of Science and Technology, Manchester, UK*
JUDI MARSHALL *Editor*	*Lecturer in Organizational Behaviour, School of Management, University of Bath, Bath, UK*
MARILYN L. DAVIDSON	*Research Fellow in Psychology, Department of Management Sciences, University of Manchester Institute of Science and Technology, Manchester, UK*
JOSEPH W. EATON	*Professor of Social Work, Graduate School of Public and International Affairs, University of Pittsburg, USA*
STEVE FINEMAN	*Lecturer in Organizational Behaviour, University of Bath, Bath, UK*
CLIVE JENKINS	*General Secretary, Association of Scientific, Technical, and Managerial Staff, London, UK*
TONY KEENAN	*Lecturer in Psychology, Heriot-Watt University, Edinburgh, Scotland*
JAMES KOCH	*Professor of Organizational Behavior, College of Business Administration, University of Oregon, USA*

CHRIS KYRIACOU *Lecturer in Education, York University, York, UK*

MATTHEW LEE *Professor of Educational Psychology, University of Texas, Austin, Texas, USA*

MIKE NOBLE *Ex-Member of Parliament and former Parliamentary Private Secretary at the Department of Prices and Consumer Protection.*

BEEMAN N. PHILLIPS *Professor of Educational Psychology, University of Texas, Austin, Texas, USA*

ROSALIE L. TUNG *Professor of Organizational Behavior, University of Oregon, Eugene, Oregon, USA*

ARTHUR VENO *Professor of Psychology, University of Zambia, Lusaka, Zambia.*

Contents

Editorial Foreword to the Series ix

Introduction xi

PART I STRESS AMONG HEALTH CARE PROFESSIONALS

1. **Dentists Under Pressure: A Social Psychological Study** 3
   Cary L. Cooper

2. **Stress Amongst Nurses** 19
   Judi Marshall

PART II STRESS IN EDUCATION

3. **School Administrators: Sources of Stress and Ways of Coping
   With It** 63
   Rosalie L. Tung and James L. Koch

4. **The Changing Role of the American Teacher: Current and Future
   Sources of Stress** 93
   Beeman N. Phillips and Matthew Lee

5. **Sources of Stress Among British Teachers: The Contribution of
   Job and Personality Factors** 113
   Chris Kyriacou

PART III STRESS AMONG COMMUNITY SERVICE WORKERS

6. **Stress and the Policeman** 131
   Marilyn J. Davidson and Arthur Veno

7. **Stress in Social Work Practice** 167
   Joseph W. Eaton

viii

PART IV STRESS EXPERIENCED BY TECHNOLOGISTS

8. Stress and the Professional Engineer 189
Tony Keenan

9. Stress Among Technical Support Staff in Research and Development . 211
Stephen Fineman

PART V STRESS AMONG PUBLIC SERVANTS

10. Occupational Stress Among Members of Parliament 235
Mike Noble

11. Only from the Outside: Stress in Trade Union Leaders 245
Clive Jenkins

Concluding Remarks 251

Index 255

Editorial Foreword to the Series

This book, *White Collar and Professional Stress,* is the third book in the series of *Studies in Occupational Stress.* The main objective of this series of books is to bring together the leading international psychologists and occupational health researchers to report on their work on various aspects of occupational stress and health. The series will include a number of books on original research and theory in each of the areas described in the initial volume, such as Blue Collar Stressors, The Interface Between the Work Environment and the Family, Individual Differences in Stress Reactions, The Person-Environment Fit Model, Behavioural Modification and Stress Reduction, Stress and the Socio-technical Environment, The Stressful Effects of Retirement and Unemployment and many other topics of interest in understanding stress in the workplace.

We hope these books will appeal to a broad spectrum of readers — to academic researchers and postgraduate students in applied and occupational psychology and sociology, occupational medicine, management, personnel, etc. — and to practitioners working in industry, the occupational medical field, mental health specialists, social workers, personnel officers, and others interested in the health of the individual worker.

CARY L. COOPER,
University of Manchester Institute of
  Science and Technology (UK)
STANISLAV V. KASL,
Yale University

Introduction

Stress-related illnesses such as coronary heart disease have been on the steady upward trend in almost all the developed world. In England and Wales, for example, the death rate in men between 35 and 44 nearly doubled between 1950 and 1973, and has increased much more rapidly than that of older age groups (e.g. 45-54). Indeed, by 1973, 41% of all deaths in the age range of 25-44 were due to cardiovascular disease. There has been an increase in other forms of stress manifestations as well, for example, admissions to alcoholism units in UK hospitals increased over 33% from the middle of the '60s to the middle of the '70s (Cooper, 1979).

Although some white collar occupations don't seem to have as high a mortality rate in respect of ischaemic heart disease and other stress-related illnesses as certain shopfloor occupations, they are becoming increasingly vulnerable to them. In addition to this, white collar and other professional workers seem to suffer more from anxiety and emotional illness than many other groups of workers. Indeed, Cherry (1978) found in her representative sample of 1,415 workers from different occupations that the following reported nervous debility and strain at work: professional 53.8%, intermediate non-manual 56.9%, skilled non-manual 44.3%, semi-skilled non-manual 50.0%, skilled manual 30.5%, semi-skilled manual 15.3%, and unskilled manual 10.3%.

The purpose of this book therefore, is to examine the plight of various white collar and professional jobs, in an effort to identify their problem areas and sources of work stress. By focusing on these particular occupations, we are not implying that they are more 'at risk' than their blue collar counterparts, but rather to circumscribe and concentrate our attention on one group at a time. It is hoped that subsequent volumes in this series of books on *Studies in Occupational Stress* will highlight the problems of other groups of workers.

In this book, we have asked a number of distinguished academics and practitioners to provide us with insights from accumulated research, their own investigations and/or their own experience about the nature and source of stress in particular white collar and professional occupations in which they have carried out research or have been associated. We have not attempted to cover all possible white collar and professional jobs, but only a sample of those of current concern or where some stress research work has been carried out. There were two occupations which we included in the book where no empirical stress work was available, but we felt that they should be included, given their importance to society, and to try and encourage more research in these fields (e.g. legislators (MPs) and trade union leaders). In these latter cases, we asked distinguished occupants of these roles to provide us with descriptive material, based on their vast experience, of the stresses and strains of their job.

In the first section, Health, we include two chapters which focus on stress among dentists and nurses. The chapter on dentists was included because it is one of the few large scale studies done in this field, using both physiological and psychological data, to assess the contribution of various sources of work stress on health care professionals. In addition, we felt that it could contribute to our understanding of the stressors experienced by medical practitioners (where little such work is available). To round off this section, we explored the particular problems of nursing staff in hospitals. This is a job of growing concern in the field of occupation health and well-being.

The second section, Education, includes chapters on teachers and school administrators. A great deal of research work has been carried out into stress among teachers, on both sides of the Atlantic. Much of the UK work has focused on classroom sources of stress and personality characteristics associated with 'teachers at risk'. The American emphasis, on the other hand, has been on the changing role of the teacher in a changing society; integration of minorities and women, teaching as an 'achieving profession', reduction in teaching force, legal status of certain aspects of schooling, etc. Since the UK and American approaches are very different in this respect, it was felt we should include one chapter on each. Later, we focus on the problems faced by school administrators (based on a large scale study) and the various coping strategies available to them for dealing with their stress.

Section three deals with occupations one might term Community Service ones, the police and social workers. Here we explore the pressures that each of these groups are currently experiencing. The data available seems to indicate that both these groups are manifesting more job-related stress than in previous decades, due in the main to their changing role in society.

The fourth section, Technology, looks at those aspects of the role of the technologist that are causing work stress. With the rapid technological developments in industry, and in Research and Development, we are finding a range of stressors or pressure points for engineers, technical support staff and the new technology recruit. These issues are developed in two chapters by prominent researchers in the field.

In the last section, Public Service, we look at the plight of two of the most vulnerable groups, legislators (e.g. MPs) and trade union leaders. Although this topic has occasionally surfaced in the popular media, little detailed empirical work or even informed descriptive accounts are available on the pressures and strains of being a public servant. It was decided therefore, to ask a former British minister and leading trade union official to assess the stressful effects of being a Member of Her Majesty's Parliament and the General Secretary of a growing and influential union respectively. They provide enlightening accounts of life at the top.

REFERENCES

Cherry, N. (1978). Stress, anxiety, and work. *Journal of Occupational Psychology,* **51** (3), 259-270.
Cooper, C.L. (1979). *The Executive Gypsy: The Quality of Managerial Life.* London: Macmillan Press Ltd.

PART I

Stress Among Health Care Professionals

White Collar and Professional Stress
Edited by C.L. Cooper and J. Marshall
© 1980 John Wiley & Sons Ltd.

Chapter 1

Dentists Under Pressure: A Social Psychological Study

Cary L. Cooper
University of Manchester
Institute of Science and Technology

According to studies (Hermanson, 1972) of occupational health among dentists, emotional illness ranked third in order of frequency while in the general population they were tenth. The American Dental Association survey of dental mortality (ADA, 1975) reported that diseases of the blood and blood forming organs were causes of death for dentists at a substantially higher rate than other people. It was also shown that dentists die from respiratory diseases more often than the general population. In addition, recent statistics (Green, 1975) revealed that dentists have the highest rate of suicide among occupational groups, although this data has recently been questioned (Gift, 1977). This information suggests that certain characteristics of the profession may be causes of stress; and that continual exposure to these stressful experiences may result in emotional as well as physical ill-health.

A study by Russek (1962) demonstrated that coronary heart disease among dentists is not linked to heredity or diet, but rather to the relative stressfulness of occupational activity. His research focussed on four categories of dentistry; periodontia, orthodontia, oral surgery, and general practice. They were ranked in order of stressfulness by seven expert independent judges (all dentists), who determined that the most stressful of the fields was general practice followed by oral surgery, orthodontia, and the least stressful, periodontia. The findings showed that general practitioners, in all age ranges, were reported to have coronary heart disease at a significantly greater rate than the other categories. The incidence of heart disease of the members of the speciality practices was also directly related to their 'stress' rank.

PREVALENT HYPOTHESES ON CAUSES OF STRESS

One hypothesis often mentioned in the literature as a cause of stress is the 'poor working conditions' of the dentist (*JCDA*, 1970). The confined space and the practitioners' restricted 'oral workfield' are considered by some as a source of 'tension build-up'. As tension mounts, the dentists can do little to relieve their anxiety, particularly in a face-to-face work context with patients and auxiliary staff. Some consider that the major source of fatigue is related to the physical position the practitioner must take while working on patients (Paul, 1969). These dentists believe that it is only by standing that a proper visual inspection of the oral cavity can be attained. A continuous standing position is regarded by some as being the primary cause of poor posture, imbalanced limb pressures and a *precursor of mental stress*. Paul (1969) suggests that the least fatiguing position for manual work is the seated one. His contention is that placing the dentist in a position of maximum comfort eliminates physical fatigue.

An empirical study (Paul, 1969) by the British Dental Association, however, indicated that that might not be the case. A sample of British dentists ($N = 2,228$) stated that their most common musculo-skeletal problem was backache. A total of 67% reported some occurrence of that ailment. Of the 1,250 who worked 'standing', 47.1% had complained of backache. Of the 205 who worked 'sitting down', 50.7% had backache. The incidence of backache, therefore, had little to do with the physical posture of the practitioner during work. Dyce and Dow (1965) concluded that backache is likely to be a 'product of living in an affluent, unstable, and highly mobile society', which is the probable precursor of spinal stiffness rather than a characteristic of the profession. Although 'poor working conditions' are a contributory factor in the etiology of stress-related illnesses among dentists, they are unlikely to be the primary or fundamental sources.

A second hypothesis related to occupational stress, concerns the 'routine and boring functions' of the profession. Some psychologists (Green, 1975) feel that the dull job of 'drilling and filling' is lonely work, which is emotionally unrewarding. According to the proponents of this thesis, as the job becomes rote the individual loses his interest, he begins to think much more about other things. The job no longer provides a release of life's pressures, instead, it acts to compound them.

Page and Slack (1969) queried 358 dentists regarding their attitude about their profession. When asked, 'what are the things you dislike most about your work', only 8% responded that they felt it was monotonous, repetitive and boring. It ranked eighth on the list of disliked items. On the contrary, however, only 6% of the sample stated that the variety of work was one of the things they liked most about their work. It ranked seventh on the list of most liked items. A comparable study by Eccles and Powell (1967) also found that only a small percentage (11%) of the sample mentioned monotonous work as being the most disliked aspect of their job; and this group, as well, was balanced by a similar number who liked its variety. Based on the research it appears, therefore, that although dentists generally do not perceive their profession as a plethora of diversity, they also do not feel it is a dull job.

One of the most highly discussed hypotheses deals with the lack of exercise among dentists (Willes, 1967). Because of the poor working conditions, the sedentary nature of the profession, and the tensions experienced in coping with resistent patients, the dentists can be physically vulnerable. A programme of exercise is often suggested in the literature to counteract the physical effects of the job and to allow an outlet for frustration.

There is evidence that suggests that exercise is an effective means of reducing tension and irritation, while at the same time stimulating mental alertness (Willes, 1967). Willes (1967) believes that participation in athletic activities improves the functioning and efficiency of the nervous system, which acts to eliminate tension.

A large scale study by Hammond (1964) showed a strong correlation between exercise and longevity. A sample of 461,440 males who participated in varying degrees of exercise was examined. A follow-up study over two time periods demonstrated that the deaths per 100 men (in all age categories) was significantly reduced as the intensity of exercise was increased. The men who received no exercise at all experienced five to six times the rate of death of the individuals who participated in an extensive exercise-based programme.

Howard et al. (1976), in an effort to examine the relationship of physical condition and stress, studied thirty-three practising Canadian dentists. The research team determined the physical working capacity (PWC) of the subjects by having them ride a bicycle ergometer. This device is considered to be a good measure of the individual's cardiovascular fitness. The dentists also completed a questionnaire which included a checklist of 40 stress symptom items. A summated scale of the number of stress symptoms reported was used as an indicator of stress levels. The results showed that 60% ($N = 18$) of the sample indicated that the make a significant attempt to get a minimum amount of exercise. This group reported a much higher average PWC score than did the non-exercise group. It was also established that the exercise group displayed a lower average number of stress symptoms (2.25) than the non-exercise group (4.90). Although the sample was small in this study, the results suggest that exercise may be a method of reducing stress. It is believed by these authors, however, that exercise is a way of providing the dentist with the facilities to cope better with stress, but not necessarily the solution to the reduction or elimination of stress-inducing aspects of a dentist's job.

A fourth hypothesis as to the cause of stress is the dentist's anxiety regarding society's expectations of his profession. Kimmel (1974) stated that the dentist receives constant criticism, is viewed as an inflictor of pain, and is not sure of his role in society (is he a doctor or only a quasi-doctor?). Witteman and Currier (1976) investigated student, practitioner and faculty motives in entering the dental profession. Their conclusions have subtle, but significant value with regard to the expectation theory. The sample included 368 dental students, 124 practitioners and 22 faculty members in the state of Virginia. One segment of the study focussed on differences between the most important motive for the private practitioner and the motive perceived by the student as most important for the practitioner. The motives perceived by dental students as important for the private practitioner were not the same as those the practitioner perceived for himself. The student perceived 'good salary' and 'a community reputation', while the practitioner perceived 'a continual educational process and freedom to carry out his ideas' as the primary motive for entering the profession. It is assumed that the practitioners' responses were related more to how they viewed their present objectives rather than their motives for entering the profession. The results, perhaps, signify that the dental students' expectation of the profession is different from the real nature of the job. The disparity that follows may be a cause of stress for the future practitioner.

Economic factors may also be another source of pressure for the practitioner. The effort involved in attempting to build and maintain a viable practice, which requires work overload, time pressures, keeping to a schedule, etc. Another component of the research by Howard et al. (1976) showed that dentists with the highest income of the sample (an average of $36,000 v. $29,800) tended to be behind schedule, worked longer hours per day (an average of 9.1 hours v. 8.9 hours), worked more evenings per week (1.9 evenings v. 1.0 evenings), and took less time for lunch (43 minutes v. 60.5 minutes) than other subjects. In addition, higher stress symptom scores (4.3 v. 3.0) were associated with 'higher income' dentists.

The evidence implies that the need for higher income is not only related to a heavy work schedule, but also to a stressful lifestyle. Will this behaviour manifest itself in physical and/or emotional illness? The likelihood, according to Rosenman and Friedman (1974), is quite high. These cardiologists have devoted several years of research to the study of behavioural patterns and their link to coronary heart disease. Their conclusion is that cardiovascular disease is more related to personality than diet, smoking, exercise, or heredity. The susceptible individuals known as Type A, are characterized by excesses of competitiveness, striving for achievement, aggressiveness, time urgency (always pushing to get more done in less time), free floating hostility, and polyphasic thought and performances (doing two or more things at the same time).

The growing use of auxiliary help has proved to be a significant benefit for the dentist in increasing productivity. Obuhoff (1974), however, suggests that the interaction and team relationship necessary to efficiently and effectively make use of the auxiliary staff can be a stressful experience. In addition to treating patients and operating an office, the dentist's job is now further complicated by having to handle a larger staff. It is often necessary for the dentist to expand the physical capacity of the office in order to accommodate the additional personnel and the increase in the number of patients. A dentist who wants to add auxiliary staff should expect to devote additional hours to management at the expense of either chairside care or leisure time. All this adds up to more responsibility for the practitioner, and, perhaps, managerial skills he currently does not possess.

Selye (1946) states that there is a relationship between work, stress, and ageing. Each period of stress, especially if it results from frustration, leaves irreversible chemical scars which accumulate to constitute the signs of tissue ageing. But successful activity, according to Selye, no matter how intense, leaves the individual with comparatively few scars. It causes stress, but little, if any, distress. On the contrary, it provides an exhilarating feeling of youthful strength, even at a very advanced age. Work wears out the individual mainly through the frustration of failure (Page and Slack, 1969).

We shall now consider where the dentist may be failing. Returning to the work of Page and Slack (1969) may provide some answers. In response to the question, 'what are the things you like most about your work', 50% of the sample said it was human contact; meeting and working with people (including children), service and welfare aspects, patient appreciation and gratitude. This reply ranked first on the list. On the other hand, when asked, 'what are the things you dislike most about your work', 21% stated it was broken appointments; patients-awkward, uncooperative, abusive, dirty, etc. — which ranked second on the dislike list.

There appears to be a conflict. The things the dentists 'most likes' — human contact — were a major problem as well. Perhaps, the dentist in an effort to please and be appreciated finds difficulty in achieving these goals, feels the pain of failure and thus, the agony of distress.

RESEARCH STUDY

Based on some of these hypotheses or speculations of the causes of stress among dentists, the author carried out a study among a group of dentists attending the California Dental Association scientific meetings in Anaheim in April, 1977. As a part of that meeting, a stress ECG health evaluation unit was provided for screening purposes. The author formed part of that unit by collecting data on two aspects of dentistry, the potential stress-related characteristics of the job of a dentist, and psychometric or personality profiles of dentists. In addition, for each dentist in the sample we were given information (anonymously) on his stress ECG results, blood pressure, and pulse rates. There were two objectives to the study. First, to find out what dentists themselves felt were their major sources of 'on-the-job' stress. And second, to find out what job characteristics and personality factors are linked to these three physiological indicators of 'dentists at risk' (from coronary heart disease).*

---

*Part of the results of this study were published by the author in the *Journal of Occupational Psychology,* **1978,** 51 (3), pp.227-234.

Sample. To collect information from the dentists about their perceptions of job stress, we sampled all the dentists who participated in the stress ECG programme at the CDA meeting. There were 150 dentists; 1 female and 149 males with a mean age of 44.7 years (median 42.7) and an age range from 27 to 73 years old.

Rated Job Pressures. All the dentists filled out a 15 item questionnaire designed to measure their perceived job pressures at work. This questionnaire was developed from a pilot study on the sources of dental stress carried out by the author among dentists at the University of Southern California School of Dental Science. The sample was asked to rate each job factor on a six-point Likert-type rating scale on the extent to which the item was a source of pressure (from 'causes no pressure at all' to 'causes high degree of pressure'). The 15 characteristics were: coping with difficult patients, job interfering with personal life, attempting to sustain and build a practice, low patient appreciation, administrative duties, too much work, organizing and interacting with the staff, coping with the routine and dull work associated with the practice, patients' perception of the dentist as an inflictor of pain, difficult physical working conditions, trying to keep to a schedule, trying to earn a living suitable to my lifestyle, inability to meet my own expectations, unsatisfactory auxiliary help, and interaction with patients.

Personality Characteristics of Dentists: 16PF Inventory. The 16PF questionnaire (Cattell, Eber, and Tatsuoka, 1970) was selected as the measure of personality for our sample of dentists. The 16PF was chosen because it was felt to be one of the most comprehensive and widely validated of the personality inventories, because it contains several subscales of personality traits that are particularly relevant to stress predisposition, and because it could be easily and quickly administered. Form C was used, which is self-administering and consists of 105 three-alternative-choice items, comprising 16 scales. Only eight of the sixteen scales were used in our study, in order to minimize the time required to fill out questionnaires and because these were the only items considered as relevant potential stress-related traits (six of them (C, H, L, O, Q3, Q4) making up the second stratum factor of anxiety). The following eight source trait personality factors were used (the first of the bipolar traits mentioned for each factor represents the low score end of the continuum): Factor C: higher ego strength *vs.* emotional instability; Factor F: desurgency *vs.* surgency or the differentiation between a sober and serious personality and an enthusiastic and happy-go-lucky one; Factor H: shy and timid *vs.* adventurous and socially bold; Factor L: trusting *vs.* suspicious personality; Factor O: self-assured *vs.* apprehensive; Factor Q1: conservatism *vs.* radicalism; Factor Q3: low self concept integration *vs.* high integration; and Factor Q4: relaxed and unfrustrated *vs.* frustrated and overwrought. In addition to these eight factors, a ninth scale was included which was developed by Cattell *et al.* (1970) as a second stratum scale of adjustment *vs.* anxiety

(QII) and was calculated by combining six of the original source traits (C −, H −, L +, O +, Q3 −, and Q4 +).

Physical Health Indices. The physical health data made available to us by the health evaluation unit (with the permission of the dentists themselves) was 'sitting' pulse rate (PR), diastolic blood pressure (DBP) and systolic blood pressure (SBP), and stress ECG results. The former three were presented numerically, while the stress ECG readings were assessed by two cardiologists and were categorized as either normal or borderline or abnormal. 83.3% were diagnosed as normal and the balance as either borderline or abnormal. The mean, modal, and median diastolic and systolic blood pressure for the sample were 78.1 (standard deviation 9.59), 70.0, 77.8, and 129.7 (standard deviation 15.99), 120.0, 127.6 respectively. 15.9% of the sample had diastolic blood pressure levels above 85 and 21.7% had systolic levels above 140. The mean, modal, and median pulse rate were 72.4 (standard deviation of 11.01), 64.0, and 72.1 respectively. 11.2% of the sample had pulse rates above 80. The correlation coefficients between the various indices were as follows: $r = 0.63$ for DBP and SBP, $r = 0.13$ for PR and DBP, $r = 0.04$ for SBP and PR, $r = -0.08$ for ECG and PR, $r = -0.05$ for ECG and DBP, and $r = 0.11$ for ECG and SBP.

Statistical Analysis. In order to analyse the relationship between our dependent variables or physical health measures (four physiological measures) and our independent variables or personality (9 scales) and job characteristic (15 scales) factors, we used stepwise multiple regression analysis. Multiple regression relates independent and dependent variables in a manner which takes interactive effects into account. This statistical technique is a method of achieving the best linear prediction equation between a given set of independent variables (in our case, personality and job factors) and the dependent variables in question (in this case the four physiological indices). In trying to isolate the independent variables (i.e. personality and job factors) which will yield the optimal predication equation, our cut off point was determined by two statistical criteria (Kerlinger and Pedhazer, 1973). First, that the overall F-ratio for the equation was significant. And second, that the partial regression coefficient for the individual independent variable being added was at a statistically significant or approaching significance level. Below this point not only is the coefficient insignificant but also the amount of variance contributed by each additional variable (R^2 change) is very small.

RESULTS

Table 1 shows the means and standard deviations for each of the fifteen job pressure variables. The results indicate that the most stressful aspects of the job were 'coping with difficult patients' and 'trying to keep to a schedule'.

Table 1.   Means, standard deviations, and rankings of the 15 stress variables

Variable	Mean	Standard deviation	Rankings of most stressful variable		
			1st	2nd	3rd
Coping with difficult patients	4.35	1.24	58	19	16
Job interfering with personal life	2.36	1.33	6	3	4
Attempting to sustain or build a practice	2.73	1.40	6	14	7
Low patient appreciation	2.57	1.25	2	4	8
Administrative duties	3.07	1.28	3	9	9
Too much work	3.28	1.35	4	17	12
Organizing and interacting with the staff	2.88	1.35	6	6	8
Coping with the routine and dull work associated with the practice	2.17	1.19	2	2	2
Patients' perception of the dentist as an inflictor of pain	2.85	1.44	7	13	10
Difficult physical working conditions	2.46	1.35	2	6	7
Trying to keep to a schedule	3.83	1.31	25	28	17
Trying to earn a living suitable to my lifestyle	2.85	1.47	5	4	12
Inability to meet my own expectations	2.93	1.40	8	9	8
Unsatisfactory auxiliary help	3.13	1.51	13	10	12
Interaction with patients	2.28	1.13	0	1	5

Also perceived as stressful, but to a much lesser degree, were 'too much work', 'unsatisfactory auxiliary help', and 'administrative duties'.

Over 53% of the sample rate 'coping with difficult patients' as a major stressor (rated at either a five or six degrees of pressure). The findings were substantiated by the rankings: 'coping with difficult patients' and 'trying to keep to a schedule' were ranked first and third respectively, as being the most stressful factors.

The least stressful items included 'coping with the routine and dull work', 'interacting with patients', 'job interfering with personal life', 'difficult working conditions', and 'low patient appreciation'. The results of both the means and the rankings (Table 1) confirm these factors as being sources of little stress.

Consideration was given to the difference in age in regard to the questionnaire responses. The sample was broken down into 5 age groups: 25-34 (18.7% of sample), 35-44 (34.0%), 45-54 (24.0%), 55-64 (13.3%), and over 64 (3.3%). In the sample, 6.7% did not provide their age. It was thought, because of an individual's experience, that certain factors might be perceived as being more stressful to older as opposed to younger practitioners, and *vice versa*. The age-related data indicates that 'coping with difficult patients' and 'trying to keep to a schedule' were considered to be the most stressful factors, regardless of age. In fact, for most items there was no significant differences in the means or rankings.

'Attempting to sustain or build a practice' was perceived by younger dentists as being relatively stressful. As the age of the practitioner increased, the mean associated with that variable declined. A *t*-test for independent samples indicates a statistically significant difference between the means.

In addition, the youngest age group of the sample (25-34) perceived the total set of job factors to be only slightly more stressful than the other age categories, while the oldest (over 64) perceived the least amount of pressure.

In order to determine the job pressures and personality variables most responsible for predicting ill health among dentists, a series of stepwise multiple regression analyses were calculated for each of the four physiological indices, beginning with diastolic blood pressure, systolic blood pressure, stress ECG, and concluding with pulse rate. Since age is (to some extent) related to some of the physical health measures, this was also included as an independent variable. Whereas the earlier analyses provided us with information about the perceptions of our sample population as a whole, the following data will tell us

Table 2. Significant differences between age groups on job stress questionnaire variables (*t*-test for independent means)

Age category	Variable	*t*-value	Probability
25-34 55-64	Attempting to sustain or build a practice	2.65	<0.01
25-34 over 64	Attempting to sustain or build a practice	2.87	<0.01
25-34 over 64	Job interfering with personal life	2.75	<0.01
35-44 over 64	Coping with difficult patients	2.54	<0.01
45-54 over 64	Job interfering with personal life	2.63	<0.01

Table 3.   Personality, job stressors, and diastolic blood pressure

Personality and rated job pressures	Multiple R	R^2	R^2 change
Age	0.36	0.13	0.13
Dentist as inflictor of pain	0.40	0.16	0.04
Coping with difficult patients	0.45	0.20	0.04
Administrative duties	0.49	0.24	0.04
Too little work	0.52	0.27	0.03
16PF factor QII 'anxiety'	0.54	0.29	0.01
Sustaining and building a practice	0.55	0.31	0.02
Job interfering with personal life	0.57	0.32	0.02

$F = 6.88 \quad p < 0.01$

something about the job characteristics and personality factors of 'dentists at risk', those with *high* blood pressure, abnormal ECG, and rapid pulse rate.

It can be seen in Table 3 that there are eight factors which significantly ($p < 0.01$) predict raised diastolic blood pressure, contributing over 32% of the total variance with a correlation coefficient of 0.57. Although it was expected that age would be such a factor, it was very interesting to discover that of the remaining seven variables, four were related to business or managerial aspects of dentistry and only one to the personality characteristics of dentists (in this case, an anxiety predisposition). The final two were linked to the wider role of dentistry, in terms of its impact on the personal and social life of the dentist, that is, that it was stressful to be perceived as an 'inflictor of pain', and the job created a certain amount of stress by interference with the dentist's personal

Table 4.   Personality, job stressor, and systolic blood pressure

Personality and rated job pressures	Multiple R	R^2	R^2 change
Age	0.21	0.05	0.05
Sustaining and building a practice	0.35	0.12	0.08
Too little work	0.40	0.16	0.03
Administrative duties	0.42	0.18	0.02
Coping with difficult patients	0.45	0.20	0.03
Unsatisfactory auxiliary help	0.48	0.23	0.02
Dentist as inflictor of pain	0.50	0.25	0.02
16PF factor QII 'anxiety'	0.52	0.27	0.02
16PF factor 0 'apprehensive'	0.53	0.28	0.01

$F = 4.70 \quad p < 0.01$

life. By far, the factors that contributed the most variance to higher diastolic blood pressure, however, were those related to the dentists' perceptions or rating of the business or managerial pressures of the job; 'trying to build and sustain a practice', 'too little work', 'administrative duties' and 'coping with difficult patients'. Curiously, the latter factor was in the opposite direction from that one would have predicted, that is, dentists with higher diastolic blood pressure levels significantly more often than those with lower levels stated that 'coping with difficult patients' was *not* a source of stress, while those with normal levels acknowledged the stress associated in interacting with difficult patients.

It can be seen in Table 4 that there were nine factors which significantly ($p < 0.01$) predict systolic blood pressure, contributing over 28% of the total variance with a correlation coefficient of 0.53. In relation to the results above, we find roughly the same factors associated with raised diastolic blood pressure; age, the four business or managerial variables (sustaining and building a practice, too little work, administrative duties, and coping with difficult patients (again in the opposite direction)), perception of the dentist as an 'inflictor of pain' and a high 'anxiety' personality trait. In addition, two other factors were included in the equation, one related to the management and organization of the practice and the other to the dentist's personality; pressure created by 'unsatisfactory auxiliary help' and an 'apprehensive personality predisposition' respectively. Job interference with the dentist's personal life was not included. Obviously, since there is a high correlation between DBP and SBP, many of the same factors appear in both analyses.

It can be seen in Table 5 that there were nine factors which significantly ($p < 0.05$) predicted borderline or abnormal stress ECG readings, contributing

Table 5. Personality, job stressors and stress ECG

Personality and rated job pressures	Multiple R	R^2	R^2 change
Sustaining and building a practice	0.19	0.04	0.04
Low patient appreciation	0.29	0.08	0.05
Age	0.34	0.12	0.03
16PF factor Q3 'controlled, socially precise'	0.37	0.14	0.02
Interaction with patient	0.39	0.16	0.02
16PF factor H 'venturesome'	0.41	0.17	0.01
Routine and dull work	0.43	0.18	0.01
16PF factor C 'less emotionally stable'	0.45	0.20	0.02
Difficult physical working conditions	0.46	0.21	0.01

$F = 3.25$ $p < 0.05$

over 21% of the variance with a correlation coefficient of 0.46. The lower level of predicted variance and significance level are probably due to the smaller range of categories on the ECG scale in comparison to the blood pressure measures. These were slightly different factors from those associated with raised blood pressure. Aside from age, they included three personality traits (i.e. 'emotionally less stable', 'controlled and socially precise', and 'venturesome'), three related to the nature of the job of dentistry (i.e. 'routine and dull work', 'difficult physical working conditions' and 'low patient appreciation'), and two associated with the managerial side of dental care (i.e. 'sustaining and building a practice' and 'stressful interaction with patients'). These results depict the dentist under stress as a person pressured not only from the business or managerial aspects of his job but also characteristics considered by many as intrinsic to the nature of the work itself; difficult physical working conditions, frequently routine and dull work, and little patient appreciation.

There were eight factors related to raised pulse rate, but these were only approaching statistical significance ($p < 0.10$), indeed, they contributed only 14% of the variance with a correlation coefficient of 0.38. Nevertheless, we found, once again, the managerial (i.e. 'sustaining and building a practice', 'keeping to a schedule', and 'coping with difficult patients' (again in the opposite direction)) and personality variables (i.e. 'anxiety', 'emotionally less stable', and 'suspicious') predominating, with two personal/social factors reappearing, pressure due to the 'job interfering with personal life' and to the dentist's 'inability to meet his own expectations'. As can be seen, raised pulse rate is less predictable than either raised blood pressure or stress ECG, nevertheless some of the same predictive characteristics are present here as in the data associated with the other physiological indices.

And finally, the authors decided to derive a single composite health index of the four physiological measures used, to examine the job characteristics and personality factors in relation to this measure by multiple regression analysis. This provided no new results and the same variables that had appeared in the earlier analyses reappeared significantly in this equation, namely, 'sustaining and building a practice', 'too little work', 'administrative duties', 'coping with difficult patients' (in the opposite direction), 'keeping to a schedule', high 'anxiety' trait, and age.

DISCUSSION OF RESULTS

Examining the data across all four health criteria measures, we find a number of interesting results. First, the only variable that consistently appears in each of the health indices as a significant source of pressure is 'the demands of sustaining and building a practice'. This supports Howard et al.'s (1976) suggestion that the 'demands of a growing practice' may be a fundamental source of job stress among dentists. Howard *et al.* (1976) also suggested the linkage between this source of pressure and a Type A behavioural pattern, namely, 'an overt behaviour syndrome or style of living characterized by excesses of competitiveness, striving for achievement, aggressiveness, etc.' This was not consistent with our findings, which suggest that our dentist 'at risk' is one who is anxiety-prone and, perhaps, somewhat less emotionally stable (or more easily upset). This may make him vulnerable to periods when there is 'too little work', or excessive 'administrative duties', or 'difficult patients to cope with'. It is this later factor which provides the second interesting, yet difficult to explain, finding, namely, that dentists at risk in our sample (in terms of three of our indices) report that they experience very little pressure in coping with difficult patients, while dentists who have normal health levels on our criteria report such pressure. This could mean that our 'dentist at risk' either does not have any such difficulties, or he has decided not to reveal them, or he has unconsciously repressed them, or he is truly unaware of the difficulty.

Because this variable reappears a number of times in the various analyses, and in the same direction, it is highly unlikely that it is not a source of pressure for our 'dentist at risk'. If he is unconscious or unaware of it, the problem will obviously be more difficult to deal with, it would be useful, therefore, for further research to explore this phenomenon in greater depth (preferably by intensive interview). Third, although it only appeared on two of the four criteria, dentists with raised blood pressure did perceive, to some extent, their image as 'inflictors of pain' and that this was a source of pressure on them. This is consistent with Kimmel's (1974) view that a major cause of stress may be the dentists' anxiety regarding society's expectations of their profession, namely, that dentists receive constant criticism, are viewed as inflictors of pain, and are not sure of their role in society. Fourth, it was interesting that, on balance, personality variables were less consistently predictive than the rated job pressures. This is contrary to the work of Friedman and Rosenman (1974) who contend that cardiovascular disease and stress-related illness is more related to personality and behavioural characteristics than work environment, diet, smoking, exercise, or hereditary. Not only were we unable to find many personality predispositions to stress but the two we did discover (i.e. anxiety and emotionally less stable) were not related to Friedman and Rosenman's Type A coronary prone personality traits. At least four of the 16PF variables could be linked to Type A behaviour, namely, Factors $F+$, $H+$, $Q1+$, and $Q3-$, but they did not appear consistently in the analyses (Factor $H+$ was the only one to appear, and only once). Fifth, it was found that our dentists also experienced some stress from their 'job interfering with their personal lives'. Howard *et al.* found that this was also one of the best predictors of job dissatisfaction among a small group of Canadian dentists. There seems to be a conflict between the feeling that work interferes with one's personal life and the low work load, which probably reflects the dentist's concern (regarding work underload) with the size and development of his practice. And finally, it seems curious to us that neither of the items ('organizing and interacting with the staff' and 'unsatisfactory auxiliary help') associated with the relationship between the dentist and his staff appeared significantly in our analyses. This does not support Obuhoff's (1974) contention that the interaction and team relationship necessary to efficiently and effectively make use of auxiliary staff is a stressful experience.

Although one would have to posit a few *caveats* about the research sample used (dentists attending a scientific meeting and seeking an assessment of their current state of health) and some of the measures used (particularly, pulse rate) it is one of the few studies that has attempted to establish a link between the working conditions of dentists (and their personality) and physical health indices associated with coronary risk factors.

REFERENCES

American Dental Association, Bureau of Economic Research and Statistics (1975). Mortality of dentists, 1968-1972, *JADA,* **90,** 195.

Cattell, R.B., Eber, H.W., and Tatsuoka, M.M. (1970). *Handbook of the 16PF Questionnaire.* Illinois: IPAT.

Dyce, J.M., and Dow, J.A. (1965). FDI special commission on dentists' health, diagnosis, and stress in dentistry, *Int. Dent. J.,* **15,** 405.

Eccles, J.D., and Powell, M. (1967). The health of dentists: a survey in South Wales 1965/1966, *Brit. Dent. J.,* **120,** 379.

Friedman, M., and Rosenman, R.H. (1974). *Type A Behaviour and Your Heart.* New York: Alfred A. Knopf.

Gift, H.C. (1977). Occupational hazards and emotional stress as related to morbidity and mortality of dentists, Report to the Division of Dentistry, U.S. Department of Health, Education and Welfare.

Green, D. (1975). Unsafe at any speed, *Dental Management,* **15,** 27.

Hammond, E.C. (1964). Some preliminary findings on physical complaints from a prospective study of 1,064,004 men and women, *Am. J. Public Health,* **54,** 1.

Hermanson, P.C. (1972). Dentistry: a hazardous profession, *Dental Student,* **50,** 60.

Howard, J.H., Cunningham, D.A., Rechnitzer, P.A. and Goode, R.C. (1976). Stress in the job and career of a dentist, *JADA,* **93,** 630.

Jenkins, C.D. (1971). Psychologic and social presursors of coronary disease, *New Eng. J. Med.,* **284,** 244-255.

Kahn, R.L., and Quinn, R.P. (1970). Role stress, in McLean A. (Ed.) *Mental Health and Work Organization.* Chicago: Rand McNally, pp.50-115.

Kerlinger, F.N., and Pedhazer, E. (1973). *Multiple Regression in Behavioural Research.* New York: Holt, Rinehart and Winston.

Kimmel, K. (1974). The expectations of the dentist, *Int. Dent. J.,* **24,** 356.

Lofquist, L.H., and Dawis, R.V. (1969). *Adjustment to Work.* New York: Appleton-Century-Croft.

Margolis, B.L., Kroes, W.H., and Quinn, R.P. (1974). Job stress: an unlisted occupational hazard, *J. Occup. Med.,* **16,** 654-661.

Obuhoff, O.N. (1974). Auxiliary utilization: increasing productivity and how to survive it, *Calif. Dent. J.,* **2,** 28.

Page, C.M., and Slack, G.L. (1969). A contented profession? A survey of old Londoner dentists, *Brit. Dent. J.,* **127,** 220.

Paul, E. (1969). The elimination of stress and fatigue in operative dentistry, *Brit. Dent. J.,* **127,** 37.

Physical and emotional demands pose problems for dentists, *J. Can. Dent. Assoc.,* **36,** 57.

Russek, H.I. (1962). Emotional stress and coronary heart disease in American physicians, dentists and lawyers, *Am. J. Med. Sci.,* **243,** 716.

Selye, H. (1946). The general adaptation syndrome and the diseases of adaptation, *J. Clin. Endocrinology,* **6,** 117.

Willee, A.W. (1967). How to avoid the occupational hazards of dentistry, *Aust. Dent. J.,* **12,** 348.

Witteman, J.K., and Currier, G.F. (1976). Motives to enter the dental profession: students, practitioners, faculty, *J. Dent. Educ.,* **40,** 265.

White Collar and Professional Stress
Edited by C.L. Cooper and J. Marshall
©1980 John Wiley & Sons Ltd.

Chapter 2

Stress Amongst Nurses

Judi Marshall
School of Management,
University of Bath, England

The word 'nurse' is derived from the verb to nourish. The profession has a long tradition of ministering to the sick, of giving both medical and emotional comfort and support. This chapter is concerned with the personal cost to the nurse of providing such a service and her needs, in turn, for 'nourishment'.

Having identified nursing as a potentially stressful occupation — recent industrial action in the UK from this otherwise passive group being a key symptom — I was unable to find anyone both able and willing to contribute a suitable chapter. I decided therefore to divert my energies to exploring the area myself. This is, then, a newcomer's impression of nurses' job stress written by someone who had previously concentrated on managerial jobs. It is incomplete, speculative in places and does not draw on personal experience of research — caveats which must be borne in mind by the reader. It does, however, take a fresh view (a sometimes surprised view!) and draws together a substantial section of the available material — these, I think, are its contributions.

My first step in exploration was to ask for a computer literature search (my thanks to Diana Stoddart for her work on this) and this has acted as my base. Most of the literature specifically about stress amongst nurses is from the United States. To supplement this I had discussion with some British nursing personnel and researchers whom I used as 'expert witnesses'. (Thanks particularly to JA, HB, AT, and AW.) I found their accounts tallied fairly closely with those in the literature. I was thus able to achieve a more rounded picture but not a sufficient base to compare the two countries. In making sense of the material I have also drawn on my own brief experience as a nursing assistant in a psychiatric hospital during a University vacation.

The literature comes from a range of sources: from academic researchers on stress amongst nurses, from those involved in nursing training, from workers

19

themselves discussing the pressures and satisfactions of their jobs and from consultants who have been called in to help staff deal with stress. Compared to literature on other occupational groups I found most of these particularly rich and evocative sources. The picture built up of the nurses' working life is also strikingly multifaceted. Discussion of work pressures leads on naturally to an appreciation of their effects; some writers point to the satisfactions which act as a balance and explain why nurses continue to do their jobs. Two special areas — death and dying and intensive care unit nursing receive separate attention. The coping strategies individuals, groups and organizations currently use to contain pressures receive considerable attention and the literature is full of suggestions for actions that may further or more productively relieve stress. Some papers also describe trials of the latter so that here I can also evaluate them in practice.

The main body of the chapter will be developed in the above order, but I should like first to set the scene by giving an overview of nursing stress as it appears in the literature and making a few 'qualifying statements' about the approach taken here.

AN OVERVIEW AND SOME DISTINCTIVE FEATURES

Most writers start by taking the existence of stress amongst nurses for granted and do not justify their concern by documenting symptoms as is more commonly the case. In fact the literature adopts a different stance from that for other occupational groups in several ways. Not only does it make assumptions of inherent stressfulness; it omits individual differences as potentially relevant contributing variables; it gives a detailed consideration of currently used coping mechanisms (which are felt to be largely inadequate) and focuses on intrapsychic rather than environmental manipulations as potential mechanisms of intervention. These biases and the job pressures identified in the literature tempt me to conclude that the job of nurse incorporates several distinctive features which set it apart as a special case in the stress literature. It appears to take to extremes certain aspects of experiencing stress which usually operate more moderately and are thus more subject to variability from individual and environmental differences. Whilst these special features of the job will become apparent as the chapter develops an overview of this argument is appropriate here as an introduction.

Perception of threat is the critical psychological process by which stress is defined by most leading writers in the stress field (e.g. Lazarus, 1966). If a nurse is fully (emotionally as well as cognitively) aware of the conditions of her patients there is reason to believe this constitutes a fundamental threat to her on two dimensions: as a skilled worker whose competence (to heal) is on trial and, even more fundamentally, as a human being who is herself vulnerable to the illnesses and death she is nursing. I see these as related to what may be termed 'primary task aspects' — core requirements of the nursing role. In order to do her job well, in fact, the nurse must fully apprehend these potential stressful stimuli. Unless coping with them takes the form of deep confrontation its effects will be superficial and transitory. The literature suggests, however, that avoidance is the primary coping mechanism at an organizational as well as an individual level and that this causes repression of emotions and leads to secondary stress effects. So, the nurse's primary task has a high anxiety-invoking potential. Her role is made more difficult both by secondary stress effects from failing to cope with this anxiety and by the failure of the primary task organization to work smoothly. This sums to a job unusually high in potential stressors. Researchers have therefore been led to concentrate on the environmental aspects and assume universal effects on nursing staff making no allowance for possible differences due to personality, ability to tolerate stress, etc.

Another extreme of relevance to stress potential is the unequivocal nature, high visibility, and importance of success and failure in nursing work. Other occupational groups measure performance on more ambiguous criteria. Many managers, for example, react only to infrequent negative feedback when they are not keeping people fully satisfied (Stewart and Marshall, 1979).

The third important extreme in nursing is the strength of sanctions against showing symptoms of stress. Whilst there are penalties for showing stress in most social settings there are often also acceptable ways to let off steam, escape into privacy or whatever. The nurse is usually denied these possibilities. A central requirement of her role is that she should show no signs of stress — maintaining a 'detached concern' and remaining calm even during emergencies. These expectations apply not only in front of patients and relatives — the 'clients' of the hospital system — but in front of other members of staff, at least whilst on duty.

Summing the above extremes we arrive at a view of the individual nurse as likely to confront daily the need to manage personal stress. At the same time she is called on to play a major part in relieving the emotional anxieties of others. Patients and, to a lesser extent, relatives demand her support. One researcher suggests that in some cases their needs for help in dealing with stress override physical factors as reasons for hospitalization: 'As we became familiar with the work of the hospital, we were struck by the number of patients whose physical condition alone did not warrant hospitalization. In some cases, it was clear that they had been hospitalized because they and their relatives could not tolerate the stress of their being ill at home' (Menzies, 1970). The nurse's role is therefore implicitly and chiefly one of handling stress. She is a focus for the stress of the patient, relatives, and doctor as well as her own.

The above outline was intended to sensitize the reader to some of the distinctive features of stress for this occupational group. It has also served to introduce the model around which this chapter is organized. The many pressures identified in the literature form the main section and can be viewed as either 'primary task aspects' or 'secondary effects' which result from the mainly avoidance-based coping strategies nurses adopt. Certain pressures — for example work overload — appear to accentuate the effects of others. Happily other aspects act as satisfactions and these help to balance and attenuate stress. Figure 1 draws together these various elements and charts their main relationships.

The literature on stress amongst nurses takes a distinctive approach to conceptualizaton as well as to exploration. It relies principally on psychoanalytic explanations (and therefore interventions). These biases seem strange to a newcomer to the area. Approaching them from my own broader base in stress research prompts me to question certain assumptions and there will be opportunities in the text for such debate. Consideration of one such topic — the role of anxiety — precedes the review of job pressures as its assumed action is a central element in so many researchers' accounts. This follows the next brief scene-setting note on 'qualifications' to this review.

QUALIFYING STATEMENTS

Several observations should be made here. Firstly whilst it is convenient to discuss 'nurses' and 'hospitals' as homogeneous categories, there are obviously important distinctions within each which must be borne in mind as potentially relevant. Pressures may be different for different kinds of nurse. Extent of experience, level in the organization and degree of specialization are the more obvious potential distinctions. The literature currently offers few opportunities to explore such differences in stress terms. Similarly wards differ, as do hospitals. (It would seem that there is a wider range in the types of care institutions in the United States than in the United Kingdom.) Miller (1976) conducted his research in three contrasting types of US general hospital. He found marked differences in organizational structure and climate, staff attitudes, and type of patient which he was able then to relate to different causes of stress. Sudnow (1967) too reports marked differences between the county and public hospitals he visited. Whilst other researchers find significant similarities between different hospitals (e.g. Jacobson, 1978), such results caution against generalizing too enthusiastically. One writer evaluating the literature from this point of view does however suggest that inter-hospital differences will be in terms of different priorities between a common set of stress factors rather than of altogether different factors (Weeks, 1978).

Secondly, in order to contain the material for this chapter to manageable proportions there were several neighbouring areas of literature which I did not explore. The expanding general literature on death, dying, and illness

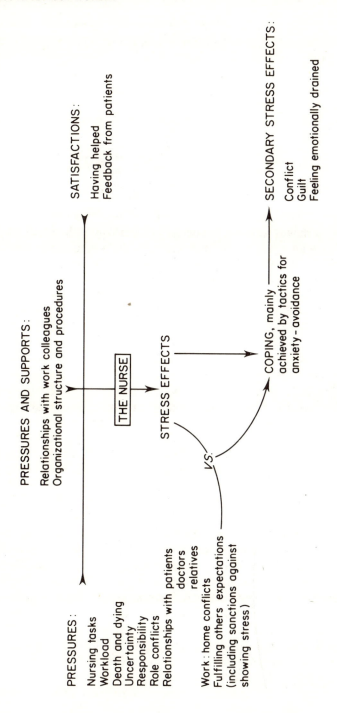

PRESSURES AND SUPPORTS:

Relationships with work colleagues
Organizational structure and procedures

SATISFACTIONS:

Having helped
Feedback from patients

THE NURSE

STRESS EFFECTS

VS.

COPING, mainly
achieved by tactics for
anxiety - avoidance

SECONDARY STRESS EFFECTS:

Conflict
Guilt
Feeling emotionally drained

PRESSURES:

Nursing tasks
Workload
Death and dying
Uncertainty
Responsibility
Role conflicts
Relationships with patients
                        doctors
                        relatives

Work : home conflicts
Fulfilling others expectations
(including sanctions against
showing stress)

Figure 2.1 The main elements in stress for the nurse

trajectories is perhaps the most obvious medical omission. I have also elaborated my own model of pressure and stress sufficiently elsewhere (e.g. Marshall and Cooper, 1979) not to discuss it here.

My final qualification is an explanation that as nursing is still predominantly a female profession, for ease (but with some reluctance) I have followed the literature convention of calling the nurse 'she' in this text. (I look forward to agreement on a joint sex singular pronoun to spare writers such dilemmas!)

THE DEBATABLE ROLE OF ANXIETY

The apparent stressfulness of the nurse's job leads many writers to take this for granted as the starting point for their work. Whilst not wishing to belittle the *pressures* involved (Marshall and Cooper, 1979) such a stand is open to criticism in that it makes assumptions about the meaning of the experience for nurses which are seldom tested out by research. A chain of assumptions which is commonly followed is that (1) nurses' jobs cause them high levels of anxiety; (2) anxiety leads to poor performance; and (3) that patient care is thus impoverished. These 'deductions' are particularly worthy of scrutiny as they form the basis for many writers' initial concern and eventually suggested actions and have significantly permeated the nursing literature.

One can firstly question whether anxiety is necessarily 'a bad thing'. It is a natural reaction to stressful conditions and is an alternative description for the general mobilization which energized the individual to do something about that condition. It is not therefore *per se* an abnormal reaction as many writers imply. Secondly there is no clear prediction from anxiety to behaviour. The resulting action may be against, and thus remove, the pressure — i.e. an adaptive coping reaction — or defensive withdrawal allowing the situation to worsen — a generally (although not always) maladaptive strategy. Just as neat *general* conclusions cannot be reached, at an individual case level the precise role of anxiety is even more difficult to predict. It will vary from individual to individual, and from environment to environment, and over time for a given individual.

With direct reference to the quality of patient care, research results suggest caution in assuming relationships for anxiety. Whilst some writers claim to show direct relationships between patient recovery rates and nursing staff morale (e.g. Revans, 1959), others have been surprised at their failure to find a direct link between these key variables. Dutton (1962) found that student teachers' effectiveness was not impaired by anxiety. The latter was however associated with less favourable attitudes toward self and others. In a similar vein Walsh (1971) cites four psychiatric studies which show that effectiveness with patients is not necessarily impaired by student nurses' negative attitudes towards them. Hay and Oken (1972) feel that stress is of some value in maintaining alertness and the ability to respond to patients. (They do however go on to conclude that in the intensive care unit studied: 'there are many signs that its intensity goes well beyond this adaptive level'.)

These findings directly challenge the above assumptions and also suggest potential areas for improvement. If it is not as necessary as has been claimed for nurses to have positive attitudes towards their charges and to be continually anxiety-free perhaps they can be freed from the straight jacket of such expectations. If this could be achieved, anxiety-avoidance will become less necessary as a coping technique and more adaptive alternatives more feasible.

SOURCES OF STRESS AND THEIR EFFECTS

I shall now describe in detail the job pressures identified in the nursing stress literature and derived from my own discussions. The main criterion by which factors are typically assessed as stressful is the writer's own evaluation of the situation. Sometimes this is substantiated by the nurses' observed reactions and these will be reported below as important additional data. Studies which ask the nurse herself to ascribe meaning to her experiences are, in fact, relatively rare. Such data which does exist is usually a by-product of the intervention of psychiatric consultants trying to alleviate stress *via* group meetings rather than the work of academically-based researchers.

The job itself

Several basic facets of nursing are identified in the literature as potential sources of stress. Nursing involves heavy physical work for much of the time and several writers note this as one of the significant if less spectacular pressures (e.g. Hadley, 1977, whose account is drawn from depth interviews with a small sample of nurses). Work overload also figures prominently in many accounts, especially when coupled with staff shortages (Jacobson, 1978). Under such circumstances desirable standards of care can be threatened causing additional pressure. Nurses are affected not only when working under such conditions but feel guilty if forced to take time off because of illness as they are then increasing the workload of colleagues. Finding time to teach patients and new staff represent additional burdens (Hadley, 1977). On some wards workload is variable and having little to do but being expected to look busy may (alternatively) cause pressure and lead to competition for the few available tasks.

The very nature of the nurses' tasks is often highly unpleasant. At the physical level, she is continually dealing with blood, vomit, noxious smells, etc. Emotionally too her environment could be described as 'hazardous'. Hadley quotes a nurse's description of the effect a patient's mood can have on the staff: 'There is a lot of sadness around a hospital . . . . . If you come in tired or depressed even the smallest thing will bother you — just as in any other kind of work. But a hospital is different because you are working around so many depressed people'. Speaking about a specific case she went on to say: 'This was very upsetting to him and us. It (his depression) made us feel like failures. Situations like that we take home at night . . . and fret about them'.

To perform her work adequately the nurse is often dependent on equipment and a ready supply of drugs. Uncertainty about these can also be pressures (Hadley, 1977; Laube, 1973).

Nurses typically work shifts and unsocial hours which can be both physically and socially unsettling. Another factor which contributes to low basic levels of job 'comfort' is low pay. This can both devalue the status of their work and cut nurses off from adequate leisure during which to recover from stress.

Returning to the work environment, a repeated complaint in the literature is the lack of privacy for the nurse. Not only can this be stressful in itself if she is always 'in public' but it means there is nowhere to get away for a few moments to cope with any stress she feels. (Obviously hosptial environments vary but my own discussions suggest that in the UK the sluice is the nurse's traditional private sanctuary.)

Uncertainty and responsibility

Several diverse accounts of stress in the literature are underpinned by two related themes — those of uncertainty and concerns about responsibility (e.g. Laube, 1973; Price and Bergen, 1977). In nursing, 'emergencies' are frequent, but this does not mean that staff are ever likely to be able to treat them as pure routine (e.g. Kopel, 1977). Staff working in the casualty or emergency ward in a hospital are reported to be continually anxious about what they might have to face. Doing night duty also represents a combination of high responsibility with uncertainty with which staff can find it difficult to cope. High absentee rates are reported for both circumstances by my 'informants' as indications that such duties are experienced as particularly stressful. Further indications of 'retreat' when faced with the potential stress of responsibility are complaints that one has been inadequately prepared and attempts to clarify 'whose responsibility it is'. The weight of responsibility in nursing is obviously heavy and appeared as a dominant concern in the literautre and my discussion. As a result clearly understood demarcations between roles are welcomed. Pressure results when these roles become blurred — on intensive care units, for example, or when an individual doctor allows or asks nurses to take on additional responsibilities. Going outside established guidelines creates tensions and there is continual awareness that if something goes wrong staff are likely to lose organizational support if they have done so. A common consequence of job stress is that its effects spill over into life outside work. Hadley's (1977) material suggests that responsibility plays a major part in this: 'If I have a really bad day, I'm ruined the rest of the night . . . . I guess it's because we are dealing with people's lives'.

A small scale but valuable study of a more unusual emergency situation is that reported by Laube (1973). He interviewed 27 registered nurses who went on duty when Hurricane Celia struck in 1970. The main stresses for this group were excessive physical demands and concern for their own and their patients' safety. Approximately a quarter of the nurses showed some effects of the stress during their period of duty and sought early relief. Two major reactions were reported: some became irritable, others cried. A significant feature of the study was the researcher's follow-up of nurses who failed to report for duty during the hurricane. Among their reasons, fear of inadequacy was a repeated concern, and again draws together the two themes identified above.

Relationships with patients and phases of illness

The nurse's relationship with the patient is obviously a key element in her working life and thus in the latter's potential to cause stress. (Its central importance is evidenced, for example, in the findings reported below which indicate that anxiety-avoidance is achieved primarily by reducing patient contact.) Weller and Miller (1977) put the point, made by many writers, most simply — the nurse is in continual attendance and so 'takes the brunt' of patient care.

The intimacy of contact alone can be a pressure, especially for the young, relatively inexperienced nurse. Sometimes issues are raised explicitly if, for example, male patients make sexual advances toward female staff (Simon and Whiteley, 1977).

Establishing satisfactory relationships with patients can be complicated by several factors. Often there is a cultural or a class difference between the nurse and the patient. The former may therefore not understand the latter's frame of reference and so may be unable to assess their suffering (Davitz et al. 1969) or level of anxiety (Schwap et al. 1970). Sudnow (1967) found that (middle class) staff were often derogatory about lower class patients. Nurses and their charges may differ in their expectations of appropriate behaviour, causing stress for both parties. Glaser and Strauss (1966) report that staff are particularly upset when patients die 'unacceptably' (for example, withdrawing and closing their eyes against the world, or screaming continually) or attempt suicide.

Personality differences may also cause tensions. The nurse is required to deal with a large, changing, and widely diverse patient population. How she treats individuals requires considerable sensitivity to how they will react. This is often very difficult to assess in a short time for someone who may anyway not be feeling or behaving 'true' to self. Often the patient's personality is not readily apparent on admission to hospital. He/she may be depressed because of their illness and be assessed negatively by the staff. Later emergence of their more typical character may even be resisted by the nurse as disconfirming her original negative (or positive) impression (Gunther, 1977). Sometimes staff read characteristics into a comatose patient and are then disappointed when the latter regains consciousness.

Compliant behaviour on the part of the patient generally makes the nurse's life easier and several writers have focused on how 'bothersome' a patient is as a factor contributing to stress. This does however ignore possible complexities. Bothersome patients can provide amusement for others on the ward and help relieve the tension by taking on the role of 'joker'. Should their behaviour become too extreme, however, they are likely to be 'brought back into line' by disapproval in the reactions of staff and of cooperative patients (the majority). Keller (1971) showed, for example, that nurses provide more services to compliant than to noncompliant patients. The staff, Roth (1972) concluded, 'feels justified in refusing services to those who complain or resist treatment or refuse to follow procedures or make trouble in any other way'. The results of a study by Miller (1976) supports a less simple view by demonstrating that organizational norms and expectations play a part in determining what is 'bothersome' behaviour and to what extent this causes difficulties for staff.

Miller's work leads from suggestions that increasing education and sophistication amongst the general population is causing a growing scepticism about the quality of professional services and a 'revolt of the client' (Haug and Sussman, 1969). He expects this to generate role strains for nursing staff, as patients increasingly fail to conform to the ideal behaviours of trust, passivity, and cooperativeness. Miller tested his hypotheses in three contrasting hospital settings. Ratings of patients' medical and hospital knowledge were compared with nurses' evaluations of them on 13 (interview-derived) strain-producing behaviours and an overall 'bothersomeness' scale. (The study has been criticized by Chen, 1977, for producing no evidence to support the assumption that more knowledgeable patients tend to make more demands on staff and for failing to investigate what the latter feels might be a more influential variable — that of patients' personality.) His results are an outstanding illustration of the complex interaction of the various factors involved. Over the sample as a whole the hypothesis that more knowledgeable patients cause more pressure for staff was not supported, but further examination revealed differential results for the three settings. In the hard-pressed county hospital with its many involuntary patients and low levels of patient knowledge and general literacy, knowledgeable patients were atypical and did cause nurse role strain. Nurses in the prepaid hospital reported much lower work load pressure: patients were seen as part of the 'team' in combating illness and were exposed to a wide array of information and literature both before and during hospitalization. In this environment patients were expected to be active and intelligent and lack of patient education was, in fact, associated with greater strain for the nurses. The third hospital was an elite private establishment with an emphasis on teaching and research activities. Again patient knowledge was high but this appeared to be taken for granted and showed no relationship, either positive or negative, with role strain measures.

These results have several implications for the study of stress amongst nurses. They point to a need to understand the organizational setting as a whole in order to interpret individual findings. They reveal the role played by expectation in translating (or not translating) a particular factor into a source of stress. They also go some way to casting doubt on the often assumed existence of nurse role strain due to diverse patient populations. This latter implication points to the deficiencies of 'outsider' studies and interpretations of the nursing role touched on above. Presumptions that particular job facets will cause stress must be tested out with nurses themselves. Certain apparent stressors may well be revealed as acceptable parts of the job, ones which can ordinarily be contained, stabilized, reduced, or prevented, even sources of satisfaction, once the jobholders themselves are consulted. Should this be the case we can achieve a more discriminating picture of job stress for nurses than is currently available.

Setting aside these methodological qualifications for the moment, there is still in the literature ample evidence of opportunities for nurse-patient relationships to develop into 'battles', as tensions lead one to displace anxiety and anger onto the other (Gunther, 1970). Relatives can also be drawn into the exchanges of complaints and antagonisms which ensue. Such developments are particularly well illustrated in the literature relating to phases of illness. Glaser and Strauss (1964), for example, describe the especially tense and complex relationships which can arise around a dying patient. From their observational data they identify four 'awareness contexts' for each of which they describe the social structural conditions, typical interactions, consequences, etc.

These contexts are (i) 'closed', in which the patient is unaware that he/she is dying and staff strive to prevent him/her finding out; (ii) 'suspicion', in which the patient suspects he/she is dying and staff try to allay these suspicions; (iii) 'mutual pretence', in which both parties are aware that death is imminent but there is an implicit mutual agreement to pretend otherwise; and (iv) 'open', in which death is faced openly and honestly by both parties. Each context has implications for patient-nurse relationships and for pressure on the latter who is the staff member who bears most of the burden for maintaining a given awareness context. In the context of suspicion, for example, there are the strains of tactics and countertactics as the patient continually tries to trap the nurse into confirming his/her worst fears and the latter offers alternative, non-malignant interpretations of signs and symptoms. Whilst it may seem ideal in some ways, the open awareness context is also potentially stressful. The nurse may find it difficult to discuss death and dying openly and may feel inadequate in the emotional care she gives.

Glaser and Strauss restrict their interest to the development of awareness between staff and patients. The more general concept of 'phases of illness' also has implications of pressure for the nurses. There is an increasing interest in identifying phases through which patients pass. The research-based paradigm of Kubler-Ross (1969) is now widely accepted as a guide to the stages of dying. His five stages (in which open awareness is assumed) are 'denial and isolation', 'anger', 'bargaining', 'depression', and 'acceptance'. The progress of patients adjusting to a major disability has also been approached from this viewpoint. Weller and Miller (1977) distinguish four stages in the development of spinal injury patients: shock, denial, anger, and depression. Strain (1978) proffers a more psychoanalytic model of a sequence of acute illness which parallels the course of early human development including separation anxiety, fear of the loss of love and approval, etc. Gunther (1977) develops a similar argument in relation to the lengthy rehabilitation patient (after an amputation, for example) for whom outcomes are typically highly uncertain and the illness is a severe threat to core identity. In such circumstances ordinary patient care problems are intensified and their study is therefore both of benefit in its own right and to illuminate more widely applicable issues.

Each of the phases identified have implications for patients' thoughts, feelings and coping activities which in turn affect nursing personnel. The literature is rich with dynamic illustrations of the form the resulting exchanges can take. The patient's reactions to his/her illness at a particular stage can, for example, help or hinder the nurse in her work. An angry patient may disrupt activities on the ward and resist the nurse's attempts to administer care. The latter may also find it difficult to follow shifts in behaviour and, it may seem, 'personality', as the patient's relationship to his/her illness develops.

There is wide agreement on what Strain terms staff's 'dual' responsibility in this context. The theme of several writers is that the patient acts as a 'mirror for medical staff portraying before them their own weaknesses, vulnerabilities, and inevitable death. The impact of this mirror is accentuated when the patient is similar to the nurse and identification occurs. As they are vulnerable to the same stresses as the patient, staff must therefore recognize and cope with their own anxieties in order to achieve the emotional stability from which to offer adequate care. Secondly they must understand the meaning (both conscious and unconscious) of the different phases of illness for the patient. Here the literature is particularly vocal on the many, and all too common, repercussions of staff's failure to understand. The nurse may become engulfed in the patient's reactions at any stage. She may find it comforting to join in denial, for example, but is most at risk during the highly 'contagious' phase of depression. She may discourage the patient from moving into an adaptive, but 'anti-social' phase such as regression (Gunther, 1977) or anger (Weller and Miller, 1977) because of the emotional repercussions for herself. This may lead to staff-patient 'battles' which the former feel they must win: 'one has the impression that each such victory is seen by the staff not only as necessary to the ultimate salvation of the patient's rehabilitation goals but is essential if some aspects of their own inner equilibrium is to be maintained' (Gunther, 1977).

Relationships with relatives, as always, add a further complicating factor. They represent a third party with their own separate attribution of meanings, reactions, and needs for support. Weller and Miller (1977) discuss the possible repercussions if the timing of the three parties is out of phase. They go on to suggest that both staff and relatives 'need to acknowledge their own feelings as reflective of, but separate from, the patient's needs (for denial)'. In the dynamic, flexible relationship between patient and care-giver what is considered acceptable and adaptive behaviour will be continually changing, for example. Staff will approve of passivity and dependence immediately after surgery, but will later require activity and independence as signs of recovery. If some detachment is not achieved both patient and staff member alike will be highly vulnerable to negative feedback from the other — exhortations to be a good, cheerful patient from the former; expressions of anger and rejection from the latter. If the nurse is unable to understand, discount and react 'appropriately' the strain of the relationship will cause her stress.

How nurses should react to patients in itself presents a critical dilemma. Gunther (1977) suggests they typically avoid empathy (with their own as well as patients' feelings) in order to shelter themselves from distress. He argues that 'In order to discover what a sick person is experiencing . . . one must split a selective part of one's own responsive self and offer it in a temporary controlled merger with that person'. In a similar vein Weller and Miller (1977) advocate authenticity in dealing with patients: 'Reacting as a real person helps the patient to feel more real and valued as a person'. They recognize however that such behaviour requires more sensitivity, involvement, and energy than does avoiding contact.

Several authors' accounts contain the idea of 'negotiations' between nurse and patient to resolve difficulties in their relationship. These may revolve around how each will behave toward the other; the way in which required hospital routines are executed or the amount of attention the nurse will give the patient, for example (Glaser and Strauss, 1964). For the nurse these represent potential pressures at two levels. In the relationship with the patient she must achieve a standard of care and involvement acceptable to both parties or suffer the tension of mismatch. She must also achieve 'balance' in terms of her wider pattern of responsibilities, duties, and activities. Sometimes agreeing to patients' demands can cause her professional conflicts. She may relax discipline, for example, but risk being disciplined herself if superiors find out.

Relationships with doctors

Relationships with doctors are another potential source of pressure. (Any tension that does exist here can also further aggravate nurse-patient conflicts as most of the issues involved centre around patient care.) The traditional role segregation between the responsible diagnosing and treating doctor and the caring nurse is not easily maintained even if both parties agree with its underlying justice. As the nurse is in constant attendance she may feel she is more aware of the patient's condition than the doctor is, yet she has no official role as his advisor. The extent to which she tries to assume such a role and the tactics she adopts are delicate issues. A repeated theme in the literature is that of the nurse feeling 'abandoned' by the doctor (e.g. Bilodeau, 1973). He is often not there when emergencies arise, according to many accounts he actively avoids more difficult or dying patients. The doctor may leave the nurse to deal with relatives. The latter are, anyway, more likely to find her approachable and to persist in questioning with which they would not trouble the doctor. In addition the doctor is not required to tell the nurse his diagnosis and prognosis for the patient and she may find acting in ignorance difficult.

These conflicts become particularly tense in relation to special cases of one kind or another. The blurring of responsibilities on the intensive care unit will be discussed below. In some circumstances nurses may disagree with the treatment a doctor is giving. This happens particularly when they feel that a patient's life, and therefore suffering, is being prolonged unnecessarily and is often associated with having become more emotionally involved than usual with the patient.

The nurse's professional status

Implicit in the nurse-doctor conflict theme above is the suggestion that the nurse's relatively low status can contribute as a cause of stress. Hadley (1977) suggests this is particularly true for the general (as opposed to specialist) nurses who the media portray as relatively lowly: 'They think if a staff nurse were any good she wouldn't just be a staff nurse'. Whilst enjoying her job she may then be made to feel inferior and that she is being cheated of appropriate social standing and salary levels.

Moves are afoot in both the US and UK to increase the professional status of nurses. Several factors combine at the moment to block the natural evolution of such developments. Clashes with the role definitions of other personnel and the threats such moves constitute are major factors. Severin and Becker (1974) focus on these as major areas of resistance to nurses taking on the new responsibilities of which they are capable. They describe an experiment in which this proved highly possible practically. Psychiatric nurses took on the role of consultant managing patient referrals. They successfully handled 66% of new patients, organizing their treatment plans, without calling for further advice. Also relevant as barriers to the future enlargement of the nursing role are nurses' own anxieties about the demarcation of responsibilities.

Relatives

As some of the above material has already implied contacts with relatives are an additional source of pressure for the nurse. The nurse's responsibilities in these relationships are poorly defined, but many authors suggest that she has a key role to play in helping relatives cope with their own stress and maintain a viable relationship with the patient. Weller and Miller (1977) note that nurses have most opportunities for observing family members' behaviour and interaction with the patient and propose a further role for them in feeding information back to other professionals (e.g. the social worker) involved in care. It is even more difficult for the nurse to get to know relatives (than patients) and she will often be faced with imparting highly charged information to them with little idea of the effects it will have.

Immediate working relationships

Working relationships with immediate colleagues and superiors are more often mentioned in the literature as positive than as negative forces in the stress-satisfaction balance of nursing. All my 'expert witnesses', however, focused on these as potential stressors. Because of the tempo of nursing life, interpersonal tensions with immediate colleagues can be accentuated. The most critical relationship, however, is that with the ward sister. A hospital is essentially organized in 'divisions' (wards) with a sister at the head of each. She plays a major part in determining how her unit is run, its organizational 'climate' and the standards of care adhered to. From a nurse's point of view, I am told, sisters are 'good' or 'bad'. Good sisters provide support for their subordinates and act as an intermediary between them and the highly bureaucratized hierarchy. Bad sisters not only neglect such 'personnel' facets of their roles, but cause additional pressures in their turn. If they are particularly individualistic and critical they represent a further factor encouraging dependence on one's superiors and the passing of responsibility up the hierarchy.

Fulfilling other people's expectations of a nurse and inherent conflicts

Many of the factors identified as causing stress relate back to the strains of fulfilling other people's expectations of a nurse — of combining expertise with detached concern. These expectations are held not only by the hospital's 'clients' — patients and relatives — but are also generally fostered by her colleagues and superiors. To question them would pose a serious threat to the often delicately-maintained balance of individual and professional identity. However much individuals may have personal doubts, therefore, they will try to maintain this image in their own behaviour and to expect it of their colleagues, particularly those in training.

These expectations can cause pressure in at least two different ways. Maintenance of this professional 'front' can be difficult, especially when it contradicts the nurses' inner feelings. Secondly there are inherent contradictions within the role requirements and the nurse may experience these as painful conflicts. That between emotional involvement and detachment is one of the more obvious. There are also opposing pressures on her to do all she can to save life yet to continually acknowledge and deal positively with death. Drotar (1976) identified 'not knowing what was right' as a major area of concern for nurses attending his staff meetings. For example, should a critically ill infant be kept alive artificially for several months, and how to react to his parents who express their own ambivalence in anger against the staff. Such conflicts appear to remain largely unexpressed and unexplored in day-to-day working and in preparatory training.

Expectations act on a further dimension to aggravate stress for the nurse. A fundamental norm of the service is that nurses' own personal needs should be ignored and are not 'legitimate' causes for concern. (Several articles about nurses' stress illustrate the power of this ordering of priorities by the ease with which they were diverted to taking the patient's or relative's perspective — e.g. Bilodeau, 1973; Strain, 1978.) This norm is fostered by all parties in the work environment and acts against nurses' own stress being seen as a 'legitimate' subject for discussion or action.

An illustration of the way in which changes in circumstances can throw the delicate balance of a nurse's identity in relation to her work into disarray is given in Char and McDermott's (1972) account of the legalization of abortion in Hawaii in 1970. The authors were called in to three hospitals as psychiatric consultants once the force of nurses' emotional reactions to this liberalization were appreciated. The problems they identified highlight causes of stress stated more generally elsewhere in this chapter and help to show their particular action.

The authors found that nurses' favourable intellectual and professional attitudes toward abortion were soon transformed into strong emotional reactions against. They overidentified with the aborted foetus, felt considerable hostility toward most of the abortion patients and were acutely aware of the conflict between their training to save life and the new instructions to 'discard' the foetus. As a result they came fundamentally to question their roles as nurses. Factors which helped to compound their reactions were their own personal 'status' in relation to the topic (whether they were themselves adopted or felt jealous of the patients' apparently liberated sex lives); the anonymity of the short-stay abortion patients; confusion about how to act towards patients (was this a happy or a sad event?); feelings of resentment towards doctors who were performing the abortions but leaving them (the nurses) to cope with patients and the lack of the ritual sanctioning document previously required.

Char and McDermott give an evocative description of the nurses' 'transient reactive disorder' to this acute pressure: 'In varying degrees they all showed symptoms of anxiety and depression. They complained about being tired and about being unhappy about their work; they cried too easily and got angry too quickly; they had difficulty sleeping and had bad dreams; during the day they found themselves preoccupied with disturbing thoughts about their abortion work; and they were overly sensitive when their friends teased them about working in a 'slaughter house' .... They were confused and uncertain about their role and function as nurses and no longer felt proud of their hospital and their work.' It is interesting that these symptoms were originally blamed on overwork rather than assigned to the later apparent root cause. (As overload is a commonly cited source of stress, it is worth contemplating whether similar 'deceptions' are happening elsewhere. Perhaps overload is presented as a 'respectable' complaint and one to which solutions are potentially forthcoming. If so, as researchers, we must learn to probe more deeply rather than take this explanation at face value.) Once the above issues had been revealed and openly addressed the nurses' problems were resolved and they regained equilibrium in relation to their work.

Conflicts appear in several contexts as sources of stress for nurses. The richness of the qualitative data typically available suggests a link between this, guilt as a resulting emotion and feeling emotionally drained — an effect of nursing to which many writers refer (e.g. Gunther, 1977; Kopel, 1977; Weller and Miller, 1977). This speculative sequence of effect is supported in practice by the 'psychic energy' oriented approach adopted by many of those called in to help alleviate nurses' stress.

Training

The above role requirements of a nurse are particularly hard for the student to meet. One contact spoke of her early experiences as a trainee nurse to whom patients and their relatives looked for reassurance — 'I was more scared than they were but I wasn't allowed to show it .... You're suddenly required to become a diplomat but you don't always feel that way'. In other ways too training is a vulnerable time for the young nurse, she is inexperienced but is faced with the full force of pressures in the nursing environment. Many stimuli cannot be 'watered down' to a suitable training level!

Several writers criticize the nature of training given and question its adequacy in preparing staff for the real pressures of the job. Kopel (1977) feels, for example, that there is insufficient and late attention to dealing with death and dying.

Menzies (1970) points to some of the more practical difficulties associated with training in the general teaching hospital she studied. Student nurses formed a large part of the general work force but the hospital's staffing was organized primarily around patient care rather than their training needs. Menzies cites disrupted and curtailed training as a further pressure for the student. She is yet another source who comments on withdrawal from duty in one form or another as a symptom of stress. A third of the student nurses did not complete training (most left voluntarily) and staff transfer and sickness rates were high.

A further potentially stressful facet of training is the tension which surrounds assessment. Besides the more obvious ways in which this can contribute to stress, an interpersonal dimension is added. The ward sister plays an important role in assessment and has the power to 'make or break' a trainee.

The organization as a source of stress

Bureaucracy, excessive paperwork, and interdepartmental demarcation disputes are features of many large organizations and hospitals are not exceptions. Such factors appear in the literature as additional pressures on nurses. There is, however, so much ambiguity surrounding the function of the highly hierarchic organization of nursing that this deserves a special qualifying note. This hierarchy is revealed as in part a reaction to stress — it reduces ambiguities about responsibility definitions — and as a source of support. Many factors have the potential to be sources of both stress and satisfaction, this is one of the more markedly 'ambiguous' elements in the profile of this occupational group.

Conflicts between work and home lives

Several of the pressures already identified contribute to conflicts between work and home for the nurses. Unsocial hours put strains on social and family relationships. Becoming emotionally involved with patients can lead to taking one's stresses home with potentially detrimental consequences (e.g. Hadley, 1977). Pressures of concern for family can spill over and affect work performance (Laube, 1973). This area is one which is likely to increase as a source of pressure. The tradition of the nurse as a single woman is fast disappearing and most now have family responsibilities which are important in the balance of their lives overall.

Satisfactions

Before proceeding to the two areas of special interest, I should like briefly to mention the satisfactions which balance pressures for nurses (these receive further attention in relation to intensive care nursing below). Compared with the complex array of potential stressors, the list of satisfactions mentioned in the literature is strikingly short. Three main themes emerge. Two focus on relationships with patients and their relatives — they are doing things to help patients and receiving feedback that one's efforts have been effective and/or appreciated. The potential for these to contribute to stress or to falter due to stress experienced from other sources must therefore be borne in mind. A further major source of satisfaction comes from relationships with colleagues, but this too is open to the same qualifications.

DEATH AND DYING

A central issue on which much of the literature focuses is the nurses' continual exposure to death and dying. Such exposure is greater on some wards and in some hospitals than in others but is part of the experience of all nurses at some time. This section covers three related areas: the problems presented by the care of such patients; nurses' reactions to patients' deaths and the concern for their own mortality with which nurses are confronted.

Because of the immediacy and continuity of their contact with patients, nurses become more involved in their fates than do any other group of medical staff. Current trends in patient care toward increasing hospitalization of dying patients (even in the United States in 1963, 53% of all deaths occurred in hospitals and many more in nursing homes; Fulton, 1964) and in nursing practice toward minimizing the number of nurses dealing with any one individual (for the latter's emotional benefit) are likely to increase these potential sources of stress in the foreseeable future.

Care of the dying

Glaser and Strauss (1964) and Sudnow (1967) give particularly valuable accounts of the social frame of interpretation which surrounds a dying patient and the ways in which 'terminality' is shown through staff behaviour and organizational procedures. The strength of feeling associated with caring for the dying is evident from the coping strategies nurses use. Glaser and Strauss (1968) suggest that an impersonal attitude is a necessary protective shield and many of the strategies revolve around maintaining this by avoiding or minimizing contact with the patient. The nurse may simply avoid the company of a dying patient (Sudnow, 1967). When she is forced to attend him/her she may concentrate on medical rather than emotional aspects of her role. She may avoid or control conversation if it is likely to stray into sensitive areas such as symptoms or the patient's plans for the future (Glaser and Strauss, 1966). Several authors suggest that nurses prefer dying patients to be heavily sedated so they are not faced with these strains.

Professional considerations also play a part. Medical staff are confronted with their powerlessness to save lives and with their responsibility to give adequate medical and emotional care even to the dying. 'Avoidance tactics' help reduce patient contact, but staff may experience conflict and guilt because they feel they are not doing enough (Schowalter, 1975).

Other pressures at this time centre on resolving the uncertainties of whether a patient is in fact 'terminal' and ascertaining the time and manner of death (Glaser and Strauss, 1966). An unexpected death is particularly 'uncomfortable' for staff, and there is the added threat that they may subsequently be charged with incompetence. Staff build up expectations about the progress of a patient's illness and it can also be upsetting to them if he/she does not die as expected, but 'lingers'.

Further pressures are the changes that take place in the previously cared-for patient at the point of death. The nurse and patient may have different expectations of how one 'should' die and the dying person's loss of personal dignity can upset and anger staff (Schowalter, 1975). The movement of the corpse to the mortuary when it is no longer treated as a human being is a critical point. Nurses are reported to be afraid of discovering a dead patient and to avoid whenever possible dealing with the corpse (Sudnow, 1967). The tension which occurs at this boundary between life and death is further evidenced in the fears nurses express at the possible premature burial of a patient (e.g. Schowalter, 1975). In several of the more personally revealing accounts nurses report 'furtive' practices of checking for vital signs in the patient even when wrapping the body or taking it to the mortuary.

Reactions to patient death

Some writers suggest that the death of a patient is not necessarily a source of stress for staff. Sudnow (1967), for example, gives an impression of detachment in his discussion of 'counting deaths'. He also discusses organizational procedures which contribute to making death 'routine'. On wards with high death rates the necessary 'morgue bundle' and forms were kept in stock, on others they were acquired individually as necessary. In a questionnaire study Shusterman and Sechrest (1973) found that nurses distinguished between the death of a friend at which they would be upset and that of a patient which would not cause them significant distress.

There is however substantial agreement in the literature that nurses find it more difficult to accept the death of some patients than of others. They become more 'attached' to children, young adults, those with whom they personally identify and those with a high 'social loss'. Several writers (for example, Glaser and Strauss, 1964) use the latter to cover a range of variables which contribute to the individual's worth to his/her relatives and/or society. Famous or beautiful people or those with family responsibilities have a high social loss. Drunks, criminals, and suicides, on the other hand, are generally disapproved of by medical staff (Sudnow, 1967). In such situations the warmth of contact is likely to benefit the patient and their family and provide the nurse with satisfaction of feedback that she has helped, but will greatly increase her sense of loss if the patient dies. Melia (1977) suggests that these feelings are accentuated if it is her duty to attend to the dead body.

Several authors give a more differentiated view still of nurses' reactions to death. Schowalter's paper (1975), for example, is highly revealing. His data is based on paediatric nurses' dreams and the weekly staff meetings in which they were used as material. Several factors accentuated nurses' emotional reactions to a child's death. The longer a nurse had known the child the more likely she was to be depressed following his/her death. She was also less likely to agree with protracted but futile attempts to save him/her, an attitude that could put her in direct conflict with doctors and hospital policy especially in institutions which pursue experimental treatments for research purposes. Schowalter found that having mixed feelings toward the patient was also associated with greater grief at their death. Dealing with patients they disliked was particularly stressful. Nurses commonly felt guilty that they had not done enough for a troublesome or complaining child and this could accentuate their conflicts about the child's death: 'When you don't like a kid who's dying and you know you're working with him, it's really hard to get up and get to work in the morning. It's like it's more than just two separate things, but as if they climb on each other to make one gigantic problem. The scariest part is, what if you want them to die? Or, does even wondering if you wish it mean that you really do? You know in your mind that your wishes don't have any power anyway, but in your heart you're not so sure, and it makes you feel like a rotten person'.

The nurses' dreams were remarkably consistent in their underlying themes. Typically a dying patient was portrayed as well or a dead patient alive. Almost always they asked something of the nurse, the latter experiencing this as a rebuke, as evidence that she had not done enough, and such doubts were often expressed openly in the dream. Sometimes death would occur during the dream, in some way reaffirming reality. Schowalter identified these themes as indicating guilt and remorse and the acting out of wish fulfillment on the nurses' parts. He also reports on the range of reactions of his paediatric nurses immediately after a death. One is confronted with her own mortality — 'I always feel that this is going to happen to me some day .... I automatically treat the body with more respect.' — one becomes angry with everything around, feeling trapped in the conflict between a natural sadness and grief and nursing training to show no emotion; another spends more time with healthier patients and another is more appreciative of her own life and vitality.

Very similar themes to those above are developed by Price and Bergen (1977) who were invited by intensive care unit nurses to help explore the latter's feelings that 'things were crazy'. The authors distinguish themselves from other writers who have portrayed death as an external event to be coped with. They feel one significant, but largely neglected source of stress comes from the internal demand nurses make on themselves to experience their relationship with death as meaningful. That nurses feel themselves in some way culpable for patients' deaths comes across strongly in the material the authors present. From their group meetings, Price and Bergen abstract two conflicting themes in nurses' accounts. The latter feel a helplessness at 'not being able to do more' for patients, revealing unrealistic (possibly unexplored) expectations of what is possible. At the same time there was the feeling that they are doing 'too much' and that their techniques and gadgetry 'prevented nature from taking its course'. Nurses directed considerable hostility toward doctors on the unit who they felt were playing a false role — 'both God and not God at the same time' — but it was readily apparent that they were in fact wrestling with their own 'false role' in these conflicts. The authors explain the nurses' dilemmas in terms of the expectations built up during training that they can in some way be held responsible for patients' deaths and of their needs to deny the fact of their own ultimate death. These are reinforced by the taboo of silence which surrounds death in medical circles just as it does in society at large.

Personal death anxiety

The third facet of involvement with death identified as a pressure is the threat it constitutes to the nurse's psychic equilibrium by confronting her with her own mortality. Weissman (1972) suggests medical staff may encourage patients to deny the possibility of death in order not to disrupt their own protective denial.

In the sub-area of literature on death anxiety the orientation of many writers is still that of ideal conditions for patient care. 'In reviewing the literature on care of the dying, it becomes evident that ... although persons around the dying may be afraid of death themselves, this should not influence the care the dying receive' (Geizhals, 1975). In terms of research methodology this is a particularly mechanistic area. Authors seem more concerned with the structure, development, and internal consistency of death anxiety scales than with achieving an in-depth dynamic understanding of relationships with death. Questionnaire studies (often with low response rates and in discussion highly critical of the tools they have used) dominate and seem particularly unlikely to achieve the latter, more valuable (I feel) objective. In view of these criticisms the results of such studies will only be briefly summarized here.

Geizhals (1975) found that intensive care nurses and occupational therapists who had only student experience of working with the dying scored higher on her death anxiety scale than did occupational therapists who had either gone on to work with dying patients or had never done so. She found her results difficult to explain by hypothesized self-selection for particular kinds of work based on concern about death as an important factor. In a more questioning paper, Denton and Wisenbaker (1977) explore the largely untested assumption that greater experience of death reduced medical staff's death anxiety. They criticize previous researchers for using a uni-dimensional concept of death experience and were able in their analysis of already existing data to relate three separate dimensions — death of a close friend or relative; experience of seeing a violent death and subjective (near) death experience — to scores on Templer's (1970) Death Anxiety Scale. Their sample was (76) nurses and nursing students. Experiences of violent and subjective death but not of a 'close' death were statistically associated with lower death anxiety scores, this partially supporting their hypothesis of a multi-faceted concept. Controlling for age and work experience did not alter these basic findings but did suggest that relationships are more complex than had appeared and warrant further research.

A further refinement of research methods is shown in the work of Shusterman and Sechrest (1973) who developed a questionnaire tapping six 'conceptually distinct' aspects of attitudes toward death. These are 'fear of death of self', 'fear of death of others', 'fear of dying of self', 'fear of dying of others', satisfaction with the nursing profession's standard care of dying patients and self confidence in ability to care for dying patients. Their target sample were (188) registered nurses in the surgical and medical wards of a general hospital, but their results are somewhat marred by the high refusal rate — nearly 50%, a sign of the sensitivity of the area under consideration. Overall the sample expressed very little anxiety about death. Their self confidence in their ability to care for dying patients was, however, unrelated to this composure and was relatively low. Satisfaction with the profession's standards of care for the dying were also very low. In this study age appeared as a significant factor. Older nurses were less personally anxious and more accepting of conventional procedures for managing the dying patient. Shusterman and Sechrest explain this in terms of self-selection for the job of nurse. Again the researchers call for 'attention to measurement problems'.

INTENSIVE CARE NURSING

A new area of nursing whose potential to cause stress is highly apparent is that of 'intensive care'. Originally attention was focused on the implications for the patient of being put in this highly restrictive and threatening environment, now concern is developing for nurses who must staff the units. I have chosen to concentrate this literature in a separate section to preserve its integrity, but its association with sections elsewhere in the chapter will be continually apparent.

An intensive care unit is a relatively small ward in which critically ill patients are kept alive and continually monitored with the aid of highly sophisticated machines. Emergencies such as cardiac arrests are commonplace, as is death. Staff are highly trained and skilled and units have relatively high staff to patient ratios. Typically a nurse will be assigned responsibility for one or two patients whom she must attend constantly.

Studies reported in this section of the literature are frequently the result of observational (participant or otherwise) research methods or direct consultation and have descriptive richness, and horror, lacking in the questionnaire studies such as those on death anxiety. They thus form an invaluable complement to the latter. In this section I shall deal firstly with the pressures apparent in the intensive care unit (ICU) and then with the methods nurses use to cope identified in the literature. Some writers have balanced the picture with a view of the job's satisfactions and these will also be briefly considered. Some of the more specific suggestions which have been made for reducing ICU stress will then be discussed.

Job pressures: the ICU environment

Hay and Oken (1972) describe their first impressions on entering an ICU graphically: 'Initially the greatest impact comes from the intricate machinery, with its flashing lights, buzzing and beeping monitors, gurgling suction pumps and whooshing respirators. Simultaneously, one sees many people rushing around busily performing lifesaving tasks. The atmosphere is not unlike that of the tension-charged strategic war bunker. With time, habituation occurs, but the evercontinuing stimuli decrease the overload threshold and contribute to stress at times of crisis.' The unit is filled with 'desperately ill people' and, they say, 'It is hard to imagine any other situation that involves such intimacy with the frightening, repulsive, and forbidden'. Many patients rely wholly on machines to stay alive and it is often difficult to maintain an appreciation that they are still 'human'. For the nurse this continual bombardment with 'affect-laden stimuli' is likely to cause distress and conflict. She may also be threatened physically by infection, inadequately screened portable X-ray equipment, etc. 'To all this is added a repetitive contact with death. And, if exposure to death is merely frequent, that to dying is constant' (Hay and Oken, 1973).

At a more specific level the sophistication, noise and potential for breakdown of vital equipment may be pressures. Lack of privacy is again a concern.

The patient and his/her care

In this situation the patient is typically wholly dependent on the nurse and may need considerable emotional as well as physical care. He/she may not, however, be able to communicate with staff, may not understand what they are trying to do and may cope with stress in ways which frighten nurses or make their jobs more difficult — by removing monitor leads, crying, or constantly asking about death, for example (Bilodeau, 1973). The high turnover of patients on the units makes it even more difficult for the nurse to build up rapport with any one individual. Frequent deaths mean the nurse is continually facing the loss of patients which may give rise to feelings of anxiety, anger, failure, or guilt. Hay and Oken (1972) suggest that the ICU nurse 'lives chronically under a cloud of latent anxiety' because of the risk of making a (life-endangering) mistake. The continuity and initimacy of care and the patient being conscious and verbal are additional factors (to those in the section on Death above) fostering attachment in this setting.

Even if the patient improves and is transferred to another ward this is unlikely to afford the satisfaction of discharge, and it is difficult to follow up patients to receive more positive longterm feedback (Drotar, 1976).

Workload

Workload on the ICU is heavy and often highly physically demanding. Patients must be constantly monitored and their hour by hour progress charted. This background of incessant repetitive routine is in direct conflict with the swift, flexible behaviour required when emergencies (the unit's other 'routine') arise. Another conflict is that whilst the nurse is expected to be highly sensitive to subtle changes in the patient's condition she is typically kept so busy collecting and charting information that she has little time to interpret it adequately (Hay and Oken, 1972). Everyday nursing tasks, such as changing a bed, become skilled and demanding activities on an ICU contributing further to the workload. Having to instruct and make allowance for new personnel can be experienced as an additional burden. There are no slack times on the ICU, no nights, weekends or holidays when the workload can be wound down. Instead the unit may become busier at such times as other wards in the hospital divert more patients to it. Staffing can thus be a problem. The specialised nature of tasks on the unit mean it cannot call in untrained temporary help.

Relatives

In this highly charged atmosphere relatives contribute an important complicating element. There are usually no set visiting times allowing them to come and go as they please. Their anxieties and needs for information and reassurance are probably even higher than those of visitors on other wards. They join in competition for the nurse's time and may misinterpret her preoccupation elsewhere. They may channel their anxieties into anger at staff and may even try to interfere actively in patient care.

Relationships within the ICU

Authors differ in the pictures of relationships between staff within the ICU they give. Hay and Oken (1972) concentrate on the beneficial aspects of group cohesion (below); Bilodeau's (1973) account is dominated by competition and conflict. The latter sugests that there is a general rivalry to master technical skills and appear competent which puts individuals, especially newcomers, under considerable pressure. On the other hand, some nurses criticize others for valuing technical skills above the quality of emotional care they give patients. Nurses who are attracted to ICU work are often more strong willed, independent, and aggressive than general nursing staff and personality conflicts may arise. Permanent rather than rotating staff on each shift can also lead to conflicts between groups.

Relationships with other hospital personnel

The ICU is special in many ways and this is reflected by distance between its staff and those on other wards and in the hospital administration. ICU nurses often see those on other wards as less competent than themselves and may even accuse them of incompetence if a previous patient relapses and is returned to the unit. In turn others see the ICU as overstaffed, a place where patients are pampered and nurses enjoy unwarranted status and responsibility.

Several writers have pointed to the 'generation gap' between ICU nurses, typically in their twenties, and hospital administrative staff (e.g. Gardam 1969). The latter are seen as failing to appreciate the 'realities' of work on the unit and so failing to listen to its staff's requests and concerns or provide sufficient support. ICU nurses may be discouraged from asking for advice from supervisors who they see as less technically competent than themselves and, anyway, unsympathetic to their problems.

The normal potential for conflicts between doctors and nurses is increased on the ICU. Some responsibilities have already been reallocated with a subsequent blurring of roles. Nurses are, for example, allowed to perform what were considered doctors' tasks such as interpreting ECGs and dealing with cardiac arrests (Melia, 1977). They are particularly well-placed to have opinions about appropriate patient care and may well disapprove of the doctor's instructions (especially if these involve fruitless prolongation of a patient's life which may upset them emotionally and also add to their workload). In addition, the doctor's immediate availability is essential to the nurse, yet he is often seen as using his prerogative to move freely to be away when crises, especially deaths, occur.

An overview of job pressures

A significant study for its several departures from those mentioned above is that by Jacobson (1976, 1978). A more systematic methodology and an orientation toward nurse rather than researcher definition of stress helps to put the contributing factors identified by other writers in context. At the same time the use of relatively qualitative research methods means her data does not lose altogether the richness of observational material. Jacobson's sample were (87) staff nurses from seven neonatal intensive care units in three American states. Whilst the environments she is describing are therefore slightly different from those studied by other researchers, her work makes a valuable contribution to the literature.

Jacobson first asked the nurses to describe the three most stressful events they had experienced professionally in the last three months. She analysed their replies and identified key elements which appeared to relate to stressfulness. These she categorized under ten headings. In order of frequency of mention these are:

1. Nurses' philosophical-emotional problems;
2. Nurse-doctor problems;
3. Understaffing and overwork;
4. Nurse-nurse problems;
5. Sudden death or relapse of an infant;
6. Insecurity about knowledge and competence;
7. Shock and impact of sights and smells; •
8. Transport (from the referring hospital);
9. Family responsibilities vs work demands; and
10. Bureaucratic-political problems.

This material was then fed back to the original sample who sorted the incidents on a scale from least to most stressful and then for frequency of occurrence. Initial analyses revealed that stressfulness and frequency were not associated. There were also no significant differences between the hospitals studied on the mean stressfulness of the items — a finding which suggests that, especially when dealing with a distinctive aspect of nursing, the results of studies may be more generalizable than might otherwise be expected.

The bulk of Jacobson's paper (Jacobson, 1978) is taken up with rich descriptions of the various stressful incidents. Most aspects have already received attention above. The distinctive contribution of her work is in suggestions of how the various factors contribute differentially to the total experience. Some categories of incidents were consistently rated as highly stressful whereas others varied between individuals and others were generally 'low stress' when they occurred. The most stressful items on these criteria were those in the three categories: *Understaffing and Overwork; Sudden Death or Relapse* and *Insecurity about Knowledge and Competence.*

A further contribution to the context in which these factors operate is the 'model' of stress which underpins Jacobson's account of her data. For a particular individual, she sees coping and adaptation as having a variable threshold which rises and falls rather than as a state which can be achieved once and for all. She thus explains her findings that even highly experienced nurses may, at times, be revolted by sights and smells to which they thought they had long-since grown accustomed: 'I was so surprised that something like this could affect me at my stage in the game'. Certain pressures may play more central roles in determining these thresholds than do others and therefore warrant particular attention. Staffing is suggested as a critical variable in the ICU environment: 'This seems to be a category of stress which warrants very close attention. One supervisor expressed the view that if adequate staffing is maintained, nurses take all other frustrations in their stride and, conversely, that inadequate staffing over a long period of time increases the nurses' sensitivity to all other stresses'.

The impact of ICU pressures on the nurse and her coping strategies

Several techniques individuals adopt to reduce stress are identified in the ICU literature. The nurse may relate more to the machines than to patients, or 'mechanize' her job by concentrating on keeping busy with the tasks. Several writers suggest that keeping active helps nurses experience a sense of control or mastery over the situation and decreases their feelings of impotence (e.g. Price and Bergen, 1977). An alternative to such avoidance behaviour is a cheerful denial which Hay and Oken (1972) claim is more common. Nurses joke, laugh, and even sing as they go about their work. The delicate balance of emotional life on the ICU is shown in several articles which give examples of tension releasing outbursts after times of crisis — hysterical giggling or intense anger after a cardiac arrest, for example (Hay and Oken, 1973). Some studies suggest that hostility, resentment, and verbal aggression are more marked in ICU than non-ICU nurses (Gentry *et al.*, 1972).

At a group level of coping, Hay and Oken (1972) pay particular attention to the strength of group cohesion on the unit. Staff are special. They volunteer, are selected and trained, come through the challenge of early days in the job and can eventually take pride in their abilities and accomplishments. They come to form an elite corps. Enforced interdependency in the unit's tasks and geographic isolation from the rest of the hospital are further cementing factors. The benefits of this group spirit are the emotional support it provides for members who understand each others experiences as 'outsiders' cannot. Typically nurses from the ICU mix together socially and reinforce these strong ties. Several writers, however, point to the potential negative consequences of such close group relationships (e.g. Jacobson, 1978). At work, group pressures for cooperation may require the suppression of anger, hostility, or conflict. Any absence increases other staffs' workload and so is avoided or accompanied by guilt. Group norms act as powerful constraints on individual behaviour and Hay and Oken report that individuals can seldom get the group to support realistic complaints. The group's strength therefore acts to perpetuate the *status quo* and the only escape for individuals is to resign completely. Outside working hours group-based activities may threaten other relationships and create conflicts for those who want to lead independent lives.

Satisfactions of intensive care nursing

Despite its many pressures, several writers (for example Bilodeau, 1973) identify satisfactions of working on the ICU. Some are the polar opposites of potential stressors; others come as a direct result of the pressures giving further evidence of the ambivalence of life on the unit (see below).

Being able to give high standards of physical and emotional care and seeing patients respond and relatives feeling helped are major sources of satisfaction. Nurses also report enjoying the challenge of the ICU's tasks and pace. Teamwork and group morale on the unit are highly prized. Satisfaction comes from relationships with those doctors who do respect the abilities of nurses and seek collaborative rather than competitive working relationships. The high status of jobs on the unit and the opportunities for independence and initiative it affords are also highly valued. Despite their sometimes horrific portrayal, Hay and Oken too feel we should recognize that nurses who work on the ICU do so by choice. Other assignments might be less gratifying for them or even more stressful.

The ambivalence of working on the ICU

Viewed as a whole the above factors testify to the ambivalence of working on an intensive care unit. Close patient contact is desirable, unavoidable, potentially satisfying, but highly potentially stressful. From a medical viewpoint, the nurses 'do too much' for the patient, but all too often they also 'do too little'. ICU nurses' additional training, skills, and responsibilities lead both to greater job satisfaction, and to tensions with other hospital staff. Group cohesion on the unit is a valuable source of emotional support but often involves sacrifices in independence from which the nurse, and eventually the group, suffer. This tension focused at the individual is (as in the wider context of this chapter as a whole) the 'point of entry' for those suggesting ways of reducing stress for nursing staff.

Recommendations for reducing stress

The literature about intensive care unit nursing makes many suggestions of ways in which the pressures involved can be reduced. Those specifically relating to ICUs are summarized here, those of more obvious general relevance appear in the 'Interventions' section below. Comments in this section reflect several different viewpoints and 'levels' of concern. Practising staff, such as Dossett (1978) and Weeks (1978) tend to concentrate on how things should be with little attention to how these, sometimes highly idealistic, states can be achieved. Overall they tend as well to be more concerned with the calibre of staff and the details of working conditions than are writers who are relative outsiders. They do, however, give an important insight into changes staff themselves would like to see occur.

Personnel selection

Several authors (Hay and Oken, 1972; Bilodeau, 1973; Dossett, 1978; Weeks, 1978) call for care in the type of person selected for ICU nursing. Ability to function under stress and to tolerate the necessary occasional boredom and repetitive work are the criteria identified. In addition, Bilodeau suggests that realistic expectations should be fostered by warning volunteers in advance of the disadvantages of such work. Adequate training is also considered important especially in developing and maintaining skills (Bilodeau) and using equipment (Dossett).

The ICU environment

Attention to the physical environment of the unit and conditions of working are also common concerns. The emphases here are on reducing the physical unpleasantness of the unit (the 'visual bombardment' for example — Hay and Oken) and providing staff with opportunities to relax and recuperate both on duty *via* rest breaks and off by attention to the duty roster (Bilodeau, 1973). Such suggestions have been implemented in some of the 'second generation' ICUs now in existence (Simon and Whiteley, 1977). Adequate staffing levels and ancillary support are also concerns (Dossett, 1978) as is the facility for nurses to ask for transfer to less stressful jobs without stigma (Hay and Oken, 1972).

Staff meetings

The most common suggestion in intensive care as in nursing generally is that regular staff meetings can help reduce stress. Their general use is discussed in detail in 'Interventions' below. Meetings are also the main method advocated to work through role conflicts between nursing staff and doctors (Dossett; Weeks). There are many calls in the literature to review roles and their boundaries and establish new guidelines (e.g. Jacobson, 1978). The attention devoted to these issues suggests that role ambiguity cannot be dismissed as lightly (or portrayed as a potential benefit) for nurses as it can for other occupational groups (e.g. Marshall and Cooper, 1979). Whether the strategy of encouraging greater role flexibility is in fact feasible is an interesting issue. ICUs are unusual wards and are serving as testing grounds in this context. In future years the results of their 'experiments' may well spill over to affect staff in more traditional settings.

ICU organization

Some writers suggest that needs for adequate leadership and coordination are currently unmet in intensive care units. Bilodeau argues for special attention to the selection and role of the unit head nurse. Others propose the creation of a unit coordinator position through which nursing staff would rotate (e.g. Hay and Oken, 1972). The coordinator could provide extra help during emergencies, but more importantly, would take on the care of new staff and visitors thus diverting major pressures from other nurses.

Increasing job satisfaction

Problems of maintaining staff morale attract some writers' attention. Hay and Oken propose that ICU nurses' already special status and therefore pride be increased further by giving them a distinctive uniform or a small pay differential or extra holiday entitlement as recognition of 'hazardous duty'. (In view of their own earlier discussion of 'elitist' conflicts with other hospital personnel such moves may well have negative as well as positive consequences.) Bilodeau and Weller and Miller point to ICU's staff's needs for opportunities to follow up patient progress both as a contribution to their further training and as a source of motivation by keeping their work and its eventual outcome in context. Bilodeau also suggests developing links with other units or professional bodies to promote discussion of problems.

The literature on death and dying and intensive care nursing illustrates special cases but also serves to highlight more general aspects of stress amongst nurses. I shall now return to the more general themes of this chapter.

PERSONAL CHARACTERISTICS AND COPING STRATEGIES
AS CONTRIBUTORS TO STRESS

Having achieved some appreciation of the contributions made to stress by tasks, relationships, environments, and working conditions, it seems appropriate to turn inward on the nurse herself and explore ways in which her characteristics play a part. The literature to which I had access paid little attention to this possibility however and most of those studies which did explore the relationship of individual differences to stress were about doctors rather than nurses (e.g. Bressler, 1976; Burrows, 1976; Strain, 1978). (It is interesting that such closely allied professions should receive such different attention. The literature on nursing focuses almost exclusively on environmental causes of stress. That on doctors blames much of their vulnerability to stress on the personality characteristics and immaturities of those who take up the profession.)

A research-based suggestion of relevance to the theme of this chapter is that personality differences may make individuals differentially suited to particular kinds of nursing duty. Quinlan and Blatt (1972) found some support for their hypothesis that 'cognitive style' was related to performance under stress. Field independent, analytical nurses performed better in surgical and field independent, global students in psychiatric assignments. (In both conditions anxiety was associated with better performance confirming the point made earlier that it cannot be taken *per se* as an index of poorer nursing care.) These results suggest that future research must be sensitive to differential aspects that may be masked by explorations at more general levels. (A conclusion I have reached in a managerial context too — Marshall and Cooper, 1979.)

A more profitable avenue in terms of currently available material about the individual's role in the stress reaction is that of the coping techniques she currently adopts and their generally acknowledged inadequacy and contribution to causing secondary stress effects. I shall next review the individual, group, and organization-level coping techniques identified in the literature, leading into an exposition of the latter argument.

The main coping technique at an individual level is that of anxiety-avoidance. This was the conclusion of Menzies (1970) in her classic study of a London teaching hospital and is no less evident in the current literature. As emotional detachment and denial of feelings are central requirements of a nurse (and are continually reinforced during training and *via* other people's expectations) this conclusion should perhaps come as little surprise. It does however have significant implications — particularly a potential decrease in the quality of patient care and the probability that it will prevent nurses developing more adaptive coping strategies in the longer term.

As patients are the major source of anxiety, the nurse can shield herself most effectively from stress by reducing patient contact. There are various means available to her. She can organize her day around tasks rather than people and so deal only fleetingly with any one patient (Menzies, 1970). Keeping busy was termed 'escape into work' by Coombs and Goldman (1976) who identified it as one of four main coping mechanisms in their participant observation study of ICU nurses. Denied complete physical separation, the nurse may seek psychological detachment from the patient. She may depersonalize the patient, for example, referring to him/her by disease rather than name. Coombs and Goldman differentiate several techniques of 'language alteration' including the use of indirect speech, euphemisms, latin derivatives, and technical terms.

Humour is a more generally-directed coping technique. Kopel (1977) refers to joking and laughter as sudden tension-release behaviours. Coombs and Goldman (1976) depict it as a routine way of maintaining a tolerable climate on the ward. They report that experienced personnel were more aware of the need for 'clowning' and 'banter' than were new staff. If a nurse became too serious others would actively try to involve her in the joking.

The fourth individual technique identified by Coombs and Goldman is that of rationalization. Nurses 'discounted' some deaths as being a welcome relief from suffering. Taking this attitude before death occurred helped prepare them for the event and often resulted in them spending more time caring for patients who they saw as having better chances of survival.

Several of Hadley's (1977) interviewees mention more specific behaviours which help relieve stress such as separating home and work lives and having someone to whom they can 'let off steam'. One of Hadley's informants revealingly identifies having coped with stress as a source of satisfaction in itself: 'Most staff nurses are aware of the stress they work under. It becomes a reward of its own sometimes — to be able to go home and say, "I did get the job done, what a courageous person I am." It can really boost a nurse's ego'.

In the UK nurses move through their training in 'sets' and these typically develop into close social as well as work groups providing support and thus alleviating stress for members. The action of similar processes amongst ICU nurses has already been discussed in detail above.

As noted above, the organization of nursing, despite its apparent rigidities, appears to operate more towards protecting staff from, than causing, stress. Well defined hierarchies clarify the distribution of responsibility, for example. The lack of acknowledgement and discussion of nursing's more distasteful aspects suggests, however, that denial is the main coping strategy at organizational as well as individual levels.

Menzies (1970) describes in detail the contributions the social structure and the organization of nursing services can make to reinforcing the dominant tactic of anxiety evasion. Several are aimed at reducing the weight of responsibility on the individual: procedures are checked and counterchecked; groups (rather than individuals) are collusively labelled 'responsible' or 'irresponsible' and there is excessive dependence on superiors to perform tasks and make decisions objectively below their station. These defensive techniques help the individual avoid the experience of anxiety, guilt, doubt, and uncertainty. Little attempt is made to confront anxiety-evoking experiences directly. Menzies suggests that it is assumed the threats involved are too 'deep and dangerous' to be confronted and that any attempt to do so would lead to 'personal disruption and social chaos'.

Secondary effects therefore, in their turn, contribute to stress and she argues that as long as avoidance is the dominant tactic 'it is to be expected that nurses will persistently experience a higher degree of anxiety than is justified by the objective situation alone'. She goes on to discuss several secondary effects which in their turn contribute to stress — for example the excessive movement of student nurses and the reduction of opportunities for direct personal satisfaction from work. The extent to which anxiety-avoidance and denial may distort research results is a further issue which should concern those working in this area.

The analysis, argument, and exhortation of Menzies supplies a fitting bridge to the final section of this chapter in which suggestions for alleviating stress will be discussed and their application in practice evaluated. The extent to which writers ignore possible actions to reduce environmental pressures and concentrate instead on techniques which support the nurse in confronting her feelings and the psychological representations of her work is striking to a newcomer to the area. The literature on managerial stress takes a very different view and typically advocates external or, for the individual concerned, purely behavioural stress control. It would seem that writers such as Menzies have been heeded and the direction of intervention (where it happens) is toward the risky psychological exploration and confrontation they recommend.

INTERVENTIONS: SUGGESTION AND PRACTICE

The close liaison between theory and practice in the literature on nursing job stress is particularly valuable when we come to suggestions for reducing stress, as accounts of attempts to implement these suggestions are usually also available. I shall briefly outline the kinds of action called for before going on to evaluate them in practice. The section on intensive care nursing has already detailed proposals specifically tailored to that environment. Before considering these proposals, however, I should like to raise a central issue which receives little attention in the literature — that stress-reduction is often competitive. Actions which improve conditions for one group on the ward may increase the pressures for others. Nurses' needs take a low priority in the hospital environment (self sacrifice is a keystone of their organizational role) and they may therefore be prevented from implementing suggestions which do not also benefit other parties.

Suggestions

Two recommendations appear more frequently in the literature than do any others; I shall therefore concentrate on these in the implementations described below. They are that nurses should have the opportunity to express and share their reactions to their work in regular staff meetings and that training should be given to help them understand and cope with anxiety about death and dying. Both are based on the implicit model that current coping is largely achieved by repression and are thus aimed at exploring and relieving emotions.

Other suggestions deal with more specific stress-related issues. As one might expect, 'training' is often advocated. Several authors suggest that training in some form can help nurses achieve greater emotional stability (Gunther, 1977) and accept their own emotions and limitations (Strain, 1978). Laube (1973) recommends regular 'disaster drills' to help prepare nurses for emergency situations. Hadley (1977) advocates staff development programmes to teach nursing supervisors to identify stress in their departments and then deal with it through counselling. Jacobson (1978) too feels that nursing management can be educated to play a more positive role.

Several authors suggest ward level organizational changes to help reduce stress. Hay and Oken (1972), Weller and Miller (1977), and Strain (1978) advocate a team approach to nursing, bringing support into the ward rather than leaving it to act behind the scenes in meetings. (They do not, however, feel this should prejudice standards of patient care and agree with the current practice that one staff member must ultimately be viewed as the primary psychological care giver by each patient.) Bilodeau (1973) proposes a form of 'self-help' which hinges on the nursing group acting as a team to identify and action a 'tangible area for intervention'. Having identified key frustrations and satisfactions in their work environment, they would plan changes to reduce the former and build on the latter. This proposal is notable for its deviation from the common emotion-venting but actionless use of group meetings but is, as far as I know, unresearched.

Expectations and role definitions were identified above as significant sources of potential stress. Hospital-based staff meetings are suggested by some authors as means of debating the issues and achieving more relevant guidelines. Others point to the need to involve 'society' in such developments. Char and McDermott (1972), for example, call for a more universal 'redefinition' of the role, philosophy, and ethics of nursing and medicine to guide us in abortion work'.

Practice: group meetings

The most frequently used method of intervention reported in the literature is that of regular consultant-led nursing group meetings in which stressful issues are aired and debated. (See Char and McDermott, 1972; Schowalter, 1975; Drotar, 1976; Price and Bergen, 1977; Simon and Whiteley, 1977.) This work has mainly been carried out in ICUs. Requests for help typically come from nurses themselves and their motivation seems generally to be high. Key benefits of this method appear to be cathartic release of repressed emotions and the realization that others have similar experiences and feelings. These interventions typically do not 'tackle' the environment in which stress is caused but rely wholly on symbolic and psychological manipulation. It would seem, however, that their effects are generally beneficial, if somewhat limited, as the following examples illustrate.

Schowalter (1975), a psychiatric consultant, was initially called in because nurses on a paediatric ward reported stress in dealing with dying children. He reports on eight years work in the Adolescent Ward at Yale New Haven Hospital during which he has facilitated two sets of weekly meetings. The first are full staff meetings in which nurses are offered an opportunity to participate in joint decisions with doctors on both the specifics and philosophy of patient care. These address issues of nurses' roles in relation to other staff. In the second, nurses are encouraged to help each other during frank, informal discussions. He reports that 'more than anything the meeting acts as an officially sanctioned time for catharsis'. During the course of early meetings he found that nurses frequently dream about dying and dead patients and subsequently used their accounts as stimuli for discussion. Unconscious material has consequently been made conscious and dealt with more effectively.

One of the dilemmas of such interventions is the threat it poses to the dominant coping strategy employed by nurses — their denial. Discussions could cause them to worry more about their jobs if there are no simultaneous opportunities to dispel the anxieties thus created. Fear of this was in fact expressed by some of the participants in Schowalter's meetings. The group however concluded that they would rather be aware of what was bothering them. It must however be recognized that, especially in the early stages, there are likely to be negative as well as positive consequences of exploring such issues. Drotar (1976) discusses the tensions this can cause in the relationship between consultant and nursing staff.

Char and McDermott (1972) report a short term intervention of the group meeting type in which they helped staff deal with a more narrowly defined problem. They were called in by Hawaiian nurses suffering unexpected and acute identity problems following liberalization of abortion laws. They felt their meetings offered opportunities for abreaction, reestablishment of positive identification with patients, and the development of self awareness through which the nurses were able to regain their objectivity about abortion work. A year after the writer's last contact with the group they understood that things remained improved and that abortion was considered a routine matter. This case study shows that intervention can take a range of forms — in it an acute problem was addressed 'acutely'. Stress was removed purely by personal insight and development on the part of the staff.

Price and Bergen (1977) report the development of weekly meetings for nurses on an eight bed ICU over a period of eight months. The fluctuation in attendance (between 3 and 8 nurses) testifies to the resistance sometimes met by this type of intervention. This account also suggests that the outcomes, even in the longterm, can be of limited benefit. Whilst the sessions did nothing to dispel the nurses' conflicts, the latter felt able to address their feelings more clearly than before and, at the very least, 'felt less crazy'.

Drotar (1976) describes the setting up of group meetings designed to improve communications both within the staff group in a paediatric intensive care nursery (in Cleveland, USA) and between staff and patients' families. His progression shows a further variation in the way such schemes originate. Drotar was called in irregularly at first when staff on the unit experienced particular problems. The first meeting was initiated by staff reactions to the death of a premature infant, for example. It went on to cover a wide range of topics, professional dilemmas, and personal concerns. The emotional climate of the ward then improved. It was three months before a second request for consultation was stimulated by the case of a child who had been maintained by a respirator for two months and the anger his parents were displaying toward staff. Following a further consultation two months later staff agreed to meet weekly. Drotar reports that over time the meetings became increasingly beneficial and broadly-based and staff's commitment to them grew. He also notes as signs of progress more direct and adaptive confrontation between medical and nursing staff and a growth in the latter's own problem solving efforts. The author reflects on the various difficulties facing a consultant involved in such work, and his sensitive account is recommended reading for those who talk glibly about the benefits of staff meetings without recognizing the obstacles involved. Keys to success, he feels, are patience, the active support of senior medical staff and social service colleagues and the continued interest of nursing staff.

The final illustration in this section also comes from a nursing group's direct request for help. Staff on an ICU (St Louis, USA) were depressed about a series of recent events and concerned that they were becoming insensitive to their patients as people. Simon and Whiteley (1977) report the development of fortnightly group meetings led by the senior author, a psychoanalyst. In their detailed account they identify three phases in the group's development. In the initial phase meetings varied greatly in quality. Typically the consultant actively offered a structure. He found the nurses' contributions insightful, but relatively random and there were often expressions of intense hostility. The midphase was characterized by greater comfort and spontaneity generally and a growing acceptance of the consultant, interspersed with periods of resistance. Informality, spontaneity and openness grew in the late phase in which participation was at a high level. Even at this stage however trust in the consultant was fragile and suffered a crisis when he suggested that the experience be written up for research purposes.

The refreshing openness of Drotar (1976) and Simon and Whiteley (1977) contributes a great deal to our understanding of the dynamics of group meetings as a method of intervention. The accounts in this section also suggest that whilst they have a contribution to make, group meetings in most cases (and particularly for continual pressures) have a limited potential for stress-alleviation.

Death and dying training

Relationship to death and the dying patient have appeared as significant sources of stress in the section above. An article which is particularly critical of staff's current preparation for dealing with death is that by Kopel (1977). He depicts the nurse as 'abandoned' by medical training which encourges only desensitization as a means of coping. The second main area of activity to relieve stress is that of training designed to reduce anxiety about death and dying.

Many institutions in the United States are now introducing 'Death and Dying Workshops' to give hospital staff information about care of the terminally ill and help them recognize their own feelings about death. Two typical examples will be described here. Laube (1977) set out to evaluate the effects of the death anxiety of registered nurses of a two-day workshop. He found firstly that his sample of (44) nurses had death anxiety scores (on a standardized scale) similar to those of the general population. The workshop had no (statistically significant) immediate effect on their death anxiety level, but a significant decrease was seen one month later. This was however not sustained three months after the close of training. In this the results agree with those of Murray (1974). The author's initial concern that nurses might not wish to participate and might have insufficient time to work through their feeling seem to be disconfirmed by their positive reactions to the experience and their requests for further training.

O'Connell et al. (1977) report the development of a one day thanatology lab aimed at exploring both personal feelings and professional problems in relationship to death. Their design is flexible but generally includes discussions between experts, experiencing sessions, and role play exercises. During the course of two years 1000 participating medical staff have completed short-course evaluation questionnaires. Of the student nurses and private hospital personnel in that number, 90% rated the lab as of 'much' or 'very much' benefit to them both personally and professionally. The authors feel that current public 'apathy' and denial of death prevents them from testing their design outside hospitals.

Whilst these two illustrations suggest valuable outcomes of such training, conceptual criticisms of this very limited approach suggests that more still could be done. Nurses' contact with death and dying is frequent if not continual and is likely to be punctuated by crises as high involvement with a particular patient or increased sensitivity for other reasons highlights particular experiences. The workshop design offers no facilities for longterm exploration and development of attitudes and feelings. Neither does it cross the gulf between the training environment and the ward, by setting up continual support facilities for example. More fundamentally, the issues of potential complexities in the roles of anxiety, denial, etc. and potential differences between individuals and environments are largely ignored. Its underlying model is simply that anxiety is a bad thing and can be reduced by greater self-awareness.

IN CONCLUSION

In conclusion I would like to draw together the more important questions about stress amongst nurses posed in this chapter. Each signposts a valuable area for further research and exploration. Are, for example, most nurses continually suffering stress as many writers imply? Nurses must be consulted about the balance of pressures and satisfactions in their lives. How do the various pressures in the work environment operate and interact? Are some central whilst others are virtually insignificant, for example? What part do individual differences between nurses play in mediating potential stressors? Is 'self-selection for the job' really the most discriminating explanation we can come to! How can active, adaptive coping strategies be integrated into the nurse's role? Finally, how are current developments in patient care affecting nurses? Current emphases on treating patients and their relatives more as whole people and moves toward decreasing restrictions in hospital procedures seem likely to increase the latters' stress unless radical changes in training, support, and coping techniques can also be achieved.

REFERENCES

Bilodeau, C.B. (1973). The nurse and her reactions to critical care nursing. *Heart and Lung,* **2,** 3, 358-363.

Bressler, B. (1976). Suicide and drug abuse in the medical community. *Suicide and Life-Threatening Behaviour,* **6,** 3, 169-178.

Burrows, G.D. (1976). Stress and distress in middle age — the mental health of doctors. *Australian Family Physician,* **5,** 9, 1203-10.

Char, W.F., and McDermott, J.F. (1972). Abortions and acute identity crisis in nurses. *Amer. J. Psychiatry.,* **128,** 8, 952-957.

Chen, M.K. (1977). Are knowledgeable patients necessarily pests? (letter), *Medical Care,* **XV,** 4, 350-351.

Coombs, R.H., and Goldman, L.J. (1976). Maintenance and discontinuity of coping mechanisms in an intensive care unit, in *Doing Social Life: A Qualitative Study of Human Interaction in Natural Settings* (J. Lofland), pp.233-249, Wiley, New York.

Davitz, L.J., *et al.,* (1969). 'Nurses' inferences of suffering', *Nursing Research,* **18,** 2, 100-107.

Denton, J.A., and Wisenbaker, V.B. (1977). Death experience and death anxiety among nurses and nursing students. *Nursing Research,* **26,** 1, 61-64.

Dossett, S.M. (1978). Nursing staff in high dependency areas. *Nursing Times,* **74,** 21, 888-9.

Drotar, D. (1976-77). 'Consultation in the intensive care nursery', *Int. J. Psychiatry in Medicine,* **7,** 1, 69-81.

Dutton, W.H. (1962). Attitude change of elementary school student teachers and anxiety. *J. Educ. Res.,* **55,** 380-382.

Fulton, R. (1964). Death and self, *J. of Religion and Health,* **3,** July, 364.

Gardam, J.F. (1969). Nursing stresses in the intensive care unit (letter), *JAMA,* **208,** 2337-8.

Geizhals, J.S. (1975). Attitudes toward death and dying: a study of occupational therapists and nurses. *Journal of Thanatology,* **3,** 243-269.

Gentry, W.D., *et al.* (1972). Psychologic responses to situational stress in intensive and nonintensive nursing. *Heart Lung,* **1,** Nov.-Dec., 793-796.

Glaser, B.G., and Strauss, A.L. (1966). *Awareness of Dying,* Weidenfeld and Nicolson, London.

Glaser, B.G., and Strauss, A.L. (1968). *Time for Dying,* Aldine, Illinois.

Gunther, M.S. (1977). The threatened staff: A psychoanalytic contribution to medical psychology. *Comprehensive Psychiatry,* **18,** 4, 385-397.

Hadley, R.D. (1977). Staff nurse cites challenge, satisfaction despite stress, *The American Nurse,* **9,** 9, 6-11.

Haug, M.R., and Sussman, M.B. (1969). Professional autonomy and the revolt of the client. *Social Problems,* **17,** 153.

Hay, D.H., and Oken, D. (1972). The psychological stresses of intensive care unit nursing. *Psychosomatic Medicine,* **34,** 2, 109-118.

Jacobson, S.P. (1976). *Stresses and Coping Strategies of Neonatal Care Unit Nurses,* Unpublished Doctoral Thesis, University of Minnesota.

Jacobson, S.P. (1978). Stressful situations for neonatal intensive care nurses. *Amer. J. Maternal Child Nursing,* **3,** 3, 144-50.

Keller, N.S. (1971). Compliance, previous access and provision of services by registered nurses, *J. Health Soc. Behav.,* **12,** 321.

Kopel, R.F. (1977). Death on every weekend. *Suicide and Life-Threatening Behaviour,* **7,** 2, 110-9.

Kubler-Ross, E. (1969). *On Death and Dying,* Macmillan, New York.

Laube, J. (1973). Psychological reactions of nurses to disaster. *Nursing Research,* **22,** 4, 343-347.

Laube, J. (1977). Death and dying workshop for nurses: Its effect on their death anxiety level. *Int.J.Nurs.Stud.,* **14,** 111-120.

Lazarus, R.S. (1966). *Psychological Stress and the Coping Process,* McGraw-Hill, New York.

Marshall, J., and Cooper, C.L. (1979). *Executives Under Pressure,* Macmillan, London.

Melia, K.M. (1977). The intensive care unit — a stress situation? *Nursing Times,* **73**, 5, Suppl. 17-20.

Menzies, I.E.P. (1970). *The Functioning of Social Systems as a Defence Against Anxiety,* Tavistock Institute, London, 1960.

Miller, G.A. (1976). Patient Knowledge and nurse role strain in three hospital settings. *Medical Care,* **XIV**, 8, 662-73.

Murray, P. (1974). Death education and its effect on the death anxiety level of nurses. *Psychol. Reports,* **35**, 1250.

O'Connell, W.E., *et al.* (1977). Thanatology for everyone: Developmental labs and workshops. *Death Education,* **1**, 305-13.

Price, T.R., and Bergen, B.J. (1977). The relationship to death as a source of stress for nurses on a coronary care unit, *Omega, J. Death and Dying,* **8**, 3, 229-238.

Quinlan, D.M., and Blatt, S.J. (1972). Field articulation and performance under stress. *J. Consult. and Clin. Psych.,* **39**, 3, 517.

Revans, R.W. (1959). The hospital as an organism: a study of communications and morale, Paper presented at the 6th *Annual Int. Mtg. of the Inst. Of Management Sciences,* Sept. 1959, Paris. Pergamon Press, London.

Roth, J.A. (1972). Some contingencies of the moral evaluation and control of clientele: the case of the hospital emergency service. *Amer. J. Sociol.,* **77**, 839.

Schowalter, J.E. (1975). Paediatric nurses dream of death. *J. of Thanatology,* **3**, 223-321.

Schwap, J.J., *et al.* (1970). The differential perception of anxiety in medical patients: sociodemographic aspects, *Psychiatry in Medicine,* **1**, 2, 151-164.

Severin, N.K., and Becker, R.E. (1974). Nurses as psychiatric consultants in a general hospital emergency room. *Community Mental Health J.,* **10**, 3, 261-267.

Shusterman, L.R., and Sechrest, L. (1973). Attitudes of registered nurses toward death in a general hospital. *Psychiatry in Medicine,* **4**, 4, 411-426.

Simon, N.M., and Whiteley, S. (1977). Psychiatric consultation with MICU nurses: The consultation conference as a working group. *Heart and Lung,* **6**, 3, 497-504.

Stewart, R., and Marshall, J. (1979). *Managers' Perceptions of the Choices in their Jobs,* Social Science Research Council Report HR 5529/1.

Strain, J.J. (1978). Psychological reactions to acute medical illness and critical care. *Critical Care Medicine,* **6**, 1, 39-44.

Sudnow, D. (1967). *Passing On: The Social Organization of Dying,* Prentice Hall, Englewood Cliffs, N.J.

Templer, D.I. (1970). Construction and validation of a death anxiety scale, *J. Gen. Psychol.,* **82**, April, 165-177.

Walsh, J.E. (1971). Instruction in psychiatric nursing, level of anxiety, and direction of attitude change toward the mentally ill, *Nursing Research,* **20**, 6, 522-529.

Weeks, H. (1978). Dealing with stress, *Maternal Child Nursing,* **3**, 3, 151-2.

Weisman, A. (1972). *On Dying and Denying,* Behavioral Publications, New York.

Weller, D.J., and Miller, P.M. (1977). Emotional reactions of patient, family, and staff in acute-care period of spinal cord injury: Part 2, *Social Work in Health Care,* **3**, 1, 7-17.

PART II

Stress In Education

White Collar and Professional Stress
Edited by C.L. Cooper and J. Marshall
© 1980 John Wiley & Sons Ltd.

Chapter 3

School Administrators: Sources Of Stress And Ways Of Coping With It

Rosalie L. Tung
University of Oregon
USA

and

James L. Koch
University of Oregon
USA

Stress is one of the most widely used and misused concepts in theoretical literature and empirical research. It has been the subject of investigation from different perspectives — physiological, psychological, and social-psychological (McGrath, 1976). This study was primarily concerned with social-psychological stress as it operated within organizational settings. This does not mean that it ignored physiological data altogether. Rather, it considered overall physical health as evidence of social-psychological states. Previous research has shown that the level of subjectively experienced social-psychological stress is strongly associated with the respondent's physical health (Russek and Zohman, 1958; Kornhauser, 1965; Wardell, Hyman, and Hahnson 1970; French and Caplan, 1973; French and coworkers, 1976; Cooper and Marshall, 1976; Cooper and Payne, 1978).

A cursory review of the literature on social-psychological stress indicates that there is a plethora of analytically independent sources of stress, implying the multi-dimensionality of the construct. In this study, following French *et al.*'s (1976, p. 3) definition, stress refers to 'any characteristic of the job environment which poses a threat to the individual — either excessive demands or insufficient supplies to meet his needs. Stress also refers to a misfit between the person and his environment'. Stressors, on the other hand, refer to the sources of stress, such as the task itself.

63

McGrath hypothesizes that there are six possible 'classes' of stressors in an organizational setting. These are task-based stress, role-based stress, stress intrinsic to the behaviour setting, stress arising from the physical environment, stress arising from the social environment, and stress within the person system (McGrath, 1976, p. 1369). However, most measures of social-psychological stress available to date fail to reflect this multidimensionality. One of the more widely used measures is the Index of Job Related Strain (JRS) developed by Indik, Seashore, and Slesinger (1964). The JRS was tested on a sample of 8,234 industrial employees representing diverse age, eductional, and occupational backgrounds. Even though Indik *et al.* (1964, p. 28) recognized the multi-dimensionality of the construct, they reported that based on their instrument and data 'the evidence of clustering is weak... Each item correlated with the index much more strongly than it correlated with any other component item.' This suggested that the JRS was only able to tap one underlying source of occupational stress. Burke and Belcourt (1974) later did a factor analysis of 14 of the 15 items comprising the JRS Index. Their sample consisted of 137 managers and managerial trainees employed by the Federal Government of Canada. While their orthogonal rotation identified two principal role-related stress dimensions (ambiguity and overload), it still suggested that the JRS taps only generic role related sources of stress. Thus, it has important limitations as an instrument for tapping the theoretically diverse nature of occupational stress within organizations.

This study sought to develop a more comprehensive measure of job-related stress, i.e. one which would reflect the multi-dimensionality of the construct. Specifically, it attempted to identify the different sources or dimensions of job-related stress experienced by administrators of educational institutions: elementary and high schools. Accordingly, the focus was upon that subset of stressors within this particular organizational setting, which became salient in the context of performing one's assigned duties and responsibilities. McGrath (1976, p. 1364) postulates that an organization can be viewed as consisting of three separate systems which are in a state of constant interaction. These three systems are: (a) the physical-technical environment of the organization or the context in which the individual performs his/her assigned tasks and responsibilities — potential sources of social-psychological stress that could arise from this context are task overload, task difficulty, and task ambiguity; (b) the social-interpersonal environment of the organization or the context in which the individual interacts with his/her superiors, peers, and subordinates in an organizational setting — potential sources of social-psychological stress that could arise from this context are role conflict, role ambiguity and role overload; and (c) the 'person-system' of the focal person — referring to the set of personality characteristics, e.g. anxiety, need for clarity, perceptual styles, etc. that the individual 'brings with him' to the organizational setting. These personality characteristics could substantially moderate the amount of stress experienced by the individual.

These potential sources of social-psychological stress, as hypothesized by McGrath (1976), have been explored by other researchers in the area of occupational stress. Guetzkow and Gyr (1954), Gullahorn (1956), Morris (1957), Nix and Bates (1962), Eckerman (1964), Kugelmass and Lieblich (1966), Cooper and Marshall (1976), McGrath (1976), Cooper and Payne (1978), Cooper (1979), and others have shown that a number of work conditions, such as task difficulty, work overload, role ambiguity, etc., can contribute to the level of subjectively experienced social-psychological stress. At the outset, it should be pointed out that the present study did not examine objective characteristics of the environment *per se*. This is not to suggest that these physical environmental variables do not influence the level of subjectively experienced stress, rather previous research indicates that the objective environment (e.g. cold) must be combined with the subject's perception or translation of such objective reality (e.g. fear of cold) before it could significantly alter the stress level experienced by the individual (McGrath, 1970).

This study sought to develop an instrument that would measure the diverse sources of social-psychological stress which arise within complex administrative organizational roles. To maximize internal validity of the instrument, the questionnaire was developed specifically for use on a homogeneous population, namely administrators of educational institutions. Although the sample included vice-principals, principals, and superintendents, all these positions involve administrative functions.

In addition, this study sought to investigate the degree and form of association between subjectively experienced stress and certain respondent characteristics, such as age, years of administrative experience, and position. Previous research has shown that all of these variables are related to stress. Stouffer and coworkers (1949), Curin, Veroff, and Feld (1960), Langner (1962), and Indik *et al.* (1964) found significant relationships between age and the amount of stress experienced. Several researchers (Farber and Spence, 1956; Pronko and Leith, 1956; Ulrich, 1957; Berkun and coworkers 1962; McGrath, 1970) have shown that past experience, either in the form of familiarity with the situation due to past exposure or practice/training to cope with the situation can significantly alter the level of subjectively experienced stress and change reactions to that stress. Finally, there is theoretical and empirical evidence to support the contention that people occupying boundary-spanning positions in an organization (i.e. those positions that seek to relate the organization to other environmental sectors and which guide the organization in its efforts to procure scarce resources, and accomplish both organizational and societal goals) do experience more stress (Kahn and coworkers, 1964; Cooper, 1979; Kast and Rosensweig, 1979). Unfortunately most of the studies cited here have involved composite samples of diverse occupational groups, thus making it difficult to separate the influence of personal characteristics from other contextual factors. The present study partially alleviates this problem by essentially controlling for occupational setting.

This study also sought to identify the mechanisms/techniques that school administrators found most useful in coping with stress.

METHODOLOGY

Instrument Development

The questionnaire developed to measure sources of administrative stress was evolved through a series of iterations designed to insure that all relevant facets of job-related strain were tapped. The fifteen-item index of Job-Related Strain (Indik *et al.,* 1964) comprised the initial questionnaire core. This index was supplemented by items suggested from a review of current publications for public school administrators, and by items suggested from stress logs which were kept by forty school administrators for a period of one week. (See Appendix A). Those participating in this initial phase of item development were asked by researchers to keep a diary of work-related stress. On a daily basis they reported: (1) the most stressful single incident occurring on the job that day; and, (2) the most stressful series of related incidents (e.g. recurring telephone interruptions, pending grievances, parent-teacher conflicts, etc.). At the end of the week, they were asked to identify other sources of stress that might not have occurred during the week in which stress logs were kept.

The pilot instrument was field tested for content validity and clarity with a group of 25 practising administrators. After revision and a second pilot test (*n* = 20) the final instrument comprised 35-items with the following five-point Likert-type response categories: 'rarely or never bothers me' (coded 1); 'occasionally bothers me' (coded 3); and 'frequently bothers me' (coded 5). This 35-item instrument was referred to as the Administrative Stress Index (ASI) (See Appendix B). Of these 35 items, 12 were retained from the JRS (Indik *et al.*, 1964). The 23 items which evolved out of stress logs and reviews of current public school administrator publications appeared to tap sources of stress which are unique to administrative roles in general, and the roles of public school administrators in particular. Thus, it was hoped that the ASI would permit a more comprehensive assessment of stress in this particular population than would be permitted by existing instruments, such as the JRS, which could tap only one, or at best two, underlying sources of job-related stress.

Use of the 'bothers me' response format in the 35-item Administrative Stress Index (as in the JRS) does raise a potential concern regarding whether such survey instruments are valid indicators of perceived environmental conditions or measures of a relatively stable personality trait which predisposes certain individuals to feel bothered by aspects of their work environment. This potential limitation will be discussed in contrasting the results for principals and superintendents, subgroups which face different objective stimulus conditions as they attend to matters associated with the institutional and managerial environments, respectively.

Sample

Data were obtained in connection with a larger study of stress among public school administrators (Swent and Gmelch, 1977). All subjects belonged to the Confederation of Oregon School Administrators ($n = 1855$). These included vice principals, principals, and superintendents and central school administrators. Every person within this population was sent a questionnaire together with a letter explaining the purpose of the study and a return envelope. Respondents were asked to complete the 35-item ASI and provide information on their age, sex, years in administration, position in organization, general physical health, number of hours worked per week, and percentage of total life stress attributed to work. Out of 1855 mailed questionnaires, 1207 were returned. Of these, 1156 useable surveys were obtained for a net response rate of 62.3%.

The average subject was 42 years old and had 9 years of administrative experience; 91% were male; 583 were principals; 191 were vice principals; 204 were superintendents; and 178 were central school administrators. The median hours worked per subject was 55, and the median percentage of total life stress attributed to work was 75%.

Analysis Method

The 35-item instrument was subjected to principal components varimax rotation. The use of orthogonal rotation was based upon the assumption that the broad ranging scale developed here permits subjects to report sources of stress differentially as between its various components. This assumption was checked by examining whether the extracted factors or derived dimensions met each and all of the following four criteria:

1. The pattern of item-factor loadings should be such that items load high on a single vector and relatively low on all other vectors. As suggested by Nunnally (1967), factor loadings of >0.30 was used as a minimally acceptable cut-off point. Items not meeting this criterion were subsequently deleted.
2. There should be higher inter-item correlations within factors than between factors; and, acceptable levels of internal consistency within each factor.
3. The dimensions derived from factor structures should have low shared variance.

4. Finally, each of the dimensions should have theoretical utility in understanding sources of administrative stress as evidenced by their relationship to selected contextual and personal characteristics.

RESULTS

Factor Analysis

Principal components analysis of the Administrative Stress Index revealed a weak general factor, suggesting that the scale was multidimensional in nature. Upon subsequent rotation, four interpretable factors were obtained. Each factor met the following criteria for extracted factors: the items comprising each factor loaded highly on a single vector; higher inter-item correlations were obtained within factors than between factors; and low shared variance existed between factors. Ten items failed to load singularly on a particular factor. These are items 3,4,8,11,14,15,17,25,28, and 33 in Appendix B. Consistent with the objective of identifying orthogonal factors, these items were deleted from subsequent analyses.

The Varimax rotated factor matrix for the remaining 25-items is reported in Table 1. This analysis indicated that the Administrative Stress Index clusters around four dimensions.

Factor 1, accounting for 52% of the common variance, appears to be very similar to Indik *et al.*'s (1964) JRS index. Six of the seven items comprising this factor were taken from the JRS index. These items pertain to sources of stress which result from the school administrator's beliefs and attitudes about his/her role in the organization. Such role expectations include preferences about what the person should do, what kind of person he/she should be, and how he/she should relate to others. Consistent with its original interpretation, this factor was labelled *role-based* stress.

Factor 2, accounting for 22% of common variance, appears to tap *task-based stress* or stress arising from the performance of one's day-to-day administrative activities. Eight of the ten items for this dimension evolved out of subject participation in pilot phases of the instrument design (stress logs) or through content analysis of relevant occupational literature. The administrator's work rests heavily on interaction involving the telephone, scheduled and unscheduled meetings, memorandums, letter-writing, and compilation of reports. Personal contacts are continuous. Contacts of this nature hinder the administrator's ability to manage time.

Factor 3, explaining for 22% of the common variance, appears to represent *conflict-mediating stress* indigeneous to the public school setting. The administrator has responsibilities and obligations to various groups or sectors both within and outside the organization. These various groups include students, parents, classified and certificated staffs, the community, etc. The demands, interests and needs of these various groups are often in conflict. The administrator has the primary responsibility for resolving the conflicts between these various groups. This attempt to satisfy responsibilities to each group results in stress on the administrator who is expected to be all things to all people.

The final dimension or fourth factor reflects *boundary-spanning stress*. Sources of boundary-spanning stress arise from the administrator's activities in relating the school to the external environment such as collective bargaining, dealing with regulatory agencies and gaining public support for school budgets. These items were also developed specifically for the present study.

Given the fairly large sample ($n = 1156$), it is possible to develop a 'hold-out' sample for cross-validation. In general, this procedure would strengthen the psychometric evidence for the scales. Given the uneven number of subjects in each of the different administrative job categories — principals, vice-principals, superintendents, and central school administrators — it was decided that the best strategy for cross-validation was to split the total sample into 2 even halves, on a random basis. Separate factor analyses were performed on each sub-sample. The varimax rotated factor matrices for the first sub-sample or validation sample ($n = 578$) and the second sub-sample or cross-validation sample ($n = 578$) are presented in Tables 2 and 3 respectively.

The factor patterns obtained in the validation and cross-validation samples are fairly consistent with that obtained when the sample was ran as a whole, except for the following: in the validation sample, factors 3 and 4 are interchanged (see Table 2). This reversal is fairly understandable from an examination of the items comprising these 2 factors. The items comprising the *conflict-mediating stress* dimension relate to resolving parent/school conflicts and resolving differences between/among students. Even though students are part of the organization (i.e. the school), they and their parents constitute part of the external environment of the organization. In dealing with the students and parents, the administrator is, in essence, trying to relate the organization to its external environment.

To provide further evidence of the multi-dimensionality of the ASI, coefficient alphas and factor correlations were calculated for the total sample, validation and cross-validation samples. These are presented in Table 4. Coefficients of internal consistency are very high. The greatest amount of shared variance between any two factors is 14% (Factor 1 $\times$ Factor 2, $r = 0.38$, $r^2 = 0.14$), indicating that the factors are fairly independent of each other. In addition, the median item correlations within factors is two and one-half times the between factor item correlations. These data, together with those presented in Tables 1, 2, and 3 provide good empirical support for conceptualizing administrative stress as a multi-dimensional construct. In this regard, they are consistent with recent theoretical treatments of occupational stress (e.g. McGrath, 1976; Cooper, 1979).

Table 1. Varimax rotated factor matrix ($n = 1156$)

Items[a]	Factor 1	Factor 2	Factor 3	Factor 4
Role-based stress				
* Knowing I can't get information needed to carry out my job properly	0.38	−0.04	0.19	0.10
* Thinking that I will not be able to satisfy the conflicting demands of those who have authority over me	0.62	0.06	0.17	0.09
# Trying to resolve differences with my superiors	0.64	0.05	0.05	0.09
* Not knowing what my supervisor thinks of me, or how he/she evaluates my performance	0.66	0.02	0.03	0.07
* Feeling that I have too little authority to carry out responsibilities assigned to me	0.63	0.03	0.13	0.07
* Being unclear on just what the scope and responsibilities of my job are	0.63	−0.02	0.16	0.11
* Trying to influence my immediate supervisor's actions and decisions that affect me	0.67	0.05	0.11	0.05
Task-based stress				
# Being interrupted frequently by telephone calls	0.03	0.46	0.06	0.01
# Supervising and coordinating the tasks of many people	0.16	0.42	0.20	0.12
# Having my work frequently interrupted by staff members who want to talk	0.00	0.48	0.11	0.03
# Imposing excessively high expectations on myself	0.21	0.41	0.01	0.11
# Writing memos, letters, and other communications	0.09	0.34	0.16	0.14
# Feeling I have to participate in school activities outside of the normal working hours at the expense of my personal time	0.12	0.41	0.22	0.08

Items[a]	Factor 1	Factor 2	Factor 3	Factor 4
* Feeling I have too much responsibility delegated to me by my supervisor	0.31	0.49	0.15	−0.06
* Feeling that I have too heavy a work load, one that I cannot possibly finish during the normal workday	0.13	0.70	0.01	0.03
# Feeling that meetings take up too much time	0.15	0.42	0.00	0.24
# Trying to complete reports and other paper work on time	0.08	0.55	0.01	0.33
Conflict-mediating stress				
# Trying to resolve differences between/among students	0.01	0.14	0.80	0.03
# Trying to resolve parent/school conflicts	0.05	0.23	0.58	0.23
# Handling student discipline problems	0.01	0.14	0.84	0.06
Boundary spanning stress				
# Preparing and allocating budget resources	0.12	0.08	0.24	0.46
# Being involved in the collective bargaining process	0.03	0.07	0.01	0.61
# Complying with state, federal, and organizational rules and policies	0.05	−0.02	0.26	0.50
# Administering the negotiated contract (grievance, interpretation, etc.)	0.10	0.12	0.06	0.64
# Trying to gain public approval and/or financial support for school programmes	0.14	0.05	0.10	0.50
Summary statistics				
Eigenvalue	4.8	2.0	1.4	1.1
Percent of Common Variance	51.6	21.7	14.7	12.0

[a]JRS items are designated by an asterisk. Others, developed in the present study, are designated by a #

Table 2.   Varimax rotated factor matrix on validation sample (n = 578)

Items[a]	Factor 1	Factor 2	Factor 3	Factor 4
Role-based stress				
* Knowing I can't get information needed to carry out my job properly	0.40	0.08	0.13	− 0.05
* Thinking that I will not be able to satisfy the conflicting demands of those who have authority over me	0.58	0.04	0.17	0.07
# Trying to resolve differences with my superiors	0.63	0.06	0.05	0.08
* Not knowing what my supervisor thinks of me, or how he/she evaluates my performance	0.61	0.04	0.06	0.02
* Feeling that I have too little authority to carry out responsibilities assigned to me	0.67	0.09	0.06	0.01
* Being unclear on just what the scope and responsibilities of my job are	0.62	0.07	0.16	− 0.05
* Trying to influence my immediate supervisor's actions and decisions that affect me	0.63	0.09	0.13	0.07
Task-based stress				
# Being interrupted frequently by telephone calls	0.03	0.47	− 0.02	0.06
# Supervising and coordinating the tasks of many people	0.19	0.40	0.16	0.20
# Having my work frequently interrupted by staff members who want to talk	0.01	0.42	0.03	0.19
# Imposing excessively high expectations on myself	0.19	0.44	0.08	0.08
# Writing memos, letters, and other communications	0.12	0.33	0.14	0.22
# Feeling I have to participate in school activities outside of the normal working hours at the expense of my personal time	0.29	0.35	0.21	0.05

Items[a]	Factor 1	Factor 2	Factor 3	Factor 4
* Feeling I have too much responsibility delegated to me by my supervisor	0.24	0.48	−0.03	0.09
* Feeling that I have too heavy a work load, one that I cannot possibly finish during the normal workday	0.09	0.70	0.17	−0.03
# Feeling that meetings take up too much time	0.16	0.38	0.25	0.05
# Trying to complete reports and other paper work on time	0.05	0.54	0.37	−0.01
Conflict-mediating stress				
# Trying to resolve differences between/among students	−0.01	0.01	0.15	0.86
# Trying to resolve parent/school conflicts	0.09	0.25	0.16	0.56
# Handling student discipline problems	0.00	0.02	0.15	0.80
Boundary spanning stress				
# Preparing and allocating budget resources	0.12	0.22	0.43	0.09
# Being involved in the collective bargaining process	0.00	−0.01	0.60	0.05
# Complying with state, federal, and organizational rules and policies	0.02	0.21	0.54	0.04
# Administering the negotiated contract (grievance, interpretation, etc.)	0.13	0.07	0.65	0.15
# Trying to gain public approval and/or financial support for school programmes	0.13	0.07	0.51	0.03
Summary statistics				
Eigenvalue	4.58	1.97	1.43	1.10
Percent of Common Variance	50.4	21.8	15.8	12.1

[a]JRS items are designated by an asterisk. Others, developed in the present study, are designated by a #

Table 3.   Varimax rotated factor matrix on cross validation sample (n = 578)

Items[a]	Factor 1	Factor 2	Factor 3	Factor 4
Role-based stress				
* Knowing I can't get information needed to carry out my job properly	0.37	0.02	0.25	0.09
* Thinking that I will not be able to satisfy the conflicting demands of those who have authority over me	0.65	0.06	0.17	0.13
# Trying to resolve differences with my superiors	0.63	0.02	0.05	0.10
* Not knowing what my supervisor thinks of me, or how he/she evaluates my performance	0.70	0.01	0.00	0.10
* Feeling that I have too little authority to carry out responsibilities assigned to me	0.61	0.06	0.17	0.04
* Being unclear on just what the scope and responsibilities of my job are	0.66	0.02	0.17	0.16
* Trying to influence my immediate supervisor's actions and decisions that affect me	0.72	0.04	0.08	0.00
Task-based stress				
# Being interrupted frequently by telephone calls	0.05	0.45	0.11	0.03
# Supervising and coordinating the tasks of many people	0.14	0.41	0.23	0.07
# Having my work frequently interrupted by staff members who want to talk	0.02	0.51	0.07	0.02
# Imposing excessively high expectations on myself	0.23	0.41	− 0.05	0.15
# Writing memos, letters, and other communications	0.07	0.35	0.13	0.12
# Feeling I have to participate in school activities outside of the normal working hours at the expense of my personal time	0.36	.31	0.15	0.22

Items[a]	Factor 1	Factor 2	Factor 3	Factor 4
* Feeling I have too much responsibility delegated to me by my supervisor	0.38	0.43	0.21	−0.07
* Feeling that I have too heavy a work load, one that I cannot possibly finish during the normal workday	0.17	0.71	0.08	0.08
# Feeling that meetings take up too much time	0.14	0.42	−0.03	0.21
# Trying to complete reports and other paper work on time	0.11	0.59	0.016	0.26
Conflict-mediating stress				
# Trying to resolve differences between/among students	0.05	0.11	0.78	0.05
# Trying to resolve parent/school conflicts	0.03	0.25	0.61	0.23
# Handling student discipline problems	0.03	0.08	0.88	0.10
Boundary spanning stress				
# Preparing and allocating budget resources	0.11	0.09	0.27	0.45
# Being involved in the collective bargaining process	0.06	0.08	0.02	0.63
# Complying with state, federal, and organizational rules and policies	0.08	0.02	0.33	0.46
# Administering the negotiated contract (grievance, interpretation, etc.)	0.07	0.08	0.05	0.62
# Trying to gain public approval and/or financial support for school programmes	0.16	0.06	0.12	0.48
Summary statistics				
Eigenvalue	5.11	2.03	1.36	1.1
Percent of Common Variance	53.1	21.1	14.2	11.6

[a]JRS items are designated by an asterisk. Others, developed in the present study, are designated by a #

Table 4. Coefficient alphas, factor correlations, median within and between for total
sample ($n = 1156$)

Analysis[a]	Factor 1	Factor 2	Factor 3	Factor 4
Factor Matrix				
Factor 1	(0.81)			
Factor 2	0.37	(0.31)		
Factor 3	0.11	0.33	(0.77)	
Factor 4	0.24	0.36	0.22	(0.70)
Median Item Correlations				
— Within	0.39	0.53	0.23	0.31
— Between	0.14	0.16	0.11	0.16

[a]Coefficient alphas are indicated in the diagonal of the factor matrix.

Coefficient alphas, factor correlations, median within and between for validation
sample ($n = 578$).

Analysis[a]	Factor 1	Factor 2	Factor 3	Factor 4
Factor Matrix				
Factor 1	(0.80)			
Factor 2	0.36	(0.80)		
Factor 3	0.12	0.32	(0.77)	
Factor 4	0.24	0.35	0.21	(0.70)
Median Item Correlations				
— Within	0.40	0.52	0.24	0.33
— Between	0.13	0.16	0.11	0.15

[a]Coefficient alphas are indicated in the diagonal of the factor matrix.

Coefficient alphas, factor correlations, median within and between for cross-validation
sample ($n = 578$).

Analysis[a]	Factor 1	Factor 2	Factor 3	Factor 4
Factor Matrix				
Factor 1	(0.83)			
Factor 2	0.38	(0.82)		
Factor 3	0.13	0.30	(0.78)	
Factor 4	0.22	0.37	0.23	(0.70)
Median Item Correlations				
— Within	0.37	0.50	0.25	.033
— Between	0.14	0.16	0.12	0.16

[a]Coefficient alphas are indicated in the diagonal of the factor matrix.

Stress and Physical Health

Previous research has shown that high occupational stress is related to poor employee health, such as coronary heart diseases, disabling ulcers, etc. (Russell and Zohman, 1958; Bresler and Buell, 1960; Kornhauser, 1965; Wardell et al., 1970; French and Caplan, 1973; Margolis, Kroes, and Quinn, 1974; Cooper and Marshall, 1976; French et al., 1976; Cooper and Payne, 1978).

Given the restrictions imposed on the collection of data that involve potential risks to subjects, it was not possible to collect more objective measures of physiological stress and strain. Consequently, the researchers had to settle for self-reported indicators of physical health. Respondents were asked to identify the state of their current physical health on a 5-point scale which ranged from '1 = poor physical health' to '5 = excellent physical health'. The administrators were also asked to identify what percentage of total stress in their life results from work. More than 60% of the administrators reported that 70% of their total life stress resulted from their jobs. Given the fairly high percentage of total life stress attributed to work itself, we would expect stress arising from the performance of one's job to have a significant impact on one's physical health.

Breslow and Buell (1960) studied the relationship between task overload (or number of hours worked) and death from coronary heart diseases. They found that employees under 45 years of age who worked more than 48 hours a week were exposed to twice the risk of death from coronary heart disease as compared with employees who worked less than 40 hours per week. Other research, such as Wardell et al. (1970) showed that 'responsibility for people', as in being different things to different people and being frequently called upon to resolve conflicts between different groups, would increase the incidences of coronary heart diseases. Other research on the subject of stress and physical health (Mettlin and Woelfel, 1974) showed that jobs which involve very extensive and diverse interpersonal communications network, as in the administrator's role of boundary-spanner, i.e. relating the school to the

Table 5.   Means and analysis of variance results for current physical health

Variable	Factor 1 (Role)	Factor 2 (Task)	Factor 3 (Conflict)	Factor 4 (Boundary)
Current Physical Health				
Poor-Average ($n = 234$)	2.26	2.74	2.44	2.63
Good ($n = 474$)	2.14	2.59	2.33	2.44
Excellent ($n = 448$)	1.96	2.38	2.07	2.26
F-ratio	12.17***	25.35***	10.59***	14.39***

***$p < 0.001$

external environment, were associated with a number of symptoms or indicators of physical and mental stress.

Table 5 reports the means and analysis of variance results for current physical health on each of the four factors or dimensions of occupational stress. Each stress dimension was strongly and significantly associated with reports of current physical health, i.e. the higher the level of experienced stress, the poorer the physical health. This is consistent with previous research findings which show the debilitating effects of stress on employee's health.

In a study of 205 volunteer engineers, scientists, and administrators at one of NASA's bases French and Caplan (1970) found that role ambiguity was positively and significantly related to low job satisfaction as well as increased blood pressure and pulse rate.

Stress and selected personal and contextual variables

This study also sought to examine the degree and form of association between various dimensions of occupational stress and certain respondent characteristics, such as age, number of years of administrative experience, and position in organization. Table 6 presents the means and analysis of variance results for age, administrative experience and position in organization.

While prior research has suggested that lower levels of stress were associated with advanced age and experience (e.g. Indik et al., 1964; McGrath, 1976), the data in Table 6 suggests a more complex perspective on this process. Although task-based stress declines with age, there was no concurrent decline in role-based stress or conflict mediating stress (the latter does drop significantly after age 50, though). Furthermore, it was discovered that boundary spanning stress actually increases with age, a factor which probably reflects growing institutional responsibilities in later career stages. This latter finding is consistent with the research of Pincherle (1972) in his study of 2000 executives. Pincherle's data showed that the probability of the presence of coronary heart disease risk factors and symptoms were substantially higher in the older executives that occupied more responsible positions. Thus, nominal declines in task-based stress appear to be offset by increases in boundary spanning stress.

As expected, results based upon years of administrative experience are similar to those for age. Respondents with 16-plus years of experience appear to be less bothered by conflict-mediating and task-based sources of stress than less experienced administrators. By contrast, boundary spanning stress increases significantly for each advanced experience group.

The stress picture for principals and superintendents is characterized by contrasts. Principals experience significantly greater role-based, task-based, and conflict-mediating stress; while superintendents report greater boundary spanning stress. The contrasts are especially sharp with respect to Factors 3 and 4. Conflict-mediation is markedly more salient to principals, while dealing

Table 6. Means and analysis of variance results for age, administrative experience and position in organization

Variance	Factor 1 (Role)	Factor 2 (Task)	Factor 3 (Conflict)	Factor 4 (Boundary)
Age				
Less than 40 ($n = 256$)	2.11	2.64	2.32	2.24
40-49 ($n = 507$)	2.11	2.54	2.30	2.40
50+ ($n = 403$)	2.09	2.47	2.13	2.54
F-ratio	.09	4.90**	1.77	9.56***
Administrative Experience				
1-5 years ($n = 264$)	2.07	2.55	2.42	2.14
6-15 years ($n = 528$)	2.12	2.59	2.28	2.42
16+ years ($n = 364$)	2.08	2.46	2.10	2.61
F-ratio	.39	4.39**	6.29**	22.98***
Position				
Principal ($n = 583$)	2.12	2.57	2.66	2.55
Superintendent ($n = 204$)	1.85	2.42	1.68	3.10
F-ratio	11.13***	4.02*	105.77***	44.39***

* $p < 0.05$
** $p < 0.01$
*** $p < 0.001$

with environmental constraints (boundary spanning stress) is of greatest salience to superintendents. This latter finding is consistent with *a priori* expectations, given objective differences in the roles and work contexts of superintendents and principals. The role of the superintendent is primarily to coordinate the activities of various schools in a given district, and to relate these schools to the community at large. On the other hand, the functions of the principal pertain more to the coordination of activities within the organization (school) of which he/she is an administrator. These differences in stress profiles between the principals and superintendents also suggest that the 'bothers me' response format used in the Administrative Stress Index (as in the JRS) is capable of tapping objective differences in stimulus conditions, i.e. the items appear to be capable of measuring differences in perceived environmental conditions (various classes of stressors) and not measuring a relatively stable personality trait (such as the respondent being a 'grouchy' person).

Finally, an overall examination of Table 6 indicates that public school administrators are more likely to be bothered by task-based, conflict-mediating and boundary-spanning stress than role-based stress. Since the items which comprise these three dimensions evolved out of administrator participation in instrument construction, this provides good support for use of similar procedures in identifying salient stress sources among various occupational groups. It also suggests that general measures, such as the JRS, are not capable of identifying and measuring the variety of job-related stress experienced by school administrators.

In addition, the findings in the present research suggest that it would be inappropriate to generalize that overall stress increases or decreases with age or position in organization. Rather overall stress should be broken down into its various components so that we could have a better understanding of the relationships between the various aspects of stress and certain personal and contextual variables.

COPING TECHNIQUES

The study also sought to identify the techniques or mechanisms school administrators have found most useful for coping with stress. The administrators were asked in an open-ended question to enumerate the ways they have 'personally found useful in handling the tensions and pressures of the job'. Approximately 77% of the administrators responded to this question.

The responses were content analysed according to the format suggested by North and coworkers (1963). The techniques reported by the administrators could be categorized into 3 general factors or areas: (1) physiological activity, (2) cognitive activities, and (3) acquisition of interpersonal and management skills. Each of these categories are examined in greater detail below.

Physiological activities

More than 50% of the respondents used some sort of physiological technique in coping with job-related stress. Physiological activities could in turn be divided into 3 sub-categories. The first sub-category involves physiological activities in which the respondents actually engage in some sort of physical work or exercise. These include jogging, competing in athletic activities, chopping wood, sex, general exercise programs, working on a farm, strolling in the woods, and gardening. The second subcategory involves activities in which the respondents purposely attempt to isolate themselves from the work environment. These include isolating oneself in one's home, having a retreat in the mountains or another area away from home, travelling for an extended period of time such as a weekend trip to the coast or to the mountains, and establishing social friendships outside the immediate educational environment, thus providing opportunities to discuss with non-educators issues and topics other than education. The third sub-category involves physiological activities designed as relaxation mechanisms. These include yoga and meditation.

Cognitive activities

Approximately 40% of the respondents indicated they used some form of cognitive activities to cope with job-related stress. Cognitive activites refer to the positive attitudes and supportive philosophies of life which were used as ways to positively cope with the tensions created by one's job. Such activities include the following: approaching all problems with an optimistic attitude; sharing problems with colleagues, spouses, and other family members; establishing realistic goals that recognize one's own limitations and the impossibility of solving all problems; attempting to keep one's emotions out of one's work; maintaining a sense of humour; believing in and practising the Christian ethic and using prayer and the help of God successfully to overcome adversity.

Acquisition of interpersonal and management skills

This last category is least frequently cited as useful in coping with stress. Less than 10% of the superintendents mentioned mechnisms relating to acquisition of interpersonal and management skills. Other administrators placed slightly more emphasis on the category. The coping techniques mentioned in this category involve updating professional skills, acquiring time management and conflict management skills, developing good human relations, and learning team management efforts.

Even though respondents in this study have placed relatively little emphasis on learning time management and interpersonal skills as means for coping with stress, it appears that greater emphasis and reliance upon these techniques could assist administrators in effectively managing stressful situations. Five of the ten stressors most frequently mentioned by the respondents were related to the control over time (interruptions, meetings, too heavy a work load, and completing reports). Since time is finite and non-expandable, the way around it would be to learn how to more effectively use and manage time. Odiorne (1973) suggests that the most successful organizations are run by administrators who are very effective and adept in managing time so that they could accomplish all the necessary activities within the given time span. The administrator's role also involves extensive interpersonal contacts with various publics — students, parents, teachers, etc. To deal successfully with these various groups, it is mandatory that the administrator develop better skills in resolving conflicts, improving communications and other interpersonal relational activities.

CONCLUSION AND DISCUSSION

Principal components analysis of the Administrative Stress Index revealed four interpretable factors of stress. Three of these four dimensions were cited as sources of stress in McGrath's theoretically derived model of occupational stress (1976). These were task-based stress, role-based stress and conflict-mediating stress.

The fourth factor or dimension of stress extracted in this study (boundary spanning stress) may be peculiar to persons occupying administrative positions (i.e. individuals whose roles involve relating their organization to the external environment or the society at large). Such positions have been hypothesized to be particularly stressful because objectives and demands of the focal organization are often in conflict with those of the external environment, and persons occupying such positions must often assume the delicate task of resolving these conflicts and satisfying organizational demands within constraints imposed by the external societal environment. In the public school system, for example, administrators must often bargain with the different government agencies and the general public for funds and support. Since educational institutions are dependent upon these external sources for financing, their objectives, policies and ways of conducting day-to-day business are often subject to scrutiny and criticism by various publics and institutional agencies. The external environment thus constitutes a challenge and poses a potential source of stress to public school administrators in the performance of their duties as boundary-spanning agents. Thus, boundary spanning stress like the other dimensions extracted from the ASI, is interpretable from a theoretical point of view as an important potential source of administrative stress.

The results of this study suggest that the ASI is a significant improvement over the JRS as a measure of stress among administrators. The latter index was only able to tap generic role-based stress (Indik *et al.*, 1964; Burke and Belcourt, 1974), whereas a general consensus exists among researchers that stress is a multi-dimensional construct.

This study also related stress to certain personal characteristics. Findings in this area were consistent with previous research in that relationships were found to exist between these two sets of variables. However, while previous research indicated increases or decreases in global stress measures with certain personal characteristics, when the present study decomposed stress into various dimensions it was found that certain dimensions of stress may covary positively with a particular personal characteristic, while others actually decrease with the same characteristic.

An interesting finding with respect to age is that task-based stress declined with age whereas boundary spanning stress actually increased with age. A possible explanation for this finding is that a person advances in years and occupies a more senior administrative position, the routine day-to-day tasks (which constitute the sources of task-based stress) would normally be delegated to subordinates or those in less senior administrative positions. Apparently, the slack which is created in this area for senior administrators is readily absorbed in increased demands to attend to pressure from the external environment, and the need to negotiate with various sectors in the community at large.

A similar explanation could be applied to findings concerning administrative experience: more experienced administrators are less bothered by conflict mediating and task-based sources of stress, but are increasingly bothered by boundary spanning stress. Presumably, once procedures and methods for handling task overloads and conflicts among students and conflicts between parent-school have been established and routinized, the administrator would be in a better position to cope with and handle such situations when they arise again in the future. On the other hand, there is empirical evidence to support the contention that the external environment of the public school system is becoming increasingly complex. The administrator has to contend with more turbulent sectors in the external environment. For example, in recent decades the general public has become more vocal in its criticism of public school operations; the spectre of tax revolts poses serious risks to institutional survival; and, the emergence of collective bargaining together with governmentally imposed employment regulations greatly increase uncertainty. Moreover, as educational institutions have become a focal point for social change, they have had to respond at an increasingly rapid rate to government pressures for program innovations. Thus, senior administrators who have to contend with multiple publics and rapid changes would find themselves increasingly bothered by stressful situations that arise from performance of their boundary spanning activities.

A priori support exists for the relationship between stress and professional position. In general, principals are more concerned with the running of day-to-day activities and dealing with problems that arise within their particular school, whereas superintendents are more concerned with coordinating the activities of several schools or relating the schools in their district to the external community. Thus, superintendents in general experience greater boundary spanning stress, whereas principals appear to be more bothered by role-based, task-based, and conflict mediating stress.

A last, and especially important finding with respect to the relationship between stress and certain personal and contextual variables is that public school administrators are more bothered by task-based, conflict mediating, and boundary spanning stress than role-based stress. This finding might be attributed to the fact that administrative positions tend to have sufficient institutionalized authority for coping with generic sources of occupational stress. It could also be an artifact of research procedures in the present study.

Most of the items comprising the task-based, conflict mediating, and boundary spanning stress components evolved out of administrator participation in instrument construction, whereas six of the seven items comprising the role-based stress dimension were borrowed from Indik *et al.*'s JRS index (1964). This suggests that the use of scales that merely measure generic work stress, such as the JRS, would greatly underestimate the ability to clearly identify the sources of occupational stress experienced by administrators. It points to the need to develop instruments with application to particular occupational groups and/or levels. To maximize internal validity, the ASI was developed specifically for use on a homogeneous population, namely school administrators of educational institutions. As Campbell and Stanley (1968) point out, it is very difficult if not impossible to maximize both the internal and external validities of a particular instrument and research design. Since the ASI was developed specifically for use on school administrators, in order to be applicable to subjects employed in other contexts many ASI items would most probably have to be modified and adapted to the unique social and cognitive realities of other work populations.

It is important to note that the findings in this study with respect to relationships between these different dimensions of administrative stress and personal characteristics point to the need for recognizing the multi-dimensionality of the occupational stress construct. As has been shown, it would be inaccurate to use scales that merely measure generic work stress and then state stress increases or decreases over various life and career stages. Rather it would be important to state specifically which components of occupational stress actually increase or decrease with age.

While the computer age of social science research appears to foster the collection of masses of data with standardized instruments, this probably contributes to many blind spots in our understanding of individual and organizational complexities. What is gained with respect to external validity may be lost with respect to more refined insights within particular occupational contexts. Perhaps instruments which involve subject groups in their design, as in the present study, will greatly add to the richness of empirical social science research. In this vein, future efforts might experiment with applications of Delphi procedures in the design of contextually-rooted instruments. Perhaps through such participative procedures researchers will gain a fuller appreciation of the phenomenological dimensions of particular occupational groups and organizational settings.

A better understanding of the behaviour sources or dimensions of occupational stress may help us arrive at suggestions of ways of coping with it. This study points to the complexity of the nature of stress and its relationship with certain personal and contextual variables. For example, older administrators appeared to be more frequently bothered by boundary-spanning stress, whereas younger administrators were more frequently bothered by task-based stress. Given these differences, it would appear more appropriate to prescribe time management training techniques for younger administrators, while it would be more appropriate to emphasize developing interpersonal relational skills among the older administrators. Also the prescription of the most appropriate stress-management training programmes would depend on other personal characteristics and contextual variables. This is consistent with the assertion made by Seyles (1975) and Cooper and Marshall (1978) that given individual differences in response to various contextual variables, there is no universal stress formula that will suit everyone. The solution to the problem lies rather in the accurate diagnosis of the sources of stress and then prescribing specific programs for reducing those particular sources. This study points to the need to analyse specific industries or organizations more intensively in order to more clearly understand the various dimensions or aspects of the job which could be potential sources of stress to the administrators involved.

REFERENCES

Berkun, M.M., Bialek, H.M., Kern, R.P., and Yagi, K. (1962). Experimental studies of psychological stress in man, *Psychological Monographs, 76,* (15, Whole No. 534).

Brummet, R.L., Pyle, W.C., and Flamholtz, E.G. (1968). Accounting for Human Resources, *Michigan Business Review, 20,* 20-25.

Breslow, L., and Buell, P. (1960). Mortality from Coronary Heart Diseases and Physical Activity of Work in California, *Journal of Chronic Diseases, 11,* 615-626.

Burke, R.J., and Belcourt, M.L. (1974). Managerial role stress and coping responses, *Journal of Business Administration, 5,* 55-68.

Campbell, D.T., and Stanley, J.C. (1968). *Experimental and Quasi-Experimental Designs for Research,* Rand McNally, Chicago.

Cooper, C.L., and Marshall, J. (1976). Occupational sources of stress: A review of the literature relating to coronary heart disease and mental health, *Journal of Occupational Psychology, 49,* 11-28.

Cooper, C.L., and Marshall, J. (1978). *Executives under Pressure,* Macmillan, London.

Cooper, C.L., and Payne, R. (1978). *Stress at Work,* John Wiley and Sons, New York.

Cooper, C.L. (1979). *Sources of Managerial (Di)stress,* Paper presented at the 39th National Meetings of the Academy of Management, August.

Eckerman, W.C. (1964). The relationships of need achievement to production, job satisfaction and psychological stress, *Dissertation Abstracts, 24* (8), 3446.

Farber, E.C., and Spence, K.W. (1956). Effects of anxiety, stress, and task variables on reaction time, *Journal of Personality, 25,* 1-18.

French, J.R.P., and Caplan, R.D. (1970). Psychological Factors in Coronary Heart Disease, *Industrial Medicine, 39,* 383-397.

French, J.R.P., and Caplan, R.D. (1973). Organizational stress and individual strain, in *The Failure of Success* (Ed. A.J. Marrow), AMACOM, New York.

French, J.R.P., Cobb, S., Caplan, R.D., Van Harrison, R., and Pinneau, S.R. (1976). *Job Demands and Worker Health,* A symposium presented at the 84th Annual Convention of the American Psychological Association, September.

Guetzkow, H., and Gyr, J. (1954). An analysis of conflict in decision-making groups, *Human Relations,* **7,** 367-382.

Gullahorn, J.R. (1956). Measuring role conflict. *American Journal of Sociology,* **61,** 299-303.

Gurin, G., Veroff, J., and Feld, S. (1960). *Americans view their Mental Health,* Basic Books, New York.

Indik, B., Seashore, S.E., and Slesinger, J. (1964). Demographic correlates of psychological strain. *Journal of Abnormal and Social Psychology,* **69** (1), 26-28.

Kahn, R.L., Wolfe, D.M., Quinn, R.P., Snoek, J.D., and Rosenthal, R.A. (1964). *Organizational Stress,* John Wiley and Sons, New York.

Kast, F.E., and Rosenzweig, J.E. (1979). *Organization and Management: A Systems and Contingency Approach,* McGraw-Hill, New York.

Kornhauser, A. (1965). *Mental Health of the Industrial Worker,* John Wiley and Sons, New York.

Kugelmass, S., and Lieblich, I. (1966). Effects of realistic stress and procedural interference in experimental lie detection. *Journal of Applied Psychology,* **50** (3), 211-216.

Langner, T.S. (1962). A twenty-two item screening score of psychosomatic symptoms indicating impairment, *Journal of Health and Human Behavior,* **3,** 269-276.

Margolis, B.L., Kroes, W.H., and Quinn, R.P. (1974). Job Stress: An unlisted occupational hazard. *Journal of Occupational Medicine,* **16** (10), 654-661.

McGrath, J.E. (1970). *Social and Psychological Factors in Stress,* Holt, Rinehart and Winston, Inc., New York.

McGrath, J.E. (1976). Stress and behavior in organizations. In *Handbook of Industrial and Organizational Psychology* (Ed. M.D. Dunnette), pp.1351-1395, Rand McNally, Chicago.

Mettlin, C., and Woelfel, J. (1974). Interpersonal Influence and Symptoms of Stress. *Journal of Health and Social Behavior,* **15** (4), 311-319.

Morris, R.E. (1957). Witness performance under stress: A sociological approach. *Journal of Social Issues,* **12** (2), 17-22.

Nix, H.L., and Bates, F.L. (1962). Occupational role stress: A structural approach. *Rural Social,* **27** (1), 7-17.

North, R.C., Holsti, O.R., Zaninovich, M.G., and Zinnes, D.A. (1963). *Content Analysis,* Northwestern University Press, Evanston.

Nunnally, J.C. (1967). *Psychometric Theory,* McGraw-Hill, New York.

Odiorne, G.s. (1973). *Management and the Activity Trap,* Harper and Row, New York.

Pincerle, G. (1972). Fitness for Work. *Proceedings of the Royal Society of Medicine,* **65** (4), 321-324.

Pronko, N.E., and Leith, W.R. (1956). Behavior under stress: A study of its disintegration. *Psychological Reports,* **2,** 205-222. (Monograph Supplement 5).

Russek, H.I., and Zohman, B.L. (1958). Relative significance of hereditary diet, and occupational stress in CHD of young adults. *Americal Journal of Medical Science,* **235,** 175-266.

Seyle, H. (1975). *Stress without Distress,* Signet Books, New York.

Shirom, A., Eden, D., Silberwasser, S., and Kellerman, J.J. (1973). Job stress and risk factors in Coronary Heart Disease among occupational categories in Kibbutzim. *Social Science and Medicine,* **7,** 875-892.

Stouffer, S.A., Lumsdaine, A.A., Lumsdaine, M.H., Williams, R.M., Jr., Smith, M.B., Janies, I.K., Starr, S.A., and Cottrell, L.S., Jr. (1949). *The American soldier: Conflict and its Aftermath,* Princeton University Press, Princeton.

Swent, B., and Gmelch, W.H. (1977). Stress at the desk and how to creatively cope, *Oregon School Study Council,* **21** (4).

Ulrich, C. (1957). Measurement of stress evidenced by college women in situations involving competition. *Research Quarterly, American Association of Health and Physical Education,* **25,** 160-192.

Wardell, W.L., Human, M.M., and Hahnson, C.B. (1970). Stress and coronary heart disease in three field studies. *Journal of Chronic Disease,* **22,** 781-295.

APPENDIX A: STRESS LOG

Stress can come from a single dramatic incident, or from a cumulation of less dramatic related incidents.

At the end of each working day next week describe:

1. The most stressful single incident that occurred on your job (confronting a staff member, etc.)
2. The most stressful series of related incidents that occurred on your job (frequent telephone interruptions, etc.)

	(1) Single Incident	(2) Series of Related Incidents
Monday Feb. 7	_____M-1	_____M-2
Tuesday Feb. 8	_____Tu-1	_____Tu-2
Wednesday Feb. 9	_____W-1	_____W-2
Thursday Feb. 10	_____Th-1	_____Th-2
Friday Feb. 11	_____F-1	_____F-2

Please indicate below other stressful incidents which usually occur but did not this week:

_____

_____

_____

APPENDIX B

School administrators have identified the following 35 work-related situations as sources of concern. It's possible that some of these situations bother you more than others. How much are *you* bothered by each of the situations listed below? Please circle the appropriate response.

		Not applicable	Rarely or never bothers me	Occasionally bothers me	Frequently bothers me	
1.	Being interrupted frequently by telephone calls	NA	1	2	3	4	5
2.	Supervising and coordinating the tasks of many people	NA	1	2	3	4	5
3.	Feeling staff members don't understand my goals and expectations	NA	1	2	3	4	5
* 4.	Feeling that I am not fully qualified to handle my job	NA	1	2	3	4	5
* 5.	Knowing I can't get information needed to carry out my job properly	NA	1	2	3	4	5
* 6.	Thinking that I will not be able to satisfy the conflicting demands of those who have authority over me	NA	1	2	3	4	5
7.	Trying to resolve differences between/among students	NA	1	2	3	4	5
8.	Feeling not enough is expected of me by my superiors	NA	1	2	3	4	5
9.	Having my work frequently interrupted by staff members who want to talk	NA	1	2	3	4	5
10.	Imposing excessively high expectations on myself	NA	1	2	3	4	5
*11.	Feeling pressure for better job performance over and above what I think reasonable	NA	1	2	3	4	5

Continued next page

Note: Items designated by an asterisk are taken from the JRS.

APPENDIX B continued

		Not applicable	Rarely or never bothers me	Occasionally bothers me	Frequently bothers me	
12.	Writing memos, letters, and other communication	NA	1	2	3	4	5
13.	Trying to resolve differences with my superiors	NA	1	2	3	4	5
14.	Speaking in front of groups	NA	1	2	3	4	5
15.	Attempting to meet social expectations (housing, clubs, friends, etc.)	NA	1	2	3	4	5
*16.	Not knowing what my superior thinks of me, or how he/she evaluates my performance	NA	1	2	3	4	5
*17.	Having to make decisions that affect the lives of individual people that I know (colleagues, staff members, students, etc.)	NA	1	2	3	4	5
18.	Feeling I have to participate in school activities outside of the normal working hours at the expense of my personal time	NA	1	2	3	4	5
*19.	Feeling that I have too much responsibility delegated to me by my superior	NA	1	2	3	4	5
20.	Trying to resolve parent/school conflicts	NA	1	2	3	4	5
21.	Preparing and allocating budget resources	NA	1	2	3	4	5
*22.	Feeling that I have too little authority to carry out responsibilities assigned to me	NA	1	2	3	4	5
23.	Handling student discipline problems	NA	1	2	3	4	5
24.	Being involved in the collective bargaining process	NA	1	2	3	4	5

APPENDIX B continued

		Not applicable	Rarely or never bothers me		Occasionally bothers me	Frequently bothers me	
25.	Evaluating staff members' performance	NA	1	2	3	4	5
*26.	Feeling that I have too heavy a work load, one that I cannot possibly finish during the normal work day	NA	1	2	3	4	5
27.	Complying with state, federal, and organizational rules and policies	NA	1	2	3	4	5
*28.	Feeling that the progress on my job is not what it should or could be	NA	1	2	3	4	5
29.	Administering the negotiated contract (grievances, interpretation, etc.)	NA	1	2	3	4	5
*30.	Being unclear on just what the scope and responsibilities of my job are	NA	1	2	3	4	5
31.	Feeling that meetings take up too much time	NA	1	2	3	4	5
32.	Trying to complete reports and other paper work on time	NA	1	2	3	4	5
33.	Trying to resolve differences between/among staff members	NA	1	2	3	4	5
*34.	Trying to influence my immediate supervisor's actions and decisions that affect me	NA	1	2	3	4	5
35.	Trying to gain public approval and/or financial support for school programs	NA	1	2	3	4	5
Other situations about your job that bother you			1	2	3	4	5

Note: Items designated by an asterisk are taken from the JRS.

White Collar and Professional Stress
Edited by C.L. Cooper and J. Marshall
© 1980 John Wiley & Sons Ltd.

Chapter 4

The Changing Role Of The American Teacher: Current And Future Sources Of Stress

Beeman N. Phillips

and

Matthew Lee
University of Texas at Austin
USA

The literature on stress of teachers is amorphous and ill-defined, and progress is uneven in understanding the nature, sources, and effects of stress on teachers and their work. In contrast, there has been considerable research on stress and anxiety of children in the classroom (e.g. Phillips, 1978), and the nature and effects of anxiety have been extensively studied in other contexts (e.g. Sarason, 1979). More closely related to the topic of stress of teachers, interest in teacher anxiety has increased recently, and Keavney and Sinclair (1978) have reviewed a substantial amount of research on this topic. However, stress is not synonymous with anxiety, which is only one of the reactions that can occur to stressful situations, as Figure 1 should make clear. The literature on teacher anxiety does have a substantive bearing on the topic of teacher stress and therefore will be incorporated in this chapter.

The purpose of the chapter is to describe the nature, sources, and effects of stress of teachers, and it will give special attention to ideas over theory, methods, and empirical results, documenting these descriptions whenever possible. In general, the potentialities rather than the actualities of stress, along with what currently appear to be the major strong and weak points of the knowledge base, will be emphasized.

RATIONALE FOR CONSIDERING STRESS OF TEACHERS

Person-situation aspects of stress

In examining teacher stress it is important to consider not only personal and situational factors separately. Person-situation interaction also needs systematic attention, a point of view emphasized by Cronbach (1957, 1975). Based on their reviews of research in several fields, Ekehammar (1974), Bowers (1973), and Endler and Magnusson (1976) have extended this point further by showing that person-situation interaction is frequently more important than individual differences or situational differences in explaining behavioural variance. Focusing on stressful situations and anxiety responses, Magnusson and Ekehammar (1975) provided additional confirmation of the interactionist viewpoint, although others have questioned these results, reporting that interaction accounts for a low percentage of behavioural variance (Sarason *et al.*, 1975). Nevertheless, it is encouraging to note the increasing number of designs in stress and anxiety research that consider interaction and at the same time recognize the need to consider the main effects of personal and situational variables in stress studies.

Aetiology of stress

The search for the specific causes of stress of teachers is a special challenge. In such an examination one needs to separate the physical and psychological factors in stress. Although teachers at times have considerable physical stress, the stress problems of most teachers will be more psychological than physical in nature. For example, it is not so much the incidence of actual violence in schools that creates teacher stress, but the fear of violence, and its correlates, that sustains stress and in some schools gives it a chronic, endemic character. One also needs to look at school parameters whose presence is associated with stress, although they may lead to knowledge of mere association or correlation of events. If one can go further and show that the presence of certain school conditions is associated with the presence of stress and absence of these conditions with the absence of stress, then a more clearcut relationship is established. The question can be put more appropriately in another way: what are the school conditions making stress reactions significantly more likely among teachers, or which create vulnerabilities within teachers that increase the likelihood of stress reactions?

   The paradigm involved here is that the teacher and the school environment are in continuous interaction, resulting in adaptive 'demands' on the teacher that can produce stress. The consequences of such stress are usually negative,

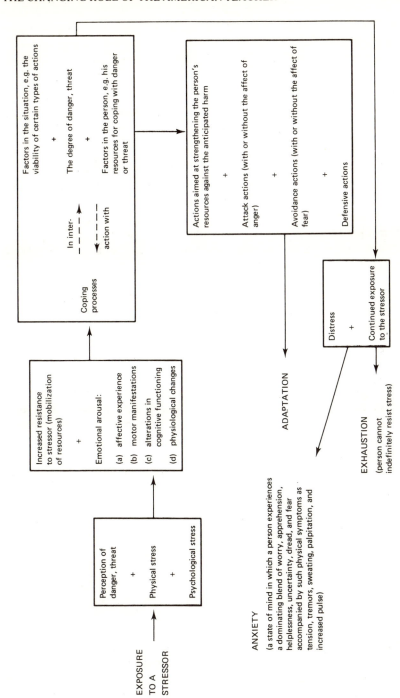

Figure 4.1 A schematic representation of the stress syndrome (after Selye and Lazarus)

although they may be positive, depending on the teacher's success in stress-mediation efforts. Unsuccessful stress mediation can result in interference with school adjustment, adaptation, and effective teaching.

SOURCES OF TEACHER STRESS

Role conflicts

In the typical American public school, teachers must deal with many expectations, including signing admission slips, issuing hall passes, taking attendance, making announcements, collecting late assignments, etc. At the same time the teacher wants to individualize instruction, foster creative thinking, personalize reinforcements, be innovative, and administer discipline fairly and effectively. During the school day, the teacher also is called upon for lunchroom duty, hall monitoring, homeroom duties, and completing state attendance registers. There also are conferences with parents, attendance at PTA meetings, sponsorship of extracurricular activities, and attendance at teacher workshops.

These activities of teachers obviously are incompatible, and viewed in the context of teacher roles, one would conclude, as Edgerton (1977) does, that the roles of the teacher are contradictory. One set of roles is made up of supervisory, directive, and other executive and evaluative functions. Another set of roles involves intellectual leadership and counselling activities, and supportive, advisory, and knowledge-oriented functions that are in basic conflict with the former set of roles. Aaron (1976) deals at length with role conflict and teacher stress in his study of the socio-psychological correlates of teacher absenteeism. He reviews role theory and models for research, including definitions of role conflict and ambiguity and the relation of role conflict to neuroticism and other personality factors. He also examines in some detail the pervasive effects of role conflict on the teacher, basing his discussion on the work of Kahn et al. (1964) and Wolfe and Snoek (1962) who studied industrial environments. They point out that role conflict and its accompanying psychological and somatic reactions lead to two types of behaviours. One is to adapt in terms of one's ego-defensive system, and the other is to utilize coping techniques. But overall, most reactions to role conflict are maladaptive, and include such emotions and behaviours as lack of job motivation and satisfaction, hostility and aggression, withdrawal and apathy, depression, loss of self-esteem, symptoms of anxiety, and psychosomatic disorders. When there are neuroticism and other dysfunctional personality factors present, these usually act as a catalyst to intensify maladaptive reactions to role conflict, which illustrates how the work environment and personal factors interact in role stress.

As Grace (1972) points out, the central component of all formulations of role conflicts and stress is incompatibility, and she elaborates this point by identifying a number of sources of role stress among teachers. One of these is role-culture conflict when essential commitments of the teaching role are in disharmony with culture. Teaching has a moral orientation and is concerned with the transmission of values (Kohlberg, 1971), but in the United States and many other advanced industrial nations there has been a deterioration in the value consensus. The teacher is in a 'confrontation' position with the reorientation of values developing in many such cultures, and these circumstances serve as a source of increased stress for teachers.

Characteristics of school systems as organizations also are determinants of role conflict and stress. In particular, the professional's emphasis on autonomy, quality of service, and application of universalistic criteria clashes with bureaucratic requirements stressing supervision, routine and particularistic criteria, and uniformity.

The community context of a role is an important dimension in conflict analysis. Role conflict and stress occur when community expectations for the teacher's role are powerful and prescriptive and run counter to teacher expectations. The principle of local control of the schools in the United States may exacerbate this problem, in contrast to the situation in many other countries. The distinction between national 'communities' also needs to be taken into account, for while there are certain continuities in the position of the teacher in the United States and other countries, there also are significant differences that are likely to be sources of differences in role stress.

The teacher's role also is articulated in a network of other roles, such as those of the pupil, the principal, and other school personnel. Others also may have different expectations for the teacher, and the teacher's perception of these differences may add to the stress on the teacher. For example, parents may expect the teacher to concentrate on the basics, while his/her principal wants more emphasis on affective development and moral education. There may be incompatibilities as well between the teacher's role expectations and his/her perception of what the role actually is. Teachers may feel, for example, that the role should have high status, but perceive that it does not. The teacher also may have role expectations that are incompatible with his/her personal characteristics.

The teacher's role, therefore, may be regarded as a prime conflict situation and an important potential source of stress. However, the potentiality for stress is not the same thing as the actuality of stress, and unfortunately there is little direct evidence on the amount of role stress actually experienced by teachers.

Teacher concerns

When teachers are asked to describe their fears, apprehensions and concerns related to teaching, student discipline usually heads the list. According to Coates and Thoresen (1976), other sources of concern, especially for beginning teachers, are motivating students, gaining the respect of students, their competence in teaching subject matter, dealing with student attitudes toward school and classwork, administrative approval, and respect from colleagues. Some of the other concerns of teachers that are frequently reported in the literature (e.g. Podrovsky, 1978; Aaron, 1976; Stinnett, 1970) include:

1. Spending too much school time filling out forms and reports unrelated to the educational needs of their students.
2. Frequent school-to-school transfers in teaching assignments, with assignments far from home.
3. Lack of supplies and materials.
4. Lack of administrative support and pressure not to 'make waves' over deplorable conditions.
5. Vandalism, violence, and generally disorderly student behaviour.
6. Seeing the casualties of the school system, e.g. promising students dropping out because of fear of crime and violence in school buildings, chronic absenteeism as a way of life, children grossly deficient in achievement for whom the school has no solution.

The concerns of teachers seem to follow a developmental sequence in that the types of concerns expressed are a function of the amount of teaching experience. According to Fuller (1969) the beginning teachers' concerns center on self, but with increasing teaching experience the nature of the concerns shift to task demands, and then to the needs of the students. There is no evidence, however, that concerns decrease with teaching experience. A difficulty with developmentally-oriented surveys of this kind, however, is that readily verbalized, self-reported concerns may not correspond well with observational and clinical data, if it were available.

Other writers have organized the concerns of teachers around personal factors. Styles and Cavanagh (1977) make an inventory of stress-producing forces experienced by teachers using the categories of expectations, self-fulfillment, ego needs, student-teacher relations, personal competence, self-relationships, conflicting values, and professional constraints. They argue that the form stress takes in the life of the typical teacher may be considered under these headings which identify personal considerations that are, in turn, the sources of teacher stress.

School factors

School-environmental conditions operate as stressors to the extent that they tax or exceed the teacher's adaptive resources. The effects of such stressors as noise and crowding have been documented. Noise, for example, is associated with elevated blood pressure and impaired task performance (Jonsson and Hansson, 1977; Weinstein, 1974; Sherrod et al., 1977). And the case can be made that the school environment has many conditions that operate as stressors, although stress research has not specifically focused on schools. While teachers may be able to adapt to school environmental stress in the short run, research implies that teachers exposed to such stressors over time are increasingly likely to develop 'after effects' leading to lower tolerance for frustration and other 'psychological' responses, as well as greater susceptibility to physical problems (Harlin and Jerrick, 1976). When the aversiveness of such events is combined with the psychological importance of these situations, their significance as sources of stress for teachers would be difficult to overestimate.

The nature of the school system also is a significant factor in the stress of teachers. Teachers frequently have little access to decision-making to influence policies under which they work, and considerable stress probably is contributed by the workload of teachers, since many teachers believe the workload is unmanageable (Stinnett, 1970). Class size, the range of intellectual and other pupil differences in class, absence of auxiliary services, the inadequacy of school facilities and teaching materials, out-of-class assignments and the inappropriateness of teaching assignments all contribute to this problem. The system's employment practices, the way a teacher's performance is evaluated, dismissal procedures, leave policies, handling of pupil discipline, and administrative procedures also are frequent sources of frustration and teacher unhappiness. They therefore are good candidates as generalized, pervasive sources of teacher stress.

Community factors

The concept of accountability has had increasing application in American education, especially at the elementary and high school level. Applying the concept to teachers and holding teachers accountable for outcomes raises issues of special concern to teachers because learning outcomes are largely the result of factors over which teachers have little control. For example, family background has consistently accounted for a large proportion of the variance in school achievement, and such factors as social class, geographic region, ethnicity, and race likewise contribute to differences in school learning outcomes (Coleman et al., 1966). Further, school populations are not randomly distributed according to such factors, so that some school districts tend to have concentrations of students that have family backgrounds, etc., conducive to school learning, while others have concentrations of students with disadvantageous combinations of such characteristics insofar as school learning is concerned. In such cases the problems and stress created by accountability are exacerbated.

The issue of crime in the schools in the United States has received increasing publicity. Although statistics are not complete, the evidence that violence, vandalism, and other crimes constitute a serious problem is convincing. It is, however, largely a problem of urban schools, with the total social system of the urban community being mirrored in the mircrocosm of the school.

In a National Center for Education Statistics (USA) survey of 8,000 public and private schools in all states in 1975 (Neill, 1978), the principal of each school was asked to provide data on the number of offences in 11 specific categories that were both committed on school premises *and* reported to the police. For the 5-month period of September, 1974, to February, 1975, a total of 280,703 offences were reported to the police, with 72% reported by secondary schools and 28% by elementary schools. The highest rate of reported offences was in schools in big cities. These figures, however, probably seriously underestimate the problem.

In a British survey (Lowenstein, 1972) of 1,065 schools, violence against property had the highest incidence, followed by violence against other students, and then against teachers. While having a lower rate of school violence overall than in the United States, the results do show that violence in the schools is not only an American phenomenon.

As to the problem from the perspective of the teacher, Neill (1978) reports that in a 1976 nationwide sampling of teachers' opinions, the NEA found that 4.3% saw student violence as a major problem. Among urban school teachers, however, the percentage was 47.3. Of all teachers polled, 24% said destruction of school property was widespread, while an additional 48% said it was present but not widespread. Similar percentages applied to serious theft.

This climate of crime in many schools has threatening effects on many teachers, with physical violence against both school staff and students being particularly stressful. But crime in the schools is only one aspect of the environmental turbulence that is a salient but pervasive aetiological aspect of stress in urban areas. The community of the urban school is not supportive of the teacher, and this is compounded by poor financing, crises generated by various single issue and special interest groups, limited interdependence among subsystems within schools, and general lack of involvement of parents in the schools.

Another important characteristic of communities is change. While no one has to the authors' knowledge scaled community changes according to their impact on schools, this has been done for a variety of life events (e.g. Rahe, 1972). Such research shows that these changes are related to emotional and physical breakdown, presumably through a mechanism of stress overload. Effects analogous to this may occur when a community changes rapidly, producing concomitant changes in the schools.

Professional factors

Teaching is a lonely profession, as Sarason (1971) and Knoblock and Goldstein (1971) have noted, and teachers are isolated in many ways from their colleagues. This creates a situation with considerable potential for stress in view of the difficulties teachers have in conducting their classes and handling the many teaching problems that arise. Utilizing the paradigm originally developed by Schachter (1959), teachers need to interact with other teachers to compare their own responses to stressful classroom events with those of colleagues. They are thereby helped to decide how they ought to feel about the problems they are having to cope with, and to obtain ideas on what they might do about them. However, teachers who are hard-driving and achievement-oriented are less likely to need this affiliative opportunity than more relaxed and easy-going teachers, although there is no evidence on whether teachers tend to fit this latter designation more often than the former. In general the need for social support gains in strength as the emotional strain of teaching increases, and since there is considerable evidence that the stress of teaching has increased, one might reasonably argue that the isolation of the teacher is more of a problem now than it was in the past.

Occupational success is also a consideration in examining the stress of teachers. How well teachers are adapting to the demands of their jobs can be determined from performance measures or the ratings of others, including school administrators, parents, and the public at large. There is the general feeling in American society that schools are not doing as well as in the past in educating children, and teachers share some of the blame in the eyes of the public. In spite of this, other factors are generally considered to be more important, e.g. lack of parental support and changes in society that have caused a lessening of discipline.

Teaching is a traditionally female-dominated profession at the public school level in American society, while the college and university level is a male-dominated occupation. This presents some contrasts and different sources of stress for men and women entering teaching at these two levels. Men entering public school teaching, especially at the elementary level, are faced with stereotypic attitudes that raise problems concerning their masculinity. In contrast, women entering college teaching face issues of sexism as well as career vs. family issues. This intertwining of sex roles and occupational roles creates conflicts between career orientation and marriage and family responsibilities that are particularly burdensome to women in higher education careers.

TEACHERS' RESPONSES TO STRESS

Stress responses viewed in terms of Selye's General Adaptation Syndrome

According to Selye (1956), the stress sequence includes alarm, resistance, and then exhaustion, which is a theory of stress that is updated, with more emphasis on adequate coping, in his more recent publication (1974). In a recent article Sylvester (1977) gives a number of examples of stress response, utilizing the categories of fighting the stressor, fleeing from it, and ignoring or tolerating it. Some examples of these categories are listed below:

1. *Fighting the stressor,* e.g. using censure or threats on misbehaving students; establishing a tight schedule to keep students busy, and thus less likely to engage in behaviour causing the teacher stress; pressuring the student to work quietly and stay seated; sabotaging disliked administrative policies, or gossiping about disliked colleagues.
2. *Fleeing from it,* e.g. calling in sick when school conditions may be especially stressful; scheduling disliked subjects late in the day so that time spent on them is shortened or eliminated; sending misbehaving pupils to the principal.
3. *Ignoring/tolerating it,* e.g. attending unnecessary meetings but using the time to correct papers; allowing pupils considerable freedom in their behaviour; following school regulations one does not approve of, but doing it unenthusiastically.

Ecologically-oriented indicators of stress response

According to Hendrickson (1979) 'burnout' is an occupational hazard for teachers that is a response to chronic stress caused by institutional and organizational factors and the immediate teaching environment. It begins with a feeling of uneasiness accompanied by being tired all the time, sleeplessness, depression, and being physically run down. Other symptoms include frequent headaches, colds, dizziness, and diarrhoea. The end result is physical and emotional exhaustion.

Teacher absenteeism is increasing dramatically in the United States (Elliott and Manlove, 1977). While this is partly a result of more generous sick leave policies, it also is an index of the effects of increased stress on the physical and mental well-being of teachers in many schools. Evidence for this is provided by Aaron (1976) who developed a rationale for absenteeism in terms of role conflict and ambiguity as stress factors. He documents the many antecedents, concomitants, and effects of role stress, and found that nine variables predicted teacher absenteeism. These included role conflict, years of teaching experience, holding summer jobs, working in inner city versus suburban schools, academic degree, psychasthenia, the Cornell Index score, hypochondriasis, and job satisfaction.

Teacher dropout is a significant problem in the United States. According to Stinnett (1970) there is an estimated 10% annual dropout rate, and nearly 50% of U.S. teachers leave the profession within 10 years of their entrance, most within the first two to three years of teaching. While teacher dropout is complex and requires sophisticated analysis, it is reasonable to believe that stress underlies many of the precipitating factors. Tosi and Tosi (1970) note, for example, that high degrees of role conflict and ambiguity are related to teacher turnover.

Anxiety as a teacher stress response

As noted in Figure 1, anxiety is one of the consequences of stress, and while it can be conceptually and operationally differentiated from stress, the two are intimately related, and sometimes used interchangeably in the literature. This conceptual distinction, however, has considerable relevance for those seeking to understand teacher stress apart from teacher anxiety. While anxiety reactions are reactions to stressful situations, not all stressful situations produce the experience of anxiety, and there are many types of responses to stress other than anxiety reactions. This distinction also is useful in dealing with the teacher anxiety literature more meaningfully. As Keavney and Sinclair (1978) point out, the failure of many writers on teacher anxiety to distinguish indications of stress from indications of anxiety has made the interpretation of the teacher anxiety literature more difficult.

This distinction between stress and anxiety having been made, the important issue of when stress is apt to lead to anxiety reactions must be considered. The paradigm presented in Figure 1 provides a conception of this problem, but does not identify the many personal and situational factors that contribute to the likelihood that anxiety will be the dominant response to stress. Such factors are described in Phillips (1978), and an example of a personal factor would be A-Trait, which is definable as the disposition to respond anxiously to threatening situations. A high trait-anxious person would be more likely to respond to threatening situations with anxiety than a low trait-anxious person, other factors being equal. A situation which is ambiguous, but perceived as threatening, is also more likely to produce an anxiety reaction. On the average, however, anxiety is not the dominant response to stress, although some degree of anxiety may occur in the context of other responses.

While the interpretation of teacher anxiety as a response to stress remains highly speculative, there are some relationships reported in the literature which bear scrutiny. For example, Parsons (1973) reports that teacher anxiety decreases as teaching experience increases, which would be expected if alternative responses to the stress of teaching increase in availability. It is possible of course that decreases in teacher anxiety as a function of teaching experience result from a change in the type and amount of stress. The findings of a number of studies (e.g. Fuller, 1969) do suggest that the *type* of stress experienced by teachers does change with teaching experience, but the evidence that there is a decrease in the *amount* of stress is more equivocal.

Other correlates of teacher anxiety have been reported that might qualify as stressors, but whether they are causes of anxiety cannot be determined due to the limitations of the correlational designs employed. For example, Petrusich (1967) reports that high teacher anxiety is related to less verbal support of students, while Doyal and Forsyth (1973) show that teacher anxiety is positively related to pupil anxiety, and Kracht and Casey (1968) found that it is negatively related to teacher warmth in relations with children. In terms of pupil achievement, Osborne (1973) reports that teacher anxiety has differential effects on the performance of high and low anxious students, and Clark (1972) found that high anxious teachers gave lower grades to pupils than low anxious teachers. In general, one might hold that teacher stress does frequently lead to teacher anxiety, and that teacher anxiety in turn does lead to lower teacher effectiveness. Although the results reported are consistent with theoretical expectations, and thus serve to underscore the importance of teacher anxiety as a reaction to stress, causation can only be assessed by experimental intervention.

FUTURE SOURCES OF STRESS

The problem futurists face is that mundane realities often undercut the chances of supplying answers. In addition to forecasting, thinking about the future can help to illuminate the present (Loye, 1978). There is value therefore in seeking to identify and evaluate future sources of teacher stress.

Integration of minorities and women

Since minorities and women (in higher education) are increasingly becoming members of the contemporary teaching profession, factors that are outgrowths of this development need consideration as future sources of stress. There is indirect evidence, for example, that the behaviour of men and women teachers may be evaluated differently due to sex role stereotypes, and there may be similar influences stemming from race and ethnic status. Another example is the impact of affirmative action on teachers in elementary and secondary schools and colleges and universities (Ornstein, 1975). While the public policy is understandable, the stressful and deleterious effects on some teachers, e.g. in being 'passed over' in order to hire a minority or woman teacher, cannot be denied. It also is likely that the stress generated in such circumstances is pervasive and widespread, reaching many aspects of a teacher's professional life.

Teaching as an achieving profession

Teacher stress can be viewed against the background of work-related attitudes and values, particularly among youth from whom future teachers will be drawn. In Yankelovich's (1974) study of job-related attitudes of American youth, for example, a strong preference was shown for careers involving self-control over one's job activities and for opportunities for interesting work and high material rewards. In a future filled with scarcities of abundance, including recognition, non-debased status, and meaningful work roles (Loye, 1978), such preferences might be considered an 'endangered species'.

In his recent review of the 'fear of success' literature, Tresemer (1977) discusses three sources of success avoidance. One is a desire to avoid putting stress on oneself by engaging in events that threaten to disconfirm self-expectancies. The others are fear of demands that accompany success and of the social ostracism resulting from success. In analysing data he pays particular attention to sex differences, but concludes that the problem touches on so many aspects of human experience, and fear of success has so many 'faces' that it is difficult to comprehend all its ramifications. In other words, there is increasing evidence that fear of success is not as sex-linked as originally thought, but rather, overall cultural influences which affect both males and females seem to be involved (Hoffman, 1974). In essence, the problem raised is related to questioning of the value of achievement itself, and a lowering of the need for achievement. With a continuing achievement 'press' in teaching, especially in higher education, this suggests a source of increasing incongruence and future stress on teachers.

Reduction in the teaching force

Another development in the teaching profession is the lower birth rate providing fewer school children and college-age youth. This trend is already clearly manifest in American society, and both public school and college enrollments are expected to decline for the next decade. At the very least this means increased job insecurity as efforts are made to bring the teaching force in line with needs. But reductions in the work force are very complex phenomena that are not susceptible to easy predictions. For example, fewer jobs for new teachers, prospective changes in the tenure system, more collective bargaining confrontations, and a general increase in adversarial relations are but some of the developments that might accompany efforts to deal with the impact of the lower birthrate on education. These factors need to be analysed and evaluated for their effects on teachers, especially since a number of these developments may produce increasing amounts of tension, stress, and anxiety among teachers.

New roles for teachers

New roles for teachers are emerging in the United States as well as other countries (Bruce, 1979) as educational systems change within changing social conditions. There is, for example, a whole complex of roles developing, in addition to the instructional role. Teachers are increasingly expected to provide guidance and counselling, and to engage in a range of social work activities (Grace, 1972). These additional roles lack specificity, partly because the role concepts are not yet well defined, and partly because they are a response to changing societal conditions. With such increasing role ambiguity, and the demands for adapting to such changing roles during the course of a teacher's career, there is likely to be increased role stress among teachers.

Legal factors

As American schools move toward the future it would appear that the legal status of certain aspects of schooling will cause increasing problems for teachers. While such developments will have greater impact on public school teachers, the effects of the intrusion of law into education also will be felt by teachers in higher education. Such intrusion at the classroom level has great potential for accentuating the ambiguities of the teacher's role. As the courts take a more active interest in classroom practice, class action suits impinging on the practices of the teacher are likely to increase (Duke, DonMoyer, and Fannon, 1978). Examples of areas where further legal action may occur include, for example, suspension from class. As student behaviour problems mushroom, teachers are demanding that discipline guidelines permit the removal of such disruptive children from class. But as this right is increasingly accorded, the issue is likely to surface more often in the courts, and the actions of the courts may well place additional constraints on this right of teachers, since the threat of legal liability will surround the 'right' with increased uncertainty. Additional teacher legal liability also may arise in regard to inconsistent rule enforcement and administration of punishment, and in relation to changing definitions of what constitutes 'equality' of opportunity. If equality of *outcome* emerges as the standard, then teachers may be accountable for providing compensating education that eliminates or minimizes initial individual differences. Teachers who are unwilling or unable to individualize successfully in this way may be subject to dismissal and malpractice suits. Another area that raises such possibilities is intraclass classification for instructional purposes. In the future the balancing of student rights and teacher responsibilities as professionals will increasingly be the subject of litigation, and the source of frustration and concomitant stress if teachers increasingly feel legalistically powerless.

STRESS INTERVENTION

There are no easy solutions for handling stress, but according to Styles and Cavanagh (1977) a definition of the forms of stress helps to bring suitable solutions into focus. Only the individual teacher or a therapist can ultimately diagnose and resolve stress, but reflections on possible ways that stress can be resolved may be helpful. They suggest the following preventive and/or remedial efforts:

1. Taking a constructive attitude toward stress, adapting positively to the pressures stress generates rather than attempting to entirely eliminate it, and thereby confusing stress which is beneficial with deleterious stress.
2. Recognize the role of one's expectations in providing feelings of satisfaction and dissatisfaction, and develop realistic expectations, which is more difficult than it appears because many teachers are idealistic and set unachievable goals.
3. Avoid procrastination and 'worrying molehills into mountains through inaction' by taking specific action, breaking king-size tasks down into bite-size chunks, since successful completion of each specific task serves as motivation to work on the next one.
4. Take time to build into one's lifestyle regular periods of stock-taking and self-evaluation. One needs to sort out the 'myriad demands, calls to duty, perceived necessities, and horrendous time restraints which flood our consciousness with a depressing sense of urgency and priority.' In other words, one needs to put things in perspective so that many of the sources of stress will not grow out of proportion and unnecessarily consume time and energy when in time the stress would have worked itself out if acted upon in the total scheme of things.
5. Make the most of the present, rather than focusing on possible future happenings and 'building unnecessary bridges that will never have to be crossed', and striking a balance between reasonable concern for and neglect of potential future problems.
6. Get adequate rest and sleep, and pursue vigorous and regular exercise which can be an excellent way to eliminate stress by switching mental stress to physical stress, and then dissipating it.
7. Learn to be more accepting of one's accomplishments and be thankful for what one has and for whatever freedom one has to decide one's own future.

In a different approach to the hazards of teaching, Harlin and Jenick (1976) stress physical and mental well-being, emphasizing that teachers cannot do an excellent job of teaching with health handicaps. While they deal with emotional and psychosomatic conditions, they give most of their attention to the physical problems which plague many teachers, discussing ten areas of health concerns which adversely affect the teacher's work. They also describe what individuals and schools can do to help teachers stay healthy. In coping with 'burnout', which has many physical symptoms, Hendrickson (1979) suggests that one needs first to recognize the symptoms, then look closely at how one is responding, recognizing the negative ways one has been trying to cope. One must also pinpoint the factors causing the stress and take appropriate action.

For those teachers whose main problem is in-class anxiety, particularly that associated with teaching itself, Richardson and Svinicki's (1979) self-instructional manual my be helpful. While it is designed primarily for college teachers, it would probably be helpful to other teachers, especially at the secondary school level. The manual is based on the principle of 'informational' learning, which they describe as the position that individuals can change their behaviour in the direction desired if they're given accurate and useful information about the task or problem faced. They state that stress in class may represent lack of preparation or motivation and interest, a reflection of other emotional and behavioural concerns, or in-class anxiety, and they point out that if a problem other than in-class anxiety is the predominant aspect of one's difficulties in class, then other remedial action would be desirable.

For teachers who need the assistance of an expert, behavioural intervention is a primary approach to stress reactions, with systematic desensitization being a popular method of treatment, although its appropriateness for all types of stress reactions is an open question. One recently developed alternative for the treatment of stress is the skills-oriented stress innoculation training of Meichenbaum and his colleagues (Meichenbaum and Cameron, 1974; Meichenbaum and Turk, 1976). This intervention incorporates education, rehearsal, and related techniques aimed at the development of insight into stress-inducing and/or maladaptive behaviours. A major advantage of this treatment strategy is its emphasis on general coping skills, and such stress innoculation training can be utilized in a group setting, which also is advantageous to working with classroom teachers. However, when poor social performance or speaking skills based on either a skills deficit or a performance inhibition model is a source of stress, systematic desensitization, while of some utility, may be less effective than assertiveness training, which combines both cognitive modification and behavioural rehearsal.

Other teachers with stress problems might benefit more from other helping-people-to-change strategies. Many examples of such techniques are provided in Carkhuff and Berenson (1976), Hammond, Hepworth, and Smith (1977), and Kanfer and Goldstein (1975). Small group interventions may be valuable tools for some teachers with stress. These can take the form of sensitivity and encounter groups (Lieberman *et al.*, 1973; Cooper 1979, or group problem solving and decision making activities (Steiner, 1972; Fisher, 1974). In still other cases, organizational interventions would be the preferred approach (Schmuck and Miles, 1971; Bowers, 1973). When serious personal problems are involved in addition to stress, then behaviour therapy, or other forms of therapy would be desirable, and usually necessary, to ensure a positive outcome.

ACKNOWLEDGEMENT

The authors gratefully acknowledge the bibliographic assistance of Vicki Caldarola, a Ph.D. student in school psychology, in the preparation of this manuscript.

REFERENCES

Aaron, D.S. (1976). *Social-psychological Correlates of Teacher Absenteeism — A Multi-variate Study,* unpublished doctoral dissertation, The Ohio State University (Xerox University Microfilm 77-10, 517).

Bowers, K.S. (1973). Situationism in psychology: An analysis and critique. *Psychological Review,* 89, 307-336.

Bruce, M.G. (1979). Notes on European education. *Phi Delta Kappan,* **60,** 530-532.

Carkhuff, R., and Berenson, B. (1976). *Teaching as Treatment: An Introduction to Counseling and Psychotherapy.* Human Resources Development Press, Amherst, Mass.

Clark, R.J., Jr. (1972). *Authoritarianism, Educational Progressivism and Teacher Trainees' Use of Inquiry,* unpublished doctoral dissertation, Stanford University, 1970, cited in *Teacher Attitudes: Their Empirical Relationship to Rapport with Students and Survival in the Profession,* R.N. Krasno (1972) unpublished doctoral dissertation, Stanford University. (ERIC Document Reproduction Center No. 067 388).

Coates, T.J., and Thoresen, C.E. (1976). Teacher anxiety: A review with recommendations. *Review of Educational Research,* **46,** 159-184.

Coleman, J.S., Campbell, E.Q., Hobson, C.J., McPartland, J., Mood, A.M., Weinfeld, F.D., and York, R.I. (1966). *Equality of Educational Opportunity,* United States Government Printing Office, Washington, D.C.

Cooper, C.L. (1979). *Learning from Others in Groups.* Greenwood Press, Westport, Conn.

Cronbach, L.J. (1957). The two disciplines of scientific psychology. *American Psychologist,* **12,** 671-684.

Cronbach, L.J. (1975). Beyond the two disciplines of scientific psychology. *American Psychologist,* **30,** 116-125.

Doyal, G.R., and Forsyth, R.A. (1973). Relationship between teacher and student anxiety levels. *Psychology in the Schools,* **10,** 231-233.

Duke, D.L., Donmoyer, R., and Farman, G. (1978). Emerging legal issues related to classroom management. *Phi Delta Kappan,* **60,** 305-309.

Edgarton, S.K. (1977). Teachers in role conflict: The hidden dilemma. *Phi Delta Kappan,* **59,** 120-122.

Ekehammar, B. (1974). Interactionism in personality from a historical perspective. *Psychological Bulletin,* **81,** 1026-1048.

Elliott, P.G., and Manlove, D.C. (1977). The cost of sky rocketing teacher absenteeism. *Phi Delta Kappan,* **59,** 269-271.

Endler, N.S., and Magnusson, D. (1976). Toward an interactional psychology of personality. *Psychological Bulletin,* **89,** 956-974.

Fisher, B.A. (1974). *Small Group Decision Making Communication and the Group Process,* McGraw-Hill, New York.

Fuller, F.F. (1969). Concerns of teachers: A developmental conceptualization. *American Educational Research Journal,* **6,** 207-226.

Grace, G.R. (1972). *Role Conflict and the Teacher,* Routledge and Kegan Paul, London.

Hammond, D.C., Hepworth, D.H., and Smith, V.G. (1977). *Improving Therapeutic Communication: A Guide for Developing Effective Techniques,* Jossey-Bass, San Francisco.

Harlan, V.K., and Jerrick, S.J. (1976). Is teaching hazardous to your health? *Instructor,* **86,** 55-58, 212-214.

Hendrickson, B. (1979). Is 'exhausted' an apt description of your present state of mind? You may be suffering from teacher burnout. But don't despair; you're not alone, and there *is* a cure. *Learning,* **7,** 37-39.

Hoffman, L.W. (1974). Fear of success in males and females. *Journal of Clinical Psychology,* **42,** 353-358.

Kahn, R.L., Wolfe, D.M., Quinn, R.P., and Snoke, J.O. (1964). *Organizational Stress: Studies in Role Conflict and Ambiguity,* Wiley, New York.

Kanfer, F.H., and Goldstein, A.P. (Eds.) (1975). *Helping People Change: A Textbook of Methods,* Pergamon, New York.

Keavney, G., and Sinclair, K.E. (1978). Teacher concerns and teacher anxiety: A neglected aspect of classroom research. *Review of Educational Research,* **48,** 273-290.

Kracht, C.R., and Casey, I.P. (1968). Attitudes, anxieties and student teaching performance. *Peabody Journal of Education,* **45,** 214-217.

Knoblock, P., and Goldstein, A. (1971). *The Lonely Teacher,* Allyn and Bacon, Boston.

Kohlberg, L. (1971). Stages of moral development with a base for moral education, in *Moral Education: Interdisciplinary Approaches* (Eds. C.M. Beck, B.S. Crittenden, and E.V. Sullivan), pp.23-92, University of Toronto Press, Toronto.

Jonsson, A., and Hansson, L. (1977). Prolonged exposure to a stressful stimulus (noise) as a cause of raised blood pressure in man. *Lancet,* **1,** 86-87.

Lieberman, M.A., Yalom, I.D., and Miles, M.B. (1973). *Encounter Groups: First Facts,* Basic Books, New York.

Lowenstein, L.F. (1972). *Violence in Schools and its Treatment,* National Association of Schoolmasters, Great Britain.

Loye, D. (1978). *The Knowable Future,* Wiley, New York.

Magnusson, D., and Ekehammar, B. (1975). Anxiety profiles based on both situational and response factors. *Multivariate Behavior Research,* **10,** 27-43.

Meichenbaum, D., and Cameron, R. (1974). The clinical potential of modifying what clients say to themselves, *Psychotherapy: Theory, Research, and Practice,* **11,** 103-107.

Meichenbaum, D., and Turk, D. (1976). The cognitive-behavioral management of anxiety, anger, and pain. In *Behavioral Management of Anxiety, Depression, and Pain* (Ed. P. Davidson), Brunner/Mazel, New York.

Neill, S.B. (1978). Violence and vandalism: Dimensions and correctives. *Phi Delta Kappan,* **59,** 302-307.

Ornstein, A.C. (1975). What does affirmative action affirm? A viewpoint. *Phi Delta Kappan,* **57,** 244-245.

Osborne, M.D. (1973). *The Influence of Teacher-Expectancy of Anxiety on Teacher Behaviour and Pupil Performance,* unpublished bachelor's thesis, University of Sydney.

Parsons, J.S. (1973). *Assessment of Anxiety About Teaching Using the Teaching Anxiety Scale: Manual and Research Report,* Research and Development Center for Teacher Education, University of Texas, Austin.

Petrusich, M.M. (1967). Separation anxiety as a factor in the student teaching experience. *Peabody Journal of Education,* **14,** 353-356.

Phillips, B.N. (1978). *School Stress and Anxiety: Theory, Research, and Intervention.* Human Sciences Press, New York.

Podrovsky, R. (1978). A teacher calls it quits. *Phi Delta Kappan,* **59,** 485.

Rahe, R.H. (1972). Subjects' recent life changes and their near future illness reports. *Annual Clinical Research,* **4,** 250-265.

Richardson, F., and Svinicki, M. (1979). *Coping with In-Class Anxiety,* unpublished report, Center for Teaching Effectiveness, University of Texas, Austin.

Sarason, I.G. (Ed.). *Test Anxiety: Theory, Research, and Applications.* Lawrence Ehrlbaum Associates, Hillsdale, N.J., 1979.

Sarason, I.G., Smith, R.E., and Diener, E. (1975). Personality research: Components of variance attributable to the person and situation. *Journal of Personality and Social Psychology,* **32,** 199-204.

Sarason, S.B. (1971). *The Culture of the School and the Problem of Change,* Allyn and Bacon, Rockleigh, N.J.

Schachter, S. (1959) *The Psychology of Affiliation.* Stanford University Press, Stanford.

Schmuck, R.A., and Miles, M.G., Eds. (1971). *OD in Schools.* National Press, Palo Alto.

Selye, H. (1956). *The Stress of Life,* McGraw-Hill, New York.

Selye, H. (1974). *Stress Without Distress,* Lippincott, New York.

Sherrod, D.R., Hage, J.N., Halpern, P.L., and Moore, B.S. (1977). Effects of personal causation and perceived control on responses to an aversive environment: The more control, the better. *Journal of Experimental Social Psychology,* **13,** 14-27.

Steiner, I.D. (1972). *Group process and productivity,* Academic, New York.

Stinnett, T.M. (Ed.) (1970). *The Teacher Dropout,* Phi Delta Kappa, Inc., Bloomington, Ind.

Styles, K., and Cavanagh, G. (1977). Stress in teaching and how to handle it. *English Journal,* **66,** 76-79.

Sylvester, R. (1977). Stress and the classroom teacher. *Education Digest,* 42(9), 14-17, from *Instructor,* (1977) **86,** 72-74, 76.

Tosi, D.J., and Tosi, H. (1970). Some correlates of role ambiguity among public school teachers. *Journal of Human Relations,* **18,** 1068-1076.

Tresemer, D.W. (1977). *Fear of success,* Plenum, New York.

Weinstein, N.D. (1974). Effect of noise on intellectual performance, *Journal of Applied Psychology,* **59,** 548-554.

Wolfe, D.M., and Snoek, D.J. (1962). A study of tensions and adjustments under role conflict. *Journal of Social Issues,* **18,** 102-121.

Yankelovich, D. (1974). The meaning of work. In *The Worker and the Job* (Ed. J.W. Rosow), Prentice-Hall, Englewood Cliffs, N.J., pp.19-47.

White Collar and Professional Stress
Edited by C.L. Cooper and J. Marshall
© 1980 John Wiley & Sons Ltd.

Chapter 5

Sources Of Stress Among British Teachers: The Contribution Of Job Factors And Personality Factors

Chris Kyriacou
University of York, England

INTRODUCTION

For the purposes of this chapter, occupational stress among schoolteachers may be defined as the experience by a teacher of unpleasant, negatively toned emotions, such as anger, anxiety, depression and tension, resulting from aspects of the teacher's job. A model of teacher stress has been presented (Kyriacou and Sutcliffe, 1978a) in which teacher stress was conceptualized as being mediated by the teacher's perception of threat to his well-being and by coping mechanisms activated to reduce the perceived threat. A discussion of this model will not be presented here, but it is important to emphasize its central argument, that whether a teacher experiences stress will depend on how he appraises his environment and on the coping mechanisms he is able to utilize.

Teacher stress will be considered in this chapter under five main headings: Prevalence, Sources, Symptoms, Personality, and Coping.

PREVALENCE

There is a great deal of anecdotal literature concerning teacher stress ranging from sensational newspaper articles to considered reporting of case studies. Dunham (1976) has reported the results of an investigation of teacher stress based on an analysis of data which included the reports of 658 teachers in primary and secondary schools in the United Kingdom. These reports were obtained from teachers attending conferences and courses who were asked to

113

describe their stress situations, how they responded to them, and what recommendations they would make for reducing stress. Dunham stated that the two major conclusions of his survey were that 'more teachers are experiencing stress' and that 'severe stress is being experienced by more teachers' (p. 19). In the absence of comparable data from earlier samples it is unclear as to how Dunham arrived at these conclusions, although a number of authors have also argued that teacher stress is on the increase (e.g. Andrews, 1977; Hargreaves, 1978). Nevertheless, his report suggests that a number of teachers are experiencing a great deal of occupational stress. Indeed, Dunham goes on to say that his investigation indicates that teacher stress can no longer be dismissed as a short term characteristic of adjustment problems during the probationary year or immediately following promotion. Unfortunately the nature of much of the anecdotal literature makes it difficult to estimate the proportion of teachers who are experiencing a great deal of occupational stress compared with those who are experiencing little occupational stress. A number of relatively recent studies conducted in the United Kingdom however can now provide some useful guidelines here.

Taylor and Dale (1971) conducted a postal questionnaire survey of 3,588 probationary teachers in primary and secondary schools in England and Wales. The probationers were asked to tick up to three items from a list of eight, those personal problems 'which you feel to be particularly relevant to your present situation'. The item 'general feeling of being under the stress of adapting to teaching (e.g. nervous fatigue)' was ticked by 36% of the probationers.

Pratt (1976) has reported some unpublished data obtained from the National Survey of Health and Development. In 1972, when the participants in the survey were 26 years old, the participants were asked to respond to the question 'Would you say/that in your work you were under severe nervous strain, some nervous strain, or little or no nervous strain?'. Of the 227 schoolteachers in the sample, 60.4% reported some or severe nervous strain. This compared with 51.1 per cent of the 311 'other professionals' and 36.1% of the total sample of 5,245.

Cox *et al.* (1978) have reported the results of a study comparing 100 schoolteachers with 100 semi-professionals matched for sex, age, and marital status. This study was conducted in the Nottinghamshire and Derbyshire areas. In response to the open ended question 'Where are the main sources of stress in your life?', 79% of the schoolteachers mentioned work whereas only 38% of the non-teachers did so.

Kyriacou and Sutcliffe have conducted four studies on teacher stress (Kyriacou and Sutcliffe, 1977, 1978b, 1979a, 1979b). Each study was based on a random sample of teachers in medium-sized (about 1,000 pupils) mixed comprehensive schools in England. The studies took the form of anonymously completed questionnaire surveys. In each study the teacher was asked to respond to the question 'In general, how stressful do you find being a teacher?' on a five-point response scale labelled 'not at all stressful', 'mildly stressful', 'moderately stressful', 'very stressful', and 'extremely stressful'. The date of the study, the number of respondents, and the percentage who rated being a teacher as either very stressful or extremely stressful for each of the four studies were as follows:

1. Spring term, 1977. $N = 109$. 29.3% (K and S, 1977).
2. Summer term, 1977. $N = 257$. 19.9% (K and S, 1978b).
3. Autumn term, 1977. $N = 130$. 30.7% (K and S, 1979b).
4. Summer term, 1978. $N = 218$. 23.4% (K and S, 1979a).

This measure of teacher stress (self-reported teacher stress) appears to have high face validity and on the basis of significant correlations with reported frequency of stress symptoms (Kyriacou and Sutcliffe, 1978b) good concurrent validity. As such, the studies conducted by Kyriacou and Sutcliffe indicate that the proportion of teachers in medium-sized mixed comprehensive schools in England who are experiencing a great deal of occupational stress is somewhere between a fifth and a third. Interestingly, Kyriacou and Sutcliffe have found no association between self-reported teacher stress and the biographical characteristics of the teachers they looked at: sex, qualifications, age, length of teaching experience, and position held in the school. This lack of association may indicate that personality rather than biographical characteristics are the more important determinants of individual differences in teacher stress. Their results also suggest that the summer term may be associated with relatively lower levels of teacher stress for their population, although this suggestion clearly requires further investigation.

Although it is tempting to use measures of occupational stress to compare teachers in different types of schools (primary and secondary, large and small, urban and rural), or indeed to compare teachers with other professional groups, it is important to note that the population that makes up any occupational group is a 'survival population', i.e. it consists of those members who have remained whilst others, for numerous reasons of which the experience of occupational stress may be one factor, have left. There is also the further possibility that 'stress-prone' individuals may be attracted to some jobs (or types of schools) and unattracted by others. Such considerations require that any between-group comparisons must be treated with caution before inferences may be drawn concerning whether jobs are equally stressful or not.

SOURCES

In looking at sources of teacher stress much of the data considered has been obtained by questionnaire. Two points should be borne in mind here. Firstly, questionnaires tend to focus attention on the relatively common sources of stress and as such underplay the importance of noting that for any individual teacher his main source of stress may not be relatively common. Secondly, it may be more likely for some sources of stress to be over-reported if they relate to salient aspects of the teacher's job, commonly attributed sources of stress, or which attribute blame outside the individual.

A number of studies of job satisfaction/dissatisfaction have been included in this section since many sources of job dissatisfaction are potential sources of teacher stress.

Gabriel (1957) has reported the results of two questionnaire studies based on data collected between 1948 and 1950 from primary and secondary school teachers in the United Kingdom. The first study was based on replies from 162 teachers in response to two open-ended questions regarding 'types of children's behaviour which tend to frustrate you, and which you therefore find annoying' and 'occasions which give rise to feeling of elation or depression'. The most frequently mentioned source of frustration and annoyance was 'disobedience or obeying slowly' and the most frequently reported source of depression was 'poor results, including exam results, lack of progress'. In the second study based on 736 teachers, the teachers were asked to rate each of twenty items (derived from the first study) on a five-point scale labelled from 'causes no feelings of worry or strain' to 'causes the utmost feelings of worry or strain'. 'Large classes' was the item with the highest median value, followed by 'slow progress', 'noise of children', 'clerical work', and 'lack of equipment'. Gabriel noted that the female teachers in the sample reported significantly greater strain for nine of the twenty items compared with the male teachers and that less experienced teachers reported significantly greater strain for 'maintaining necessary discipline to carry on work' compared with their more experienced colleagues. However, in view of the fact that these subgroups were confounded with type of school, any conclusions must be treated with caution.

A study conducted by Rudd and Wiseman (1962) focused on the sources of job dissatisfaction among 590 teachers in institutions ranging from infant schools to further education establishments. The teachers in their sample had all qualified as teachers five years earlier. By means of a postal questionnaire they were asked to list their 'chief sources of professional dissatisfaction'. Rudd and Wiseman categorised the most frequently mentioned sources of dissatisfaction as 'teachers' salaries', 'poor human relations among staff', 'inadequacies of school buildings and equipment', 'teaching load', 'teacher training', 'large classes', 'feelings of inadequacy as a teacher', 'more time needed', and 'status of the profession in society'. Further analyses of the data separately for sex of teacher and type of school however revealed different underlying patterns. For example, salaries stood out as a particular source of dissatisfaction for male teachers in junior and secondary schools, while large classes was the major source of dissatisfaction for female teachers in infant and junior schools. Rudd and Wiseman went on to argue that their results indicated that 'women are more pre-occupied with day-to-day classroom problems and stresses whilst men appear to find their frustrations in a wider context' (p. 289).

Payne (1974) reported the results of a postal survey of 274 teachers in educational priority area (EPA) primary schools in England regarding job satisfaction. The teachers were asked to compare their jobs with (a) the jobs of friends of approximately the same age and with equivalent qualifications, and (b) the jobs of teachers they knew in other schools. Although there were numerous ways in which the EPA teachers rated their jobs worse than those in both comparison groups (notably the neighbourhood in which they worked, the physical conditions, the pressure of work, and the salary level), nevertheless they rated their general satisfaction as better than for both the comparison groups. Payne however argued that 'this satisfaction is evidently not sufficient compensation for many, for we have seen above that teacher turnover in the inner city project schools was extremely high' (p. 54). One interpretation of these findings is that the EPA teachers reported greater satisfaction than for the comparison groups owing to their evaluation of the greater worthwhileness of their work, while at the same time being subject to greater teacher stress. In the presentation of the results of the survey Payne appeared to assume that the ways in which the EPA teachers rated their jobs worse than for the comparison groups were the sources of dissatisfaction and discontent. However, for some items this assumption may be incorrect. For example, the EPA teachers rated their jobs worse than for teachers in other schools with respect to the ability of the children they taught. However this may have been an aspect of the teaching situation that attracted them to such schools and contributed to the evaluation of their jobs as more worthwhile rather than a source of dissatisfaction and discontent.

Numerous problems are faced by teachers in dealing with difficult pupils (Caspari, 1976; Dunham, 1977a; Laslett, 1977). Indiscipline in the classroom may range from cheek (Hargreaves, 1976) to violent and disruptive behaviour (Lowestein, 1975). Maxwell (1974) has reported the results of a survey of primary school teachers in the Inner London Borough of Southwark. She found that 10% of the teachers surveyed suffered daily anxiety about behaviour problems and a further 32% felt anxious at least once a week. Lawrence et al. (1977) have focused their attention on disruptive behaviour occurring in one particular secondary school in London. They argued that their study corroborated the finding of Dunham (1976) that 'stress is not confined to probationers but may be felt by teachers of all degrees of experience' and furthermore that their study 'makes it clear that disruptive behaviour is an important area of potential stress for many teachers' (p. 55). Lawrence et al. illustrate with reference to case studies the different ways in which disruptive behaviour can precipitate teacher stress.

Comber and Whitfield (1979) have recently reported the results of a survey of 642 members of the National Association of Schoolmasters and Union of Women Teachers. The respondents included teachers in primary, middle, and secondary schools, and about half the respondents held promoted posts (head of department or higher). The teachers were asked to 'Please describe briefly (but including any important detail) a recent school incident which caused you considerable stress and personal difficulty'. The replies of nearly half of the respondents indicated that their school work never caused them considerable stress although Comber and Whitfield noted that by asking for incidents causing 'considerable' stress, it is possible that a number of minor, day-to-day incidents were not mentioned, and as such the overall picture of indiscipline in schools indicated by the respondents may be distorted. In addition, the authors formed the impression that there is a great reluctance on the part of most teachers to admit to any discipline problems, perhaps because of the stigma attached to not being able to keep order. Of the 342 respondents who did describe a recent school incident causing considerable stress and personal difficulty, 202 incidents concerned indiscipline (133 minor to moderate; 69 major, e.g. assault, damage to property, theft, truancy, drug taking), 92 incidents concerned conditions in the school, and the remainder concerned inter-pupil problems (15), curriculum, standard of work, examinations (13), emotional outbursts (11), and safety, hygiene, accident (9). Comber and Whitfield also noted that a very disturbing feature of the incidents reported was that the heads of schools were not perceived by many teachers as giving a sufficiently strong lead against indiscipline in their schools. In their report Comber and Whitfield present accounts of eighteen critical incidents based very firmly upon incidents reported by respondents, together with a discussion of each incident in terms of possible causes of the incident, how the incident could have been avoided and dealt with, and possible short term and long term solutions.

A number of authors have argued that discipline problems are the major source of teacher stress. Caspari (1976) for example has argued that 'the exhaustion felt by most teachers at the end of term is more closely linked to the demands made on the skills and personality of a teacher in keeping discipline over the children he teaches than to any other aspect of his work' (p. 29). It is interesting to note however that in a number of studies reviewed, maintaining classroom discipline was not identified as the most important source of stress. If the contribution of maintaining classroom discipline to teacher stress is indeed greater than that indicated by many studies, then at least three explanations may be advanced: (1) that teachers distinguish between aspects of the job which are regarded as an integral part of the job (e.g. teaching children, maintaining discipline) and those aspects of the job which can be changed (e.g. salary levels, size of classes); although both aspects may contribute to teacher stress, the latter may be given greater emphasis as sources of discontent; (2) that ego-defensive processes lead to the under-reporting of sources of stress which imply personal failure or deficiencies; (3) that the contribution of maintaining classroom discipline to teacher stress may be subtle; for example, maintaining discipline may involve constant monitoring of the pupils' behaviour and as such teachers may not be fully aware of its significance, particularly if their classes appear to be well behaved.

Taylor and Dale (1971) in their survey of 3,588 probationary teachers asked the probationers to identify from a list of thirteen items up to three teaching problems they felt 'to be particularly relevant to their present situation'. The major teaching problem identified was dealing with groups of wide ability. However when head teachers were asked to identify the teaching problems associated with the work of probationers from the same list of thirteen items, the head teachers rated classroom discipline as the major teaching problem.

Dunham (1976) has identified three common stress situations: (1) reorganization, (2) role conflict and role ambiguity, and (3) poor working conditions. Dunham used extensive quotations from the reports of the teachers in his study to illustrate various stress situations. He identified three possible sources of stress associated with reorganization: 'leaving the security of familiar environments in grammar or secondary schools', 'working in large schools', and 'teaching pupils who have a much wider range of abilities and attitudes'. In the discussion of role conflict and role ambiguity, Dunham has linked many sources of stress to poor communications between teachers within the school or between teachers and other adults outside the school. In the discussion of poor working conditions, Dunham focused on inadequate buildings and high noise levels as important sources of stress.

The role of the teacher has received much attention (e.g. Grace, 1972; Hoyle, 1969), and a number of authors, like Dunham, have focused on role conflict and role ambiguity as important sources of teacher stress. Dodds (1974) in a study of 86 schoolteachers who had taken part in comprehensive school reorganization reported that the teachers felt their role had become more diffuse and exacting. Blackie (1977) has argued that the need for teachers to assume several roles is a major factor in teacher stress.

Clwyd County Council (1977) has reported the proceedings of a conference on teacher stress attended by 65 people concerned with teacher stress, ranging from heads of schools and teachers to members of the Council's Department of Education and the Area Health Authority. Cox and Dunham monitored the conference and contributed to the conference report (Cox, 1977; Dunham, 1977b). Cox grouped the sources of teacher stress/dissatisfaction considered by the conference participants under five headings: (1) training and career development (e.g. inadequate induction, unfulfilled ambitions), (2) nature of work (e.g. excess workload, disruptive pupils, constraints on resources, rate of educational change), (3) working environment (e.g. ill-designed, noisy), (4) school organization (e.g. size of school, poor administration, bad man-management, role conflict), and (5) school and community (e.g. lack of support from parents, excessive demands made by society). Dunham, utilizing reports on stress situations elicited from the participants identified six categories of stress situations: (1) educational and social change, (2) role conflict and role confusion, (3) poor physical and social working conditions, (4) problem pupils, (5) poor inter-professional communication and co-operation, and (6) problem teachers. The conference report also included six fictitious case studies which served to 'highlight' some of the situations that cause stress in teaching'.

Cox et al. (1978) have reported a study of 200 primary and secondary school teachers in Gwynedd, Wales. Part of the study utilized a questionnaire consisting of 59 items each of which the teachers were asked to rate on a five-point scale labelled from low to high as sources of job dissatisfaction. A factor analysis revealed five factors which were identified as (1) school organization, (2) job demands, (3) teaching resources and job environment, (4) career and training, and (5) pupil behaviour. When the types of schools were divided into primary, small comprehensive (1,000 to 1,500 pupils) and large comprehensive (more than 1,500 pupils), it appeared that male teachers in large comprehensives reported the greatest overall job dissatisfaction whilst female teachers in primary schools reported the least. This study also utilized the General Well-being Questionnaire designed by Cox et al. which consists of 44 items regarding affective, cognitive, and somatic aspects of stress which subjects rate on a frequency scale labelled from 'not at all' to 'very often'. Cox et al. reported that the factor structure of the questionnaire consists of one general factor. Of the five sources of dissatisfaction factors indentified above, only 'pupil behaviour' correlated significantly with 'poorer health' as indicated by the General Well-being Questionnaire, indicating that dissatisfaction with pupil behaviour was positively associated with poorer health. Interestingly, poorer health appeared to be greater for female compared with male teachers and for teachers in primary and small comprehensive schools compared with those in large comprehensive schools, although possible confounding between sex of teacher and type of school was not discussed. Comparison between subgroups for age, experience, responsibility, and marital status did not reveal further differences.

Pratt (1976, 1978) has reported the results of a study of 124 primary school teachers drawn from a northern education authority. The teachers were asked to complete a Teacher-Event Stress Inventory (TESI) which consisted of 43 items describing potentially stressful occurrences. Teachers were asked to rate each event that had occurred during the day on a seven-point scale ranging from 'this event occurred, but did not cause me to feel any stress' (rated 0) to 'extremely stressful' (rated up to a maximum of 6). The TESI was completed on five, usually consecutive days. The items with the highest mean values, in descending order of means, were 'the weather made the children restless', 'some children did not do as they were told straight away', 'a child did not do as I told him to', 'there was one difficult child in my class', 'the children did not listen to what was said', 'children had difficulties in learning/understanding', and 'I was interrupted by other people/events'.

A cluster analysis of the 43 TESI items indicated six clusters which were labelled (1) staff relations, (2) non co-operative children, (3) inadequate teaching, (4) aggressive children, (5) extra jobs, and (6) concern for children's learning. Perceived stress, as indicated by mean daily TESI scores, and the six item-clusters were compared for biographical subgroups of the teachers for the variables sex, age, length of service, and posts of special responsibility. None of the comparisons however revealed significant differences. A consideration of perceived stress in relation to the age of the children taught and the financial hardship of the home background of the children in each school, as indicated by the percentage of the pupils receiving free school meals, revealed an interesting and significant interaction between the variables of financial hardship and age of children. For teachers in schools where a comparatively small proportion of pupils were receiving free school meals, perceived stress appeared to be unrelated to the age of the pupils taught; however, for teachers in schools where a comparatively large proportion of pupils were receiving free school meals, perceived stress increased with the age of the pupils taught. This interaction was also significant for the two item-clusters non co-operative children and aggressive children, where again each of these clusters increased with the age of children taught for only for those teachers where a comparatively greater proportion of pupils were receiving free school meals.

Kyriacou and Sutcliffe (1978b) in a study of 257 teachers in medium-sized mixed comprehensive schools asked the teachers to rate 51 sources of stress in response to the question 'As a teacher, how great a source of stress are these factors to you?' on a five-point scale labelled from 'no stress' to 'extreme stress' (scored 0 to 4). The items with the highest mean values, in descending order of means, were 'pupils' poor attitudes to work', 'trying to uphold/maintain values and standards', 'poorly motivated pupils', 'covering lessons for absent teachers', 'too much work to do', 'lack of time to spend with individual pupils', and 'individual pupils who continually misbehave'. A principal components analysis of the sources of stress revealed four factors which together accounted for 52.0% of the total variance. These four factors (with items loading highly in brackets) were labelled 'pupil misbehaviour' (noisy pupils, difficult classes, difficult behaviour problems), 'poor working conditions' (poor career structure, poor promotion opportunitites, inadequate salary, shortage of equipment), 'time pressures' (not enough time to do the work, too much work to do, administrative work) and 'poor school ethos' (inadequate disciplinary policy of school, lack of consensus on minimum standards, attitudes and behaviour of the headmaster). Kyriacou and Sutcliffe also noted a number of differences in sources of stress between biographical subgroups.

A number of authors have focused their attention on particular sources of teacher stress and as such complement those studies which have attempted to present a more general overview of sources of teacher stress. Hanson (1971) has argued that teachers spend too much time actually teaching and that more preparation periods would help reduce the overall stress experienced. Hargreaves (1972) has focused on staffroom relationships and has identified a number of possible sources of conflict there. Hinton (1974) has discussed the problems of teaching in large schools and Kelly (1974) has considered the problems associated with mixed ability classes. The problems and pressures faced by heads of schools (e.g. Jackson, 1977) and heads of departments (e.g. Dunham, 1978) have also been considered. Indeed, heads of schools have also received attention as sources of stress for other teachers (e.g. Lawrence, 1974).

SYMPTOMS

Many studies have investigated the association between sources of occupational stress and the resulting manifestations of stress. The manifestations of stress identified may be psychological (e.g. depression, anxiety), physiological (e.g. increased heart rate) and behavioural (e.g. deterioration in work performance, deterioration in interpersonal relationships). The long term effects of occupational stress may include both physical and mental ill-health (Cooper and Marshall, 1976).

The purpose of this section will be to consider a number of studies which have sought to identify the most common manifestations of teacher stress. A few points should however be borne in mind here. The distinction between sources of stress and the manifestations of stress may often be unclear. For example, poor relations with other members of staff may be the result of a heavy work load, and thus can be considered a manifestation of stress, or they may be the primary sources of stress themselves. Indeed, failure to deal with one source of stress may quickly lower one's ability to tolerate another source of stress. Furthermore, the primary sources of stress may arise outside the work situation, such as marital difficulties, although home and work situations undoubtedly influence each other.

Dunham (1976) has argued that there are two main types of common stress responses among teachers. The first is frustration, and is associated with headaches, stomach upsets, sleep disturbances, hypertension and body rashes, and in prolonged cases, depressive illness. The second is anxiety, and is associated with feelings of inadequacy, loss of confidence, confusion in thinking, and occasionally panic. Cases of severe anxiety may lead to psychosomatic symptoms such as a twitchy eye, a nervous rash, loss of voice, and weight loss. Prolonged stress can lead to a nervous breakdown. It is unclear however as to how Dunham has arrived at this clinical dichotomy of an 'anxiety' and a 'frustration' dominated response syndrome and clearly more research is needed here to substantiate this dichotomy. Dunham has further argued that absenteeism, truancy, leaving teaching and early retirement are forms of withdrawal associated with situations which become too stressful to tolerate.

Hargreaves (1978) has discussed some of the long term effects of teacher stress. Hargreaves has argued that many teachers experience a progressive state of total emotional exhaustion. This total exhaustion may lead to out-of-school apathy, alienation from their work, and withdrawal into a number of defensive strategies.

In Clwyd County Council's (1977) conference report, both Cox and Dunham deal with the manifestations of teacher stress. Cox makes the point that no one symptom is diagnostic of occupational stress, since each symptom has a variety of causes. Cox argued that a teacher experiencing occupational stress will be characterized by a number of symptoms which together will form that person's 'individual' syndrome. Dunham used quotations from the conference participants to illustrate the range of symptoms of teacher stress. These included 'increasing lack of self-confidence', 'increasing cynicism, pessimism, irritability', 'inability to relax — to the extent of affecting home life' and 'suspicion of other teachers' intentions, acts and motives'. Dunham also attempted to provide a checklist of stress responses based on the most frequently reported symptoms of teacher stress indicated by 47 of the conference participants. The most frequent responses, in descending order, were tension headaches, general irritability and bad temper, hypersensitivity to criticism, moodiness, frequent forgetfulness, inability to concentrate, depression, loss of a sense of humour, excessive aggressiveness, feverish activity with little purpose, insomnia and excessive smoking.

Kyriacou and Sutcliffe (1978b) in their study of 257 schoolteachers, asked the teachers to rate 17 items regarding symptoms of stress in response to the instruction to 'Please estimate how frequently during the school term you feel in these ways' on a five-point scale labelled from 'never' to 'many times a day' (scored 0 to 4). The items with the highest mean frequencies, in descending order, were exhausted, frustrated, under stress, very angry, very tense, anxious, and depressed. A principal components analysis of the 17 symptoms of stress revealed one factor accounting for 34.8% of the total variance. This factor appeared to be largely defined by reported frequency of feeling very tense.

Cox et al. (1978) in their study of 100 schoolteachers and 100 matched semi-professionals utilized three questionnaires. The first was a General Health Questionnaire (GHQ) which requested information concerning specific complaints (e.g. diabetes), hospitalizations, risk factors associated with coronary heart disease, estimated general health, smoking, drinking, sleeping, and obesity. The second was the Jenkins Activity Survey, a personality test used to identify 'type A' individuals who are characterized as hard driving, ambitious, time-oriented, impatient, and highly job involved, in contrast to 'type B' individuals who lack these characteristics. A number of researchers have attempted to demonstrate that type A individuals are more vulnerable than type B individuals to heart disease (e.g. Jenkins *et al.*, 1968). The third was the General Well-being Questionnaire designed by Cox *et al.* and described earlier. A comparison of the responses of the teachers and non-teachers on the three questionnaires revealed only two significant differences, both on the GHQ. These were that female teachers compared with male teachers and non-teachers reported sleeping longer, and that teachers compared with non-teachers reported drinking less!

Pratt (1978) in his study of 124 primary school teachers reported a significant association between perceived stress reported by the teachers and an index of mental ill-health (Goldberg's General Health Questionnaire) ($r = 0.41$, $P < 0.001$). A high score on the General Health Questionnaire indicates the probability of psychiatric illness. Pratt reported that an inspection of the teachers' scores indicated that about 25% of the sample appeared to be 'at risk'. Overall however, there appears to be little evidence to indicate that teachers as an occupational group have a greater incidence of mental ill-health compared with other occupational groups.

Similarly, there is little evidence to indicate that schoolteachers display a higher incidence of physical ill-health that may be associated with occupational stress (e.g. coronary heart disease, stomach ulcers, hypertension) compared with other occupational groups (Registrar General's Decennial Supplement, 1971; Venning, 1978). Nevertheless, Hodges (1976) has reported that the number of male teachers dying whilst approaching the end of a career in teaching had doubled in the previous ten years and the number qualifying for a breakdown pension had more than trebled.

Three widely attributed consequences of teacher stress are lower job satisfaction, absenteeism, and leaving the profession. Simpson (1976) has argued that sickness absence allows teachers to withdraw temporarily from stress at work without having to make a distinct break. Such occasional withdrawals enable teachers to readjust continually to stressful work situations while continuing to develop the necessary skills to deal with the sources of stress. However, a full understanding of the relationship between teacher stress and absenteeism will require a distinction to be made between absence due to stress related physical illness and absence of a more psychological and to some extent voluntary nature (such as being depressed or feeling in need of a break).

Kyriacou and Sutcliffe (1979a) have recently investigated the association between self-reported teacher stress and job satisfaction, absenteeism, and intention to leave teaching. They reported significant associations between self-reported teacher stress and job satisfaction ($r = -0.27$, $P < 0.01$), total days absent (rho $= 0.12$, $P < 0.05$) and intention to leave teaching ($r = 0.18$, $P < 0.01$) for a sample of 218 secondary school teachers. The sizes of these correlations however indicate that the association between teacher stress and job satisfaction, absenteeism, and intention to leave teaching is not nearly as large as that implied in many of the discussions of teacher stress considered.

PERSONALITY

Surprisingly few authors have attempted to investigate the role of the teacher's personality in the experience of occupational stress. The results of two studies are of note here. Pratt (1976) in his study of 124 primary school teachers employed the Eysenck Personality Inventory and reported significant correlations between his measure of reported stress and both neuroticism ($r = 0.21$, $P < 0.01$) and extraversion ($r = 0.15$, $P < 0.05$). However, caution must be expressed concerning the association between neuroticism and stress since there is evidence to indicate that neuroticism scores increase when the individual is experiencing stress (Humphrey, 1977), and as such the two variables cannot be considered independent.

Kyriacou and Sutcliffe (1979b) in a study of 130 secondary school teachers have investigated the association between self-reported teacher stress and Rotter's Internal-External locus of control (I-E) scale (Rotter, 1966). A number of authors (e.g. Chan, 1977; Geen, 1976) have argued that the degree to which a person experiences stress is related to the degree to which he perceives himself to lack control over a potentially threatening situation, either by being unable to deal with the demands made upon him or by not having adequate coping mechanisms available. Furthermore, it has been argued that the degree to which individuals have a generalized expectancy that they will be unable to deal with potentially threatening situations will be associated with their degree of experienced stress (Lazarus, 1966; Lefcourt, 1976). Certain authors (e.g. Anderson, 1977; Lefcourt, 1976) have argued that Rotter's I-E scale provides a measure of such a generalized expectancy that can account for some of the variance in experienced stress.

Rotter (1966) developed the I-E scale to measure individual differences in the generalized expectancy that 'rewards' are perceived to be contingent on one's own behaviour or independent of it. Individuals who believe that reinforcement is contingent on their own behaviour are said to have a belief in internal control; those who believe reinforcement is the result of luck, chance, fate, the action of powerful others or is essentially unpredictable are said to have a belief in external control.

In their study Kyriacou and Sutcliffe employed a Likert scale format of the I-E scale and obtained a significant correlation between self-reported teacher stress and externality ($r = 0.36$, $P < 0.01$), i.e. those teachers who reported greater teacher stress tended to have a belief in external control. This finding may indicate that teachers with a belief in external control may be more likely to appraise their environment as threatening and thereby may be more likely to experience greater occupational stress.

COPING

Very little research has been undertaken to investigatge the coping mechanisms utilized by schoolteachers in dealing with occupational stress. Coping with stress involves two components. The first is directed at dealing with the sources of stress (direct-action); the second is aimed at dealing with the experience of stress (palliation). Palliative devices include intrapsychic processes such as denial, detachment and attention deployment, and somatic-oriented devices, such as drugs and relaxation training, which are aimed at moderating the bodily concomitants of stress. Whether a teacher will employ direct-action or palliative devices is largely a function of the characteristics of the situation and the teacher's personality.

A consideration of the ways in which teacher stress can be reduced involves two perspectives. The first focuses on alterations to the teacher's environment. The second focuses on the coping skills (both direct-action and palliative) which the teacher may utilize. In focusing on alterations to the teacher's environment both Cox (1977) and Dunham (1977b) have discussed the need for a social support system. Cox argued that forms of counselling may enable a teacher to improve his coping skills particularly by altering his perception of his own capabilities and the consequences of his actions. Dunham, in discussing social support, has emphasized the importance of the support coming from colleagues and senior staff rather than from a professional counselling system. Although Dunham also provides a list of a number of ways in which the teacher's environment may be altered to reduce stress, it is important to bear in mind the fact that effective measures to reduce teacher stress may well have to be 'tailored' to the circumstances of each teacher. In focusing on coping skills Cox and Dunham both emphasize intrapsychic processes rather than somatic-oriented devices. Although intrapsychic processes may well be important determinants of whether a teacher will experience stress, there is nevertheless a need to consider the extent to which somatic-oriented devices may be useful in reducing the deleterious effects of stress on physical health, particularly those devices which may enable the teacher to dissipate any excessive tension which may have built up during the course of a school day.

CONCLUDING REMARKS

Case studies and surveys have now yielded a wealth of data concerning the sources of teacher stress. Studies of a number of occupational groups are exploring the relationship between the experience of stress and both the resulting short term and long term effects. The major area for further research into teacher stress is clearly that of the coping strategies teachers utilize in dealing with stress. Advances in this area may be slow but the value of focusing more attention into ways occupational stress may be reduced is evident.

REFERENCES

Anderson, C.R. (1977). Locus of control, coping behaviors, and performance in a stress setting: a longitudinal study. *J. Appl. Psychol.,* **62,** 446-451.

Andrews, A.G. (1977). Ground rules for 'the great debate'. *Cambridge J. Educ.,* **7,** 90-94.

Blackie, P. (1977). Not quite proper. *Times Educ. Suppl.,* No. 3259 (25th Nov.), 20-21.

Caspari, I.E. (1976). *Troublesome Children in Class,* Routledge and Kegan Paul, London.

Clwyd County Council (Ed.) (1977). *The Management of Stress in Schools,* Clwyd County Council Department of Education Conference Report, Clwyd, Wales.

Chan, K.B. (1977). Individual differences in reactions to stress and their personality and situational determinants: some implications for community mental health. *Social Science and Medicine,* **11,** 89-103.

Comber, L.C., and Whitfield, R.C. (1979). *Action on Indiscipline: A Practical Guide for Teachers,* National Union of Schoolmasters and Union of Women Teachers, Hemel Hempstead.

Cooper, C.L., and Marshall, J. (1976). Occupational sources of stress; a review of the literature relating to coronary heart disease and mental ill health. *J. Occup. Psychol.,* **49,** 11-28.

Cox, T. (1977). The nature and management of stress in schools. In *The Management of Stress in Schools* (Ed. Clwyd County Council), pp. 5-29, Clwyd County Council Department of Education Conference Report, Clwyd, Wales.

Cox, T., Mackay, C.J., Cox, S., Watts, C., and Brockley, T. (1978). Stress and well-being in schoolteachers. Paper presented to the Ergonomics Society Conference *Psychophysiological Response to Occupational Stress,* Nottingham University, Nottingham (September).

Dodds, C. (1974). Comprehensive school teachers' perceptions of role change. *Research in Education,* No. 12, 35-45.

Dunham, J. (1976). Stress situations and responses, in *Stress in Schools* (Ed. National Association of Schoolmasters and Union of Women Teachers), pp.19-47, NAS/UWT, Hemel Hempstead.

Dunham, J. (1977a). The effects of disruptive behaviour on teachers. *Educ. Rev.,* **29,** 181-187.

Dunham, J. (1977b). The signs, causes, and reduction of stress in teachers, in *The Management of Stress in Schools* (Ed. Clwyd County Council) pp. 30-41, Clwyd County Council Department of Education Conference Report, Clwyd, Wales.

Dunham, J. (1978). Change and stress in the head of department's role, *Educ. Res.,* **21,** 44-47.

Gabriel, J. (1957). *An Analysis of the Emotional Problems of Teachers in the Classroom,* Angus and Robertson, London.

Geen, R.G. (1976). *Personality,* Mosby, St. Louis.

Grace, G.R. (1972). *Role Conflict and the Teacher,* Routledge and Kegan Paul, London.

Hanson, D. (1971). The strain of front line service. *Times Educ. Suppl.,* No. 2954 (31st Dec.), 4.

Hargreaves, D. (1972). Staffroom relationships. *New Society,* **19,** 434-437.

Hargreaves, D. (1976). The real battle of the classroom. *New Society,* **35,** 207-209.

Hargreaves, D. (1978). What teaching does to teachers. *New Society,* **43,** 540-542.

Hinton, M.G. (1974). Teaching in large schools. *Headmasters' Association Review,* **62,** 122-128.

Hodges, L. (1976). Why teaching is a dying profession. *Times Educ. Suppl.,* No. 3206 (12th Nov.), 7.

Hoyle, E. (1969). *The Role of the Teacher,* Routledge and Kegan Paul, London.
Humphrey, M. (1977). Review: Eysenck Personality Questionnaire. *J. Med. Psychol.,* **50,** 203-204.
Jackson, A. (1977). *Heading for What? — A Study of the Role of the Head As Seen by the Person in the Job,* University of Leeds Department of Psychology Counselling and Career Unit, Leeds.
Jenkins, C.D., Rosenman, R.H., and Friedman, M. (1968). Replicability of rating the coronary prone behaviour pattern. *Br. J. Prev. Soc. Med.,* **22,** 16-22.
Kelly, A.V. (1974). *Teaching Mixed Ability Classes,* Harper Row, London.
Kyriacou, C., and Sutcliffe, J. (1977). The prevalence of stress among teachers in medium-sized mixed comprehensive schools. *Research in Education,* No. 18, 75-79.
Kyriacou, C., and Sutcliffe, J., (1978a). A model of teacher stress. *Educ. Studies,* **4,** 1-6.
Kyriacou, C., and Sutcliffe, J. (1978b). Teacher stress: prevalence, sources and symptoms. *Br. J. Educ. Psychol.,* **48,** 159-167.
Kyriacou, C., and Sutcliffe, J. (1979a). Teacher stress and satisfaction. *Educ. Res.,* **21,** 89-96.
Kyriacou, C., and Sutcliffe, J. (1979b). A note on teacher stress and locus of control. *J. Occup. Psychol.,* **52,** 227-228.
Laslett, R. (1977). Disruptive and violent pupils: the facts and the fallacies. *Educ. Rev.,* **29,** 152-161.
Lawrence, E. (1974). The head and his teachers. *New Society,* **30,** 201-203.
Lawrence, J., Steed, D., and Young, P. (1977). Disruptive behaviour in a secondary school. *University of London Goldsmiths' College Educational Studies Monographs,* No. 1.
Lazarus, R.S. (1966). *Psychological Stress and the Coping Process,* McGraw-Hill, New York.
Lefcourt, H.M. (1976). Locus of control and the response to aversive events. *Canadian Psychol. Rev.,* **17,** 202-209.
Lowenstein, L.F. (1975). *Violent and Disruptive Behaviour in Schools,* National Association of Schoolmasters and Union of Women Teachers, Hemel Hempstead.
Maxwell, M. (1974). Stress in schools, *Centrepoint,* **7,** 6-7.
Payne, J. (1974). *Social Priority, Vol. 2: EPA Surveys and Statistics,* HMSO, London.
Pratt, J. (1976). *Perceived Stress Among Teachers; An Examination of Some Individual and Environmental Factors and their Relationship to Reported Stress,* Unpublished M.A. thesis, University of Sheffield, Sheffield.
Pratt, J. (1978). Perceived stress among teachers: the effects of age and background of children taught. *Educ. Rev.,* **30,** 3-14.
Registrar General's Decennial Supplement, (1971). *Occupational Mortality Tables: England and Wales, 1961,* HMSO, London.
Rotter, J.B. (1966). Generalized expectancies for internal versus external control of reinforcement. *Psychol. Monogr.,* **80** (1, Whole No. 609).
Rudd, W.G.A., and Wiseman, S. (1962). Sources of dissatisfaction among a group of teachers. *Br. J. Educ. Psychol.,* **32,** 275-291.
Simpson, J. (1976). Stress, sickness absence, and teachers. In *Stress in Schools* (Ed. National Association of Schoolmasters and Union of Women Teachers), pp. 11-17, NAS/UWT, Hemel Hempstead.
Taylor, J.K., and Dale, I.R. (1971). *A Survey of Teachers in their First Year of Service,* University of Bristol, Bristol.
Venning, P. (1978). A healthier future in teaching. *Times Educ. Suppl.,* No. 3271 (24th Feb.), 3.

PART III

Stress Among Community Service Workers

Chapter 6

Stress And The Policeman

Marilyn J. Davidson
University of Manchester
Institute of Science and Technology UK

and

Arthur Veno
University of Zambia
Zambia

INTRODUCTION

In recent years, many authors have proposed that occupational stress can be fully comprehended only by taking a multidisciplinary approach (e.g. Beehr and Newman, 1978; Caplan *et al.,* 1975; Cooper and Marshall, 1976, 1978; Davidson and Veno, 1978; Veno and Davidson, 1978). That is, by investigating the whole arena of problems — occupational, sociological, psychological, and physiological — in which individuals in the environment are taxed by stimulus demands up to the limits of their potential ability to adapt and cope. This approach allows for factors such as how different personality types respond in different ways to stress, in that a particular event may or may not be seen as stressful depending upon the myriad of other relationships in which an individual is involved.

Occupational stress in the police has been a topic of research in the United States (US) for over a decade, and numerous studies have indicated that the job of policing is an extremely stressful occupation (e.g. Heiman, 1975; Kroes, 1976; Nelson and Smith, 1970; Niederhoffer and Niederhoffer, 1978). In fact, concern over the high incidence of occupational stress in the police in America, has reached such proportions that an 'International Law Enforcement Stress Association' (ILESA) has been formed and publishes its own quarterly magazine entitled *Police Stress*. It is of interest to note that it

131

was in the first issue of this magazine that the father of stress research — Hans Selye — in his opening address, suggested that the police are in a uniquely high stress occupation. According to Selye (1978, p.7):

> Unlike most professions, it ranks as one of the most hazardous, even exceeding the formidable stresses and strains of air traffic control.

The implications of the police being an extremely high stress occupation are numerous and complex. For example, besides there being a high cost in terms of impaired psychological, social, and physical functioning of members of the police force, stress can also impair job performance which in turn can lead to poor response to community needs.

To date however, with the exception of a small number of authors (e.g. Davidson, 1979; Davidson and Veno, 1977; Hurrell, 1977), researchers have failed to develop a multifaceted, multidisciplinary paradigm of the concept of occupational stress in the police. Another feature characteristic of research in the police stress area, is that the attempted reviews are often uni-cultural. In view of this, it is the aim of this chapter to provide readers with a multicultural, multidisciplinary approach to stress in the police.[1] We provide this review in the hope that future researchers in the field of police stress, will utilize the constructs set out in this chapter as issues for further research, the ultimate goal being to develop a 'picture' of occupational stress in police.

While our primary interest is stress in police, we have structured our review of the literature to include the following four major categories which we see as relevant to any review of occupational stress: (a) extra organizational stressors, (b) stress and individual differences, (c) occupational sources of stress and, (d) occupational stressors and stress-related outcomes. Before turning our attention to the first of the major categories, there are two issues which require clarification. Firstly, while we acknowledge that police women are probably being exposed to the same quantity of stressors as their male counterparts, unfortunately due to the scarcity of relevant research literature, we are forced to limit our review to male police oficers. Secondly, for the same reason, although our review of stress and the policeman aims to be a crosscultural review, we have been confined to investigating the American, British, and Australian situation.

EXTRAORGANIZATIONAL STRESSORS

Research in social and cultural factors related to stress tend to use incidences of chronic disease and mortality rates as the main measurement variables (e.g. Dodge and Martin, 1970; Levine and Scotch, 1970; Selye, 1976). Authors such as Frankenhaeuser (1974, 1976) and Dodge and Martin (1970) view the extent of socially induced stress in a population as being dependent on such variables as status integration, role conflict, frustration, and goal attainment struggles.

They maintain that their hypotheses can be substantiated by the fact that affluent industrial societies have a higher incidence of chronic stress-related disease, such as coronary heart disease (CHD), than do non-affluent societies.

Numerous authors (e.g. Hayton, 1975; Jirak, 1975; Lewis, 1973) maintain that the complex need structure and societal pressures inherent in affluent societies have particularly adverse effects on members of the police service (due also to certain unique occupational factors), resulting in such states as role conflict, powerlessness, alienation, and anomie (i.e. a condition of normlessness). In order to measure the degree of alienation among members of the New York City Police Department, Jirak (1975) administered the Dean Scale of Alienation to 736 New York City police. He hypothesized that police feel alienated as an occupational group due to lack of support from institutions such as political groups, press, courts, and the community at large.

Jirak's findings substantiate hypotheses previously proposed by Niederhoffer (1967), in that police tend to feel more isolated than powerless or normless but that alienation generally rises throughout their career, reaching a peak at their 15th year of service — at which point retirement and pensions are within sight and, subsequently, feelings of alienation diminish. Jirak's research findings have more recently been supported by Lotz and Regoli (1977) who studied police in nine American police departments, and also found that cynicism (a factor of alienation proposed by Jirak) peaks in mid career.

These studies do suggest that there may be definite career phases within the police service in which police are more likely to be exposed to stressors resulting from aspects of alienation; e.g. officers with less than five years' police service may be more prone to feelings of normlessness and isolation than other officers. As well, there may be differences in degrees of alienation not only during different career periods, but also between large *vs*. small police departments, as well as between different ranks (Regoli and Poole, 1978).

Taking into account an obvious need for further research in order to identify some of the reasons for different degrees of police alienation, along with other extra-organizational stressors, it seems relevant to review some of the 'cause and effect' areas which previous research findings (e.g. Chappell and Wilson, 1972; Heiman, 1975; Munro, 1975) have isolated. These include: (a) police-community relations, (b) social/cultural and geographical influences, (c) police family and social life, (d) police suicide and, (e) life events and their relation to stress.

Police-community relations

It appears from numerous crosscultural studies (e.g. Banton, 1964; Cain, 1973; Skolnick, 1973) that poor police-community relations are instrumental in enhancing police alienation and subsequent increased stress. Critchley (1967) and O'Connor (1974) among others have suggested that the United States, England, and Australia have modelled their different types of police forces on common origins based on the 18th and early 19th century English notions of policing.

Several authors have noted that, in Britain, due to such factors as shortages of personnel and crime increases, Sir Robert Peel's ideal of the police being servants of society has mutated such that they take on a more oppressive role (e.g. Cain, 1973; Clark, 1965; Critchley, 1971), which results in lowered police-community relations. However, research by Belson (1975) strongly suggests that public trust in the police (in London) was comparatively quite high, in that 73% of adults surveyed were reported as having 'a lot of respect' for the police. As well, Punch and Naylor (1973) have indicated that British police still respond largely as a community service agency, since roughly one half of the calls received by British police are requests for service-related functions.

Police duties in the US have been found to parallel British trends in that the vast majority of calls received are likely to involve service requests rather than requests for police action against activities (e.g. Bard, 1971). Radelet (1973) suggests these data indicate that the American police role has returned toward Peel's original model of maintaining order and peace in the community. However, the fact that service calls represent such a high proportion of police activities should not be interpreted as meaning that the police actively encourage such duties. Unlike Britain, crime rates in the U.S. tend to be higher and of a more violent nature, which creates a demand within the community for the police to carry out a deterrence role (Wilson, 1968). Wilson suggests that this conflict between community demand for deterrence and police activities being largely directed toward service-oriented activities, results in worsened police-community relations and increased police alienation, due to this role discrepancy. Despite numerous police-community relations programmes, the recent extensive survey of over 2,000 US police patrolmen carried out by Hurrell (1977), found that only 36% of the police respondents agreed that police-citizen relations were good. Whatever the reasons, it is clear then, that police-community relations in the U.S. are less than ideal (e.g. Banton, 1964; Chappell and Meyer, 1975).

In Australia, as in America, early settlers attempted to structure a police system based on the English model. However, as Chappell and Wilson (1972) suggest, Peel's model was not realized — due to the fact that many of the early settlers tended to be law-breakers rather than law-abiders. Consequently, the role of police in Australia from the early years of settlement, was characterized as being the protection of security and enforcement of the laws — the same as in America.

Research by Belson (1975), Chappell and Meyer (1975), Davidson (1979), and Hurrell (1977), using interview and survey methods, indicates that police-community relations are best in England and worse in the U.S., with Australia occupying the middle position but tending towards the American situation than the British. This hypothesis was supported by a recent survey of a random stratified sample (*via* rank) of 25% of the Northern Territories police (*N* = 75), in which only 38% of the Australian police respondents agreed with the proposition that police-citizen relations were good (Davidson, 1979).

If, as Kroes (1976) maintains, negative public image and poor police-community relations are the stressors which are most difficult for the police to live with, this is surely an area which requires further research. In fact, there are a number of reports of collaboration between police and social scientists in the US, Britain and Australia which suggest that police-community relations can be substantially improved through *controlled exposure techniques*, e.g. controlled interaction with minority groups (Allen *et al.*, 1969; Bard, 1969; Bell *et al.*, 1969; Gardner and Veno, 1976; Krocker *et al.*, 1974; Sikes and Cleveland, 1968; Veno and Gardner, 1979).

Social/cultural and geographical influences

Numerous studies (e.g. Averill *et al.*, 1971; Lazarus *et al.*, 1966; Matsumoto, 1970) indicate that physiological and psychological stress reactions to technologic change, economic, or physiologic deprivation, epidemics, war, and even movie films, are very different for people of differing cultural and ethnic backgrounds. Selye (1976) maintains that social and cultural stressful agents are also influenced by many other factors such as diet, climate, genetics, religion, social class, overcrowding, and isolation; all of which vary with culture and geography.

These crosscultural variances are also important variables which must be considered when hypothesizing about differences in chronic disease mortality rates among various segments of a population in the same society. Consequently, any proposed study of stress among police should take into account social and cultural background factors which appear to influence certain stress-related outcomes such as disease.

Another variable influencing lifestyles and relationships is frequent moving. According to Cooper and Marshall (1978), mobile families are unable to make meaningful ties with the local community. This may prove particularly stressful for the police family, who are not only susceptible to frequent 'transfers', but also face more difficulties in integrating into the immediate community (Niederhoffer and Niederhoffer, 1978).

An additional demographic variation relative to the prevalence of stress disorders has been found to exist between urban and rural areas. Levine and Scotch (1970) state the prevalence of hypertension is higher in urban than in rural areas, and Dodge and Martin (1970) claim that CHD is persistently higher along the North American eastern and western seaboards than in the inland rural farm states. However, Levine and Scotch (1970) propose that the factors associated with city living, e.g. noise, overcrowding, and fast living, could just as easily be counteracted by stressful factors in country living, e.g. isolation, lack of privacy, and social control. Furthermore, the long held belief that better mental health is experienced by rural dwellers compared to their urban counterparts, has recently been challenged by Srole's (1977) research findings. It is apparent that the literature on the overall health differences between urban and rural populations is somewhat inconsistent and it is still difficult to demonstrate a causal relationship as to why any of these differences occur.

Although there is a lack of empirical findings which would enable us to compare stress disorders for urban police with those for rural police, there have been numerous studies (e.g. Cain, 1973; Levine and Scotch, 1970; Munro, 1975) showing that rural police report different types of occupational inconveniences and stressors when compared with their urban counterparts. In general, the findings of such studies indicate that rural police appear to be far more affected by transfer problems, delays on duty (e.g. accidents, poor car allowance), social callers and lack of social privacy. Urban police on the other hand, appeared to be affected more than rural police by inconveniences stemming from working hours, holiday systems, long hours, and shift work. Having suggested that rural police will be facing differing occupational stressors than their urban counterparts, it is also relevant to consider Munro's (1975) hypothesis that urban-born police have different personalities than rural-born police. In his investigation of personality perceptions of South Australian police, Munro found that place of birth was the most pertinent variable, as urban-born police saw themselves as more competitive and rebellious than those born in the country.

Even though it is impossible to derive conclusions from a single study, the data do appear to reflect the differences that often exist between the city and country perspectives on life. The results from Munro's (1975) study appear to support the hypothesis that social background and early life are more important in shaping a policeman's attitudes to citizen, criminal, and self, then his current location and its associated experience.

Police family and social life

When investigating the disruption of homelife and family as a direct stress outcome resulting from occupational stressors, one has to be aware of a multitude of interrelating variables. Firstly, there is an interaction with stressors at work being able to affect family life and *vice versa*, with one often exacerbating the other. Secondly, actuarial statistics, such as separation and divorce rates, do not give absolute indications of family disruption patterns, and influencing factors such as religion, availability of legal aid, etc., all need to be considered (Kunzel, 1974).

Finally, when attempting to investigate the correlation between occupational stress and its effects on family life, it is important to be aware of the fact that the family life cycle is a U-shaped curve with a decline in satisfaction over the earlier stages followed by an increase over the later stages of married life (Rollins and Cannon, 1974; Rollins and Feldman, 1970). Davidson (1979) administered the Rollins and Feldman (1970) *Family Life Cycle and Marital Satisfaction Scale* to the married police officers in her Northern Territories survey and found similar shallow U-shaped trends of general marital satisfaction over the family life cycle. However, there appeared to be a tendency towards lower marital satisfaction in the marital stages one and two (i.e. the first five years of marriage) in the Australian police respondents compared to Rollins and Feldman's (1970) sample. It appears therefore that the first few years of police marriages tend to be high risk in terms of marital disruption compared to other marriages; a finding which has been substantiated by previous research findings (e.g. Paulson, 1974; Rafky, 1974; Reiser, 1978; Stratton, 1976).

A recent study by Niederhoffer and Niederhoffer (1978) investigating police families in America concluded that police divorces occurred no more frequently that divorces in other families. However, other research findings in the US have indicated that police on the whole have one of the highest divorce rates in the country (Hurrell, 1977; Stratton, 1976). Similarly, there are indications that there are high divorce rates in Australian police marriages compared to the general population (Davidson, 1979).

Even though one has to acknowledge that divorce rates are on the increase in the general population, Stratton (1976) maintains that the common high rate of divorce in police marriages compared to other occupationally sorted marriages, is due specifically to specialized occupational stressors which can create difficulties that do not exist in other marriages. Certainly, limited interview surveys by such authors as Kroes *et al.* (1974) and Rafky (1974) on American police families have produced consistent results. Rafky's (1974) survey of 100 police wives revealed that one fifth to one quarter were dissatisfied with their husbands' career generally and reported that particular aspects of the job resulted in family arguments. Kroes *et al.* (1974), in their survey of 81 married police officers, found 79 of them felt police work had an adverse effect on their homelife in that, among other things, being a policeman, (a) retarded nonpolice friendships, (b) made one less able to plan social events, (c) meant that one was more likely to take the pressures of the job home, (d) the effects of negative public image on the family, and (e) wives' concern over their husbands' safety. This concern over safety was subsequently verified by Hurrell (1977), who reported that 79% of his US police sample maintained their family were very concerned for their safety.

More recently, Niederhoffer and Niederhoffer (1978) have substantiated the majority of these findings and go as far as to propose that the traditional role of the police requires an officer to be unmarried in order for him to be able to perform his duties adequately. In more realistic terms however, they pinpoint particular stressors including those related to the wives' feeling threatened by the 'police groupie' syndrome, their husbands having policewomen partners and frustrations related to rotated shift work. In relation to problems encountered by police children, the Niederhoffers see these emerging when the children reach adolescence and become susceptible to peer attacks due to their father's occupation or conversley, preferential treatment by persons who want to stay friendly with the police.

Several American police departments, according to Paulson (1974) and Stratton (1976), have found three consistent factors in their members. They noted: (a) there appears to be a correlation between poor job performance and poor marital relations; (b) police cynicism appears to have a particularly adverse effect on the officers' first 3 years on the force (Rafky, 1974, maintained that one third of the married cadets were divorced within their first 2 years on the force); and (c) the high divorce rate among police generally. In addition, marital disharmony has been associated with police suicide and Danto (1978) discovered that 50% of his surveyed Detroit police suicide victims had marital problems as precipitating events for the suicides.

However, there are indications that in America at least, police officers appear to be becoming aware of these problems themselves. For example, a recent national survey investigating the need for psychological services as perceived by US urban police departments, reported that the most requested service by police officers (i.e. 82% of the sample) was for personal and family counselling (Rios *et al.*, 1978). Furthermore, some American police departments have introduced orientation programmes for the police families (Stratton, 1976). According to Stratton (1978) his follow up study of two such programmes run by the Los Angeles County Sheriff's Department have shown them to be beneficial for both the officer and the spouse.

Similar occupational stressor influences have been found in British and Australian police families. In a detailed British study by Cain (1973), in which she interviewed policemen and their wives in both rural and city areas, asking questions concerned with particular occupational sources of inconvenience, most of the results suggested tension between home and work, suggesting that family life suffered because of work. Police wives from both rural and urban areas felt their children suffered from the constantly changing shifts as they rarely saw their fathers. In Australia, the stressors associated with family concern for safety appear to be prominent, with 72% of Davidson's (1979) Northern Territories police sample reporting this issue of primary concern.

Perhaps one of the major factors which crosscultural studies (e.g. Banton, 1964; Cain, 1973; Davidson, 1979; Hurrell, 1977; Kroes, 1976; Skolnick, 1973) have demonstrated is that increased family conflict is related to the social isolation often felt by a policeman and his family. Various studies have shown that police are often regarded with reserve, suspicion and sometimes hostility even when off duty and at private social functions (Banton, 1964; Skolnick,

1973). Consequently, due to these strong negative pressures, both British, American, and Australian studies (e.g. Cain, 1973; Davidson, 1979; Kroes *et al.*, 1974) have found that police family conflict increases in proportion to their growing feeling of isolation and that policemen and their wives are more likely to make friends with other police families, who understand and share their problems.

Both the American and Australian police surveys conducted by Hurrell (1977) and Davidson (1979) found that overall the police felt that their occupation had quite a negative effect on the following aspects of their social activities: holding a second job and/or going to college; social life; holidays; friendships with persons who are not police officers; and recreation. Kroes (1976) believes this effect on home and social life is probably greatest for the young policemen who, besides having to face problems of negative community contact and isolation, may also be having to adjust to the new rigors of police work itself.

Cain (1973) found a difference in social isolation between British country and city police. Although, when questioned, both country and city police felt they had fewer nonpolice friends than they would have in another occupation, the results indicated that country police tended to hold themselves aloof to avoid difficult conflict situations when they had to exert authority. Isolation, where it existed, with city police stemmed from the community rather than being voluntarily imposed by the police themselves.

Police suicide

The concept of anomie (i.e. feelings of normlessness) has been postulated as one of the major influencing variables in the psycho-social theory of suicide (Durkheim, 1951; Wenz, 1975). Given that feelings of alienation and anomie appear to be common in police, it is perhaps not surprising that police suicide has been investigated as a measure of anomie (e.g. Heiman, 1975; Lewis, 1973; Nelson and Smith, 1970; Niederhoffer, 1974). Certainly, the literature tends to indicate that the police profession may well be a high risk population in relation to suicide rates. Nelson and Smith (1970), for instance, found that in the US State of Wyoming, the 1960-1968 suicide rate for police was almost twice the rate of physicians, the next highest group.

This type of uniquely high suicide rate is not universal in all police forces and not only varies from state to state in the US but also from country to country. Dash and Reiser's (1978) recent survey of police suicide rates in Los Angeles County illustrates this point, as they found the police suicide rate to be significantly below both the national average and the Los Angeles County rates. The authors credit these findings to the rigorous screening and evaluation given to prospective police recruits, along with good psychological and mental health services made available to this particular police force. Heiman's (1975) comparison of police suicide rate between 1960 and 1973 in the New York City Police Department and the Metropolitan Police Force of London typifies crosscultural differences. Hieman found that the London police suicide rate differed only slightly from that of its white male, urban population, whereas the New York City police suicide rate was almost twice that of its white male, urban population (Heiman, 1975).

In attempting to isolate the societal causal factors for these differences, Heiman (1975) attributes the sparse use of firearms by London police, their higher degree of role acceptance, and their higher morale, compared to their New York counterparts, as being major influences. Interestingly, the American research (e.g. Danto, 1978; Heiman, 1975) has shown that 90% of police suicides used their own service revolvers, and in Danto's (1978) survey of Detroit police suicides, none of the officers were in uniform at the time of their death.

Although there are no official published statistics for the suicide rates in the Australian police, there are indications that they may be higher than the general population rates (*The Australian*, Feb.16, 1979, p.3). Obviously, individual psychological multidetermined aspects of police suicide patterns are relevant, as are differential rates of access to firearms. Also, as with a certain number of suicides in the community at large, many police suicides according to Kroes (1976), are never reported as such. Very often the first people to reach the scene are the suicide victim's police colleagues who, showing concern for the widows and children in respect to insurance policy claims as well as social stigma, report the incidence as 'accidental death' (Kroes, 1976).

Life events and their relation to stress

Extensive empirical research over the past few years has shown that stressful life events may play a role in the etiology of various somatic and psychiatric disorders (e.g. Dohrenwend and Dohrenwend, 1973). The utilization of a life events measure appears to be an important measure which should be included in any study of stress in the police. Besides proving to be an additional indicator of the kinds of stressors that may lead to illness in the police community, according to Danto (1978), high risk police suicide profiles could also be developed from analysis of life crisis inventory scores.

To date, the only known survey of police which has utilized the life events questionnaire is Davidson's (1979) survey of Northern Territories police officers. Although this pilot study was retrospective in nature, Davidson adopted the assessment scoring proposed by Rahe (1978) and administered the *Occurrences of Life Events Social Readjustment Rating Questionnaire* (Dohrenwend and Dohrenwend, 1973), to her Australian police sample. The results were compared with those attained in a study undertaken by Hurst *et al.* (1978), in which they administered an almost identical 39 item life occurrences scale to 416 male US air traffic controllers; an occupation which research (e.g. Cobb and Rose, 1973) has similarly shown to be a very high stress occupation.

The results illustrated that the Australian police sample reported on average nearly three times as many total life event changes in the previous year, compared to the US air traffic control group. Consequently, in the Australian police sample, the high number of life event scores proved to be an important extraorganizational stressor influence; especially in view of the finding that this police sample had higher levels of illnesses compared to Australian males of similar age and locality (Davidson, 1979).

Conclusions

Occupational stress can only be adequately investigated by taking a multidisciplinary approach. Consequently, when investigating stress in police, the extraorganizational cultural and social influences have to be accounted for, as they can affect the mental and physical health and behaviour of an individual at work and *vice versa*.

STRESS AND INDIVIDUAL DIFFERENCES

Although we are reviewing aspects of stress in a specific occupational group, i.e. police, we are still dealing with individuals who will have their own unique life histories, experiences, and personalities. According to such authors as Appley and Trumbell (1967), Sells (1970), and Selye (1976), it is an individual's personality profile, past experience, and variables such as age and history of family health, which can be instrumental in determining performance under certain stimulus conditions. Therefore, in any analysis of occupational stress in police, specific individual responses to stress which involve complex interdependence among physiological, psychological, and behavioural variables must be taken into account. For the purposes of a study of stress in the police, there appear to be two main variables which research has identified as discriminant in relation to individual differences in response to stressors: (a) stressor types as related to personality, and (b) stress behaviour patterns.

Stressor types as related to personality

Numerous studies (e.g. Finn *et al.*, 1969; Jenkins, 1971; Schalling, 1975; Welford, 1974) have been carried out on individual personality differences associated with stress-related diseases. Thus, it is essential to try to isolate the types of individuals (in our case, police) who may be more characteristically predisposed to stress.

Welford (1974) maintains that individual differences in the degree of anxiety to stressors related to personal dimensions are due to variations between extremes of stability and instability linked to Eysenck's (1958) concept of neuroticism and to Spence and Taylor's (cited in Welford, 1974) measure of anxiety. From linking personality scores and autonomic indications of arousal and performance, Welford concludes that introverts represent greater chronic arousal than do extraverts. Therefore, introverts tend to perform better under monotonous conditions where arousal tends to sag and to be less affected by loss of sleep and by narcotic drugs than extraverts. However, unlike introverts, extraverts tend to seek stimulation in order to sustain optimal arousal and tend to remain stable under pressure and perform well under such conditions. These assumptions have been verified more recently by Schalling's (1975) anxiety studies. Another important finding evolving from Schalling's (1975) studies is that self reported sensitivity to different types of stressors was related to different personality dimensions, e.g. extraverts reported fewer unpleasant feelings than introverts to anticipatory situations. Also, Kahn et al. (1964, cited by Cooper and Marshall, 1978) investigated the personality variables in managers as related to job stress and found that extraverts were more highly reality-oriented and adaptable than introverts.

According to Eysenck and Eysenck (1964) there appear to be some occupational differences between overall scores of extraversion/introversion and neuroticism. As well, these authors postulate that the reaction to neurotic breakdown is different in introverts and extraverts, with the former developing dysthymic symptoms and the latter developing psychopathic and hysterical ones (Eysenck and Eysenck, 1964).

Although there have been many studies which have attempted to define the 'police personality' (e.g. Balch, 1972; Sheppard et al., 1974), to date the only known study which has attempted to investigatge individual police differences in degree of anxiety to stressors, as related to personality dimensional variations between the extremes of stability and instability and extraversion vs. introversion, is Davidson's (1979) Australian survey. Due to the outgoing nature of the job with the heavy emphasis on fitness and versatility, especially at recruit level, one might expect the police occupation to attract more extraverted types as opposed to introverts. However, Davidson's (1979) results did not meet this expectation and analysis of the Eysenck Personality Inventory Scores of all her Northern Territories police subjects indicated that this police sample at least, was no more extraverted or introverted than the general population.

Nevertheless, an important finding emerged in relation to the Northern Territories police sample's neuroticism scores. According to Eysenck and Eysenck (1964) the mean neuroticism score for the normal population was 10.523, with the skilled working class population having the highest neuroticism score of 11.786. The mean neuroticism score for the Australian police sample however, was an even higher 11.96 (Davidson, 1979).

Consequently, assuming Schalling's (1975) hypothesis that anxiety is higher in individuals possessing high levels of neuroticism using Eysenck's scale, the Northern Territories police appeared to be a more anxious population compared to the norm, which in turn may have made them more susceptible to stress-related maladies.

When examining the relationship between MMPI and 16PF and other psychometric measures and stress-related disease, the findings do tend to be consistent. Cooper and Marshall's (1976) article provides an extensive review of these studies. The authors conclude that before the onset of their illness, CHD patients differed from individuals who remained healthy on several MMPI scales including hysteria, hypochondriasis, and depression. Another important issue they emphasized was that the studies also indicated that after the onset of potentially fatal diseases, survival rates were lower and mortality rates were higher for those who showed greater neuroticism (especially depression).

Psychometric measures have been administered to police populations in an attempt to define both the 'police personality' and the 'ideal police personality' (Fabricatore *et al.*, 1978; Sheppard *et al.*, 1974). Fabricatore *et al.* (1978) for example, attempted to isolate predictors of successful police performance on the basis of personality factors as measured by the 16PF Questionnaire. Consisting of a sample of 333 young white Los Angeles patrolmen, the results of their study indicated that aggressiveness and tough-mindedness were the two consistent predictors of superior performance (based on police supervisor ratings, fewer car accidents, peer ratings, and least number of official reprimands — Fabricatore *et al.*, 1978). Even so, it should be taken into account that as with most police studies, the research was focused on one particular police force in one particular culture and may not be applicable to all policemen.

Recently, Murrell *et al.* (1978) have proposed that the 'police personality' label should be abandoned, having found few differences between the personality scores of American prison guards, security guards, and police officers. However, they did find that police officers were high in heterosexuality but low in abasement, succorance, and counselling readiness.

While not proposing a 'police personality' *per se,* Skolnick (1973) maintains that the pressures and stressors of the police job itself generates specific cognitive and behavioural responses in police which he refers to as a 'working personality'. Even though there are vast variations in this so called 'police working personality', some of the basic attitudinal similarities which have been attributed to it include suspiciousness, conformity, rigidity, cynicism, and authoritarianism (Balch, 1972; Niederhoffer, 1967; Radelet, 1973; Skolnick, 1973). It has been proposed that higher education for police would help to neutralize these personality trait effects, however recent research is now questioning this assumption (e.g. Vastola, 1978).

Indeed, these traits, rather than being an inherent personality construct, tend instead to be developed by the work situation and, therefore, vary not only between cultures but also between police forces in the same society. Vastola (1978) presents a 'sub-culture model' of the police personality which develops this approach and attempts to explain individual differences. According to Vastola (1978, p.52):

> Simply put, the police personality is merely a reflection of the dominant cultural personality of citizens with whom police primarily interact.

However, we must not assume that this so-called 'police working personality' will always have adverse attributes when subjected to stressful situations. In relation to conformity and rigidity, for example (by its very nature, police work implies the maintenance of the *status quo* of law and order), Reiser (1976) maintains that flexible people experience more conflict than rigid ones when exposed to severe conflict stress situations.

Stress behaviour patterns

According to Cooper and Marshall (1976) research investigating individual stress differences and behaviour patterns began in the early 1960s, being influenced by the work of Friedman *et al.* (1958), and has since shown a relationship between prevalence of CHD and behavioural patterns. More recently, Rosenman and Friedman (1974) believe they have isolated two main types of behaviour patterns — Type A and Type B. Type A behaviour is characterized by high achievement, motivation, striving, hard driving competitiveness, time urgency, and many other activities which involve a tendency to suppress fatigue in order to meet deadlines. Therefore, the kind of life style associated with this type of behaviour pattern is implicated in the aetiology of CHD. Type B behaviour is characterized by relative absence of Type A behaviour patterns and significantly lower incidences of CHD.

Thus, it appears appropriate to assume that police with Type A behaviour traits will be more prone to stress-related disease. This assumption is of specific importance when one considers that recent American and Australian police stress surveys have both found over 75% of their respective police samples to fit into the Type A category (Davidson, 1979; Hurrell, 1977).

If then, the majority of police are Type A personalities, there are certain important factors to be considered in relation to occupational stress. Firstly, it would seem necessary to ascertain whether the police as an occupation either *attracts* Type A persons or *facilitates* Type A behaviour in people. McMichael (1978) asserts that Type A persons possess personality traits which actually facilitate self-selection into occupations that involve greater exposure to stressors. However, other authors such as Frankenhauser (1976) suggest that occupational stressors can in fact encourage Type A behaviour patterns. Unfortunately, until Type A questionnaires are administered to appropriate samples of new police applicants and recruits, the questions regarding Type A behaviour in police populations remain unanswered.

The second relevant issue which requires discussion, in relation to Hurrell's (1977) and Davidson's (1979) police survey findings, centres around the behavioural responses of Type A subjects to stressful situations. McMichael (1978) for example, proposes that Type A persons are more likely to perceive and exaggerate potentially stressful conditions, and consequently experience more stress at work. An alternative view is presented by Dembroski and MacDougall (1978). After reviewing the relevant literature, they suggest that Type A personalities preferred to work alone when put under high threat and complained more often than Type B persons about heavy work responsibilities and conflicting work demands. Dembroski and MacDougall (1978) go on to propose that Type A behaviour causes self-imposed pressure and increased work loads (i.e. enhanced threatening situations), which in itself may increase stress by reducing the opportunity for support from co-workers. This assumption may in fact explain why so few of Hurrell's (1977) and Davidson's (1979) American and Australian police samples sought social support from colleagues.

Conclusions

It appears evident that variables such as psychometric and behavioural measurements of individual differences play an important role in police stress research. In particular, issues relating to Type A behaviour patterns in the police population require further research.

OCCUPATIONAL SOURCES OF STRESS

Extraorganizational variables, personality characteristics, and individual differences as well as negative community attitudes, alienation, crisis intervention situations, and subsequent role conflicts are all acknowledged as being important stressors to police. In this section we will concentrate on a number of possible environmental sources of stress in police work hitherto not discussed. In order to do this we utilize the main sources of stress at work, which are commonly stated as stressors in occupational environments (e.g. Cooper and Marshall, 1976; Davidson and Veno, 1977): (a) factors intrinsic to a particular job, (b) role in the organization, (c) career development, (d) relationships at work, and (d) organizational structure and climate.

Factors intrinsic to the job

Sources of stress intrinsic to the job across a variety of occupations include poor physical working conditions, work overload, time pressures, and physical danger (Cooper and Marshall, 1976, 1978). In relation to police careers, stressors intrinsic to the job have been isolated as including poor equipment, long hours and shift work, job overload, job underload (due to such factors as paper work resulting in boredom), the courts, and threatening duty situations (Chposky, 1975; Davidson, 1979; Hurrell, 1977; Kroes, 1976; Margolis, 1973).

Equipment. Both American and Australian studies (e.g. Davidson, 1979; Eisenberg, 1975; Hurrell, 1977; Margolis, 1973) have stated that police report discontent due to poor equipment and continual equipment failure. Approximately 60% of Hurrell's (1977) US police officers, and 78% of Davidson's (1979) Australian police sample reported dissatisfaction with work equipment. This concern over equipment satisfaction is, according to Eisenberg, not surprising when one considers that both the quality and safety of police work is partly dependent on having efficient equipment, which includes communication equipment, vehicles, safety material, and so on.

Shift work. Numerous occupational studies have found that shift work is a common occupational stressor as well as affecting neurophysiological rhythms within man such as blood temperature, metabolic rate, blood sugar levels, mental efficiency, and work motivation — which may ultimately result in stress-related disease (Cobb and Rose, 1973; Colquhoun, 1970; Hurrell and Kroes, 1975; Selye, 1976). A particular occupational study by Cobb and Rose (1973) on air traffic controllers (a particularly highly stressed occupation) found there was four times the prevalence of hypertension and also more mild diabetes and peptic ulcers than in their control group of second class airmen. Although these authors considered other job stressors as being instrumental in the causation of these stress-related maladies, a major job-stressor was isolated as shift work.

There has been no empirical association found between stress-related maladies in the police and shift work. However, surveys have indicated that police report shift work as being a major occupational stressor (Eisenberg, 1975; Hilton, 1973; Kroes, 1976; Margolis, 1973). Hilton (1973), Margolis (1973), and Kroes (1976) report police as complaining that rotating shift work not only disrupts their family life and health but can also affect their performance on the job, especially when they are suffering from fatigue due to their inability to sleep during the day. Eisenberg (1975) suggests that inconveniences related to shift work in the police are further enhanced by the necessity to make irregular and lengthy court appearances, a stressor Kroes (1976) maintains is a unique police stressor.

Although stressors associated with shift work require investigation in police cohorts, we need to take note of Selye's (1976) conclusion that shift work becomes physically less stressful as individuals can (and do) habituate to the condition. Even so, being 'excluded from society' is a common complaint among shift workers. Research may indicate, as Knowles and Jones (1974) found in their US police population, that police training skills override their biorhythm ratings and subsequent shift work effects.

Job overload. French and Caplan (1972) see work overload as being either quantitative (i.e. having too much to do) or qualitative (i.e. being too difficult) and, although empirical evidence demonstrating that work overload is a main factor in occupational ill health is not available, certain behavioural malfunctions have been associated with job overload (Cooper and Marshall, 1976, 1978; Kasl, 1978). For example the French and Caplan (1972) research indicated a relationship with quantitative overload and cigarette smoking (an important symptom in relation to CHD), and Margolis *et al.* (1974), in their sample of one and a half thousand employees, found that job overload was associated with such stress-related symptoms as lowered self-esteem, low work motivation, and escapist drinking.

Similar findings have been reported by Kroes (1976) in his US police surveys. Kroes (1976) suggests that qualitative job overload among police is often due to expectations placed on the police officer by the police department and society, with quantitative overload being dependent on the particular police department and the population of the area. However, more recent American and Australian studies have found that stress associated with quantitative job overload does not appear to be as important an issue. In fact over 70% of the police surveyed maintained that they were satisfied with their workload quantity (Davidson, 1979; Hurrell, 1977).

Nevertheless, American, British, and Australian studies — by Rubinstein (1973), Martin and Wilson (1969), and Wilson and Western (1972) respectively — have indicated that shortage of manpower causes major problems in a police force, especially when it involves longer working hours. In view of this, it is of importance to note that there are indications that in some parts of America and Australia, the average hours overtime worked by policemen is approximately four hours per week, with over two of those overtime hours being nonvoluntary (Davidson, 1979; Hurrell, 1977).

Job underload. Job underload associated with repetitive, routine, boring, and understimulating work environments (e.g. paced assembly lines) has been associated with ill health (Cooper and Marshall, 1976, 1978). In relation to the police situation, there appears to be conflicting opinions in the literature. Rubinstein (1973) for example, found that periods of boredom such as routine patrolling are a common situation inherent in police careers which he suggests not only causes fatigue, but the resulting sensory deprivation may possibly result in psychological regression (a state characterized by psychological deterioration).

Eisenberg (1975) substantiates these hypotheses and maintains these periods of boredom are especially detrimental to health when they are suddenly disrupted due to a crisis call for instance, therefore giving a sudden jolt to the physical and mental state of the police officer. Kroes (1976) proposes that besides health, the actual performance of police can be influenced by boredom and suggests that police will occasionally engage in marginal activities such as questioning 'suspicious' characters in order to break the monotony.

On the other hand, more empirically based findings by such authors as Davidson (1979), Harrison (1975), and Hurrell (1977), challenge some of these assumptions. Harrison's (1975) questionnaire data from four US occupational groups (policemen, administrators, assembly line workers and scientists) illustrated that compared to other occupations (with the possible exception of assembly line workers), work underload appeared to have little effect on the policemen's job satisfaction. McMichael (1978) suggests these findings may be due to the police being less concerned about factors associated with job satisfaction. A more feasible explanation however, is presented by Van Harrison (1978) who suggests that routine activities and possible work underload are probably seen by police as being an integral part of their job (while being prepared for sudden emergency situations), and subsequently have less effect on their overall job satisfaction *per se*.

Van Harrison's explanation would seem to be verified by Davidson's (1979) and Hurrell's (1977) findings, as only approximately 19% of US police officers reported feeling frequently bored while on duty compared to 25% of the Northern Territories police sample. In terms of the popularity of routine activities which included pedestrian and car checks, routine patrol and staying alert to the police radio, on average, approximately 76% of US officers and 73% of Australian police respondents expressed a liking for these situations (Davidson, 1979; Hurrell, 1977).

Even so, a particular complaint inherent in police work and related to boredom and routine, has been shown to be excessive paperwork. In the US, Kroes *et al.* (1974) reported that police felt they were spending too much time on paperwork, and approximately 73% of Hurrell's (1977) police officers stated a dislike for the routine paperwork they had to do.

These findings have been replicated in Australian studies. Chappell and Wilson (1969) for example, found that paper work was a particular area of concern among Queensland police with 55% of respondents feeling that this time and effort would be better channelled into such areas as crime prevention and detection. As well, Swanton (1974), in a survey of the police association of South Australia, found that excessive paperwork was considered by noncommissioned members as being second only to pay and allowances, as a cause for concern. More recently, 75% of Northern Territories police surveyed professed to disliking routine department paperwork (Davidson, 1979). Therefore, frustrations associated with paperwork appear to be common in all police forces. Eisenberg (1975) maintains these frustrations are enhanced by the fact that a majority of police fail to see the need or purpose of this task as being part of their job.

In conclusion, it would appear that both job overload and underload may have detrimental effects on police. A particularly relevant physiological study undertaken by Frankenhaeuser *et al.* (1971) found that student policemen, when subjected to both overstimulation (a complex sensorimotor test) and understimulation (a vigilance test), secreted increased norepinephrine in both situations when compared to controls operating under conditions of medium stimulation. However, subjects excreting relatively more epinephrine performed better during understimulation, whereas efficiency was greater during overstimulation in those releasing small amounts of epinephrine.

Obviously then, as in most cases, individuals react differently to the same conditions. However, if we agree with Coburn's (1975) assumption — in which he suggests that the closer one is to the job the greater the detrimental effects from job overload or underload — the police who can rarely escape their work role are probably highly susceptible to certain maladies related to job underload and overload; especially factors intrinsic to the job which they deem as being unnecessary.

Courts. Kroes (1976) suggests that stressors associated with the courts are specific occupational stressors unique to police careers and not shared with other occupations. Most of the relevant research regarding this issue is American. Chposky (1975), for instance, refers to earlier work by Kroes in which 50% of the police interviewed (total being 100) reported they were bothered by the amount of time they had to spend in court and the general lack of consideration given in the scheduling of appearances; approximately 61% of Hurrell's (1977) US patrolmen maintained similar court inconveniences.

With regard to Australian cohorts, research by Wilson and Western (1972) indicated that 10% of time was taken up with court work in their police sample and 54% of Davidson's (1979) Northern Territories police respondents complained of frequent court delays. Besides court appearances being time consuming, police are often frustrated over judicial procedure, inefficiency, and court decisions (Eisenberg, 1975; Margolis, 1973). This was recently verified by Hurrell's (1977) and Davidson's (1979) American and Australian studies, both of which reported that approximately 86% of their police samples maintained that the courts were often too lenient with offenders.

Physical danger. According to Kroes (1976), physical danger — which can result from line of duty/crisis situations and racial situations between minority group members, in which a threat to an officer's physical wellbeing may overwhelm him emotionally — is a specific police stressor not shared by any other occupational groups. While we support Eisenberg's (1975) claim that danger, fear of serious injury and disability, and even death, can make police work a hazardous environment in which to work and are probably major job stressors, we cannot agree with Kroes' assumption that such conditions are unique to police careers. Kasl (1973), for instance, isolates other occupations which share similar physical dangers as including mine workers, soldiers, and firemen.

We believe that the similar American and Australian research findings by Hurrell (1977) and Davidson (1979) throw the most light on the controversy regarding the effects of physical danger in police careers. In both studies, the situations found to be most tense (as ranked by the police officers themselves), where those which involved the possibility of danger or violent confrontation, e.g. 'a person with a gun'. However, a surprising finding was that overall, neither study found a significant negative relationship between the perceived level of tension of a situation and the extent to which the police officers liked the situation (Davidson, 1979; Hurrell, 1977).

The only situations which were found to be viewed as very tense and were also disliked by a high majority of police in both the American and Australian samples, were those situations involving — 'a person with a gun', 'child beating', 'delivering death messages', 'domestic disturbance', and 'shootings' (Davidson, 1979; Hurrell, 1977). Consequently, these could perhaps be classified as potential stressor variables if one accepts the contention that high anxiety situations plus negative feelings are more detrimental than high anxiety plus positive feelings. Many other situations which police in both samples found most tense, were in fact positively evaluated by the officers, which indicates that perhaps men in police careers are stimulated by certain aspects of police work and indeed, may even be stress seekers.

However, one has to keep in mind that Davidson's (1979) Northern Territories police study also substantiates Hurrell's (1977) conclusion that the greatest amount of a policeman's time is spent in low tense and hence not particularly stressful situations with the highly tense situations occurring very infrequently (some of the latter being regarded favourably by most police officers). Rather than assuming that the threat of physical danger is unique to police, we suggest that future investigations should concentrate more on both the clustering of the various dimensions of physical threat (e.g. brawls, domestic interventions, impersonal violence) and the implications of the officers' actions in responses to physical danger (e.g. litigation, liabilities, court appearances). Thus, the policeman — unlike the fireman, prison guard, or military man — is likely to have a unique set of stressors with regard to physical danger.

Role in the organization

Other sources of occupational stress are role ambiguity (i.e. a lack of clarity about the work), role conflict (i.e. conflicting job demands), and responsibility for people, as well as conflicts stemming from organizational boundaries (Cooper and Marshall, 1976). Authors such as French and Caplan (1972), Beehr *et al.* (1976), and Shirom *et al.* (1973), have indicated that these organizational stressors stemming from role ambiguity and conflict can result in such stress-related maladies as CHD.

Neither Davidson's (1979) or Hurrell's (1977) Australian and American police stress studies found high incidences of role conflict *per se;* with only 30% and 23% of their respective police respondents reporting frequent feelings of role conflict. Even so, degrees of responsibility for people and their safety, appear to be a potentially viable occupational stressor in policing, although not to the extent it is for air traffic controllers (Kroes, 1976). However, Kroes posits that in some ways this stressor can be as great for police, as their guidelines are more varied and the decisions they have to make (e.g. stopping suicide attempts or deciding when to shoot) are less clearly defined.

Eisenberg (1975) has isolated the police role related to stopping the rise in crime as causing most role conflict, the conflict existing between maximizing the efficiency in enforcing law on the one hand and guaranteeing constitutional rights and civil liberties on the other. There are indications that these types of frustrations may be present to some degree in the Northern Territories police, as 55% of the officers surveyed stated they were often unable to utilize their abilities (Davidson, 1979).

Perhaps one of the major organizational role conflicts found in police careers, and which we have already discussed, stems from negative community attitudes. On this particular occupational stressor we agree with Kroes (1976) who maintains this is a unique police stressor not found in other occupations. Stress resulting from role expectation and conflict between police and the community can lead not only to isolation but also to low morale, which in turn may lead to overly aggressive police work; especially when the police regard the public as their enemy, and *vice versa* (Clark, 1965). Ward (1971) goes one step further, believing that if the police service is to be improved, and the ambiguity of the police role clarified, we must begin to look at it in its perspective to society.

Career development

The next group of environmental stressors is related to career development which, Cooper and Marshall (1976, p.18) maintain, refers to 'the impact of over-promotion, under-promotion, status incongruence, lack of job security, thwarted ambition, etc.' Certainly, police hierarchy, promotion restrictions, and pay inadequacies have all been attributed to police job stress (e.g. Cain, 1973; Hurrell, 1977; Punch and Naylor, 1973; Reiser, 1974; Rubinstein, 1973; Wilson and Western, 1972). Status congruency, or the degree to which there is job advancement (including pay grade advancement), was found by Erickson *et al.* (1972) — in their large sample of navy employees — to be positively related to military effectiveness and negatively related to the incidence of psychiatric disorders. In relation to stress resulting from promotion, Brook (1973) found that overpromotion (i.e. beyond maximum level of competence) and underpromotion caused job stress; thereby causing some individuals to progress from minor psychological symptoms to psychosomatic complaints, and finally to mental illness.

Both Eisenberg (1975) and Kroes (1976) state that in the US limitations on police promotional opportunitites and career mobility are another major occupational stressor. This was recently substantiated by Hurrell's (1977) study which indicated that 71% of the surveyed patrolmen were dissatisfied with the promotion system and 50% were uncertain about their job future. Eisenberg (1975) blames this particular stressor as being a contributing factor behind police leaving the force for career-related professions such as firemen and probation officers. Hurrell and Kroes (1975) believe poor promotional opportunities in policing also create disruptive competitiveness which hinders true group cohesion.

Slow promotion through the ranks also appears to be a particular problem facing Australian police, with Wilson and Western's (1972) survey indicating a large proportion of police were dissatisfied with the present system, e.g. 37% gave lack of opportunity for promotion as the major reason for leaving the force. However, due possibly to recent promotional policy changes in the Northern Territories police force, this potential stress source appears to have been alleviated as over 63% of the police recently surveyed were satisfied with their promotion system (Davidson, 1979).

Inadequate pay is another area of concern for police. Approximately 90% of Hurrell's (1977) US police sample believed their pay was unfair compared to other occupations, and about 51% reported dissatisfaction with their pay. Recently in England, the police have been awarded a massive 40% increase in an attempt to improve the quality of policemen (less than 1% of the total 120,000 men in the police force have degrees), and to stop members from leaving the force (in 1977 for the first time in 20 years more men left the force than joined it — *Guardian Weekly,* July 30, 1978, p.1).

In Australia, police earn more throughout their years of service than public servants, but Wilson and Western (1972) suggest their pay is not commensurate with their difficult and responsible (not to say dangerous) job. The Northern Territories policemen themselves appeared to agree with this suggestion as 64% maintained their pay was less fair then other comparable occupations and 55% were dissatisfied with their pay (Davidson, 1979).

Moreover, Miller *et al.* (1973) found that 40% of US police had second jobs, which were mainly in security fields. Although Australian police are not officially allowed to have second jobs, Chappell and Wilson (1969) found that these rules were often ignored by administrators. Objections to police personnel working at second jobs include fatigue, adverse job efficiency, and the fact that they may be placed in a compromising situation through their civilian employment (Chappell and Wilson, 1969).

Relationships at work

Relationships at work which include the nature of relationships with one's colleagues, boss, and subordinates, have also been related to job stress. According to French and Caplan (1972), poor relations with other members of an organization may be precipitated due to role ambiguity in the organization, which in turn produces psychological strain in the form of low job satisfaction. Empirical data as to whether this occupational stressor actually contributes to mental and physical ill health are limited. However, Caplan *et al.* (1975) found that high social support from peers relieved job strain and was also shown to condition the effect of job stress on cortisone, blood pressure, glucose, and the number of cigarettes smoked as well as cigarette smoking quit rate. Hurrell and Kroes (1975) propose that although extreme competitiveness between police peers can be disruptive, loyalty and fear of letting a fellow police officer down often drive police to continue performing their duty. Both Rubinstein (1973) and Reiser (1974) emphasize the importance of hierarchical and peer-group good relationships, and support, in police working environments in which cultural norms, values, and attitudes are overriding. Furthermore, conflict and anxiety can be generated in officers if dissonance exists with regard to identifying with or conforming to peer-group expectations (e.g. Reiser, 1974; Rubinstein, 1973).

Kroes *et al.* (1974) suggest that a police officer is better able to cope with the stress he faces if he feels that his superiors understand and know his problems and will support him. It is of interest to bear in mind that poor relationships with one's supervisor did not seem to be a common occurrence in either Davidson's (1979) Australian, or Hurrell's (1977) US police samples.

Besides relationships *per se*, lack of social support has also been associated with stress outcomes (Caplan *et al.*, 1975; McMichael, 1978). In fact, recent Australian and American police survey findings (i.e. Davidson, 1979; Hurrell, 1977) have indicated that lack of social support may be an important stressor inherent in police careers, and requires further investigation. Both studies found that the vast majority of police respondents reported not being able to often seek social support from either their supervisor or from persons other than their spouse (Davidson, 1979; Hurrell, 1977). Indeed, this lack of social support appears to be often facilitated by the policeman himself, as some of the Australian respondents were of the opinion that personal matters should be kept to oneself and not discussed outside the family (Davidson, 1979).

Organizational structure and climate

The final potential source of occupational stress is related to organizational structure and climate and includes such factors as office politics, lack of effective consultation, no participation in the decision-making process, and restrictions on behaviour (Cooper and Marshall, 1976, 1978). Margolis *et al.* (1974) and French and Caplan (1972) both found that greater participation led to higher productivity, improved performance, lower staff turnover, and lower levels of physical and mental health (including such stress-related behaviours as escapist drinking and heavy smoking).

With regard to the police, the main occupational stressor related to organizational structure and climate appears to be dissatisfaction with administration. Kroes *et al.*'s (1974) survey reported that 51% of police respondents, when asked what areas of their job they were most dissatisfied with, said administration and related policy, assignments, and procedures. A greater proportion, i.e. 65% of Hurrell's US police officers, complained of feelings of dissatisfaction with management, 60% thought the departmental policies were too rigid and 48% reported communication of department policies to be poor (Hurrell, 1977).

Similar strong feelings of dissatisfaction relating to organizational factors were found in Davidson's (1979) survey of Northern Territories police. A high 68% of the Australian sample were dissatisfied with management, 63% believed the departmental policies were too rigid, and 63% maintained that the communication of department policies was not good (Davidson, 1979). Related to this, both Kroes (1976) and Rubinstein (1973) have found that police officers often complain of not being asked to provide any professional input in the decisions and policies that directly affect them, as well as having little knowledge of police or governmental policies.

A final issue which emerged from both Hurrell (1977) and Davidson's (1979) police surveys concerns the dissatisfaction of police training. Over 68% of the Australian police sample compared to 50% of their American counterparts professed to not being satisfied with their training (Davidson, 1979; Hurrell, 1977). Surely, this is an important area requiring more research. We believe that police training programmes should aim to cover all aspects of police work, including stress awareness and stress coping programmes.

Conclusions

By reviewing relevant occupational research, we have attempted to isolate possible occupational stressors which may be inherent in the police service. Rather than police being subjected to unique stressors, what we suggest is that it is the components of the stressors which may define the police as a 'unique' occupation in the way that they cluster.

OCCUPATIONAL STRESSORS AND STRESS-RELATED OUTCOMES

Occupational stressors and health

Aldridge (1970) refers to the report of the British Department of Health and Social Security (1968), in which the sum of incapacity for men suffering from psychoneurotic, mental, and personality disorders, headache, and nervousness, accounted for 22.8 million days off work, thereby placing mental illness in second place after bronchitis, and before accidents and heart disease. As well, Cooper and Marshall (1976), in their extensive literature review of occupational sources of stress, point out that Felton and Cole (1963) found that in the US all cardiovascular diseases accounted for 12% of lost working time in their sample. In Australia, current research indicates this figure may be even higher (Byrne and Henderson, 1976).

Selye (1976) reports that these diseases, i.e. psychiatric disturbances, cardiovascular disease, and bronchial maladies, as well as diabetes and gastrointestinal malfunctions, are stress induced. What is of even greater relevance is that there is substantial evidence suggesting that occupational stress is a causal factor in these diseases (Margolis *et al.*, 1974; Selye, 1976). Within this growing body of evidence relating occupational stress and disease, certain occupations, including police (Eisenberg, 1975; Kroes, 1976; Selye, 1978), are identified as being particularly high risk occupations in relation to susceptibility to stress-induced mental and organic diseases.

Occupational stressors and mental health

According to Kasl (1973), mental health indices of functional effectiveness in varying occupations have tended to rely on absence from work, hospitalization, quitting the job, and spouse desertion. Indices of well-being concentrate on measuring self-esteem, depression, life satisfaction, job satisfaction, and needs satisfaction. Finally, other indices aimed at ascertaining mastery and competence have relied on measures of adequacy and coping, attainment of valued goals, and psychiatric signs and symptoms indices.

Mental health disturbances associated with occupational stress have also been found in dentistry, medicine, nursing (Selye, 1976), and post office employees (Ferguson, 1973). A particularly interesting finding in relation to stress factors in the medical occupations is that a specific occupational stressor appears to be the constant necessity to be ready to act in unexpected, emergency situations (Selye, 1976) — a common occupational hazard found in police careers (Kroes, 1976).

Recent research by Davidson (1979), Eisenberg (1975), Hurrell (1977), and Kroes (1976), indicates that occupational stressors inherent in police careers are causal agents in such mental health problems and outcomes as severe nervous conditions, neurosis, job dissatisfaction, high rates of divorce, marital discord, high suicide rates, increased incidences of alcoholism, and other drug abuse. Unfortunately, the majority of these data to date are subjective in nature (relying on questionnaire surveys and personal experiences within the field) with few or no empirical medical indices to substantiate their claims. However, two indices of behavioural and attitudinal/mental disorders which have been associated with occupational stress in relation specifically to the police, hitherto not discussed, include alcohol and drug abuse (including smoking), and job dissatisfaction.

Alcoholism

Margolis *et al.* (1974), after interviewing over one and a half thousand workers in the United States in varying occupations, found a positive relationship between escapist drinking and number of specific job stressors. Those experiencing high job stress drank more than those in occupations experiencing less job stress. The following year, Hurrell and Kroes (1975) suggested that the presence of high levels of stress at work can facilitate some individuals to resort to heavy drinking as a coping technique. Further, they posit that men in policing are especially vulnerable to alcoholism. They go on to state that some US police officials have reported informally, that as many as 25% of officers in their respective departments have alcohol abuse problems. In the Northern Territories police survey, while fewer police actually drank alcohol compared to the same age and sex Northern Territories male population, of those police who did drink, a higher percentage were 'medium' and 'heavy' drinkers (Davidson, 1979).

Besides occupational stress *per se,* Rubinstein (1973) blames the alcohol abuse problem in police as being due to emphasized drinking opportunitites open to police in their work, and it is of interest that Heiman (1975) has linked alcoholism with police suicide in America. Although there is a lack of empirical research on this issue (especially in Britain), there are subjective indications that alcoholism may be a problem in police forces both in the US and Australia. Future research needs to record police alcohol usage in a controlled fashion with records relying on actuarial pathological reports (e.g. diseases of the liver). As well, if research findings indicate that alcoholism is a problem in any particular police force, police alcoholic counselling services should be established.

Smoking and job stressors

Not only is smoking related to incidence of CHD (Selye, 1976), but it has also been found to be associated with neuroticism and anxiety (McCrae *et al.*, 1978), and to be most frequent in stressful occupations, along with other drug abuse behaviours and high fat diets (Russek, 1965; Selye, 1976). As well, Russek (1965) and Ikard and Tomkins (1973) maintain that cigarette smoking quit rate is greatest under low occupational stress.

Recent Australian and American data indicates that approximately 49% of police sampled were cigarette smokers (Davidson, 1979; Hurrell, 1977). Although Hurrell (1977) presented no comparative American smoking consumption statistics, Davidson (1979) discovered that while the percentage of smokers in her Northern Territories police sample was lower than in the Northern Territories male population, a greater percentage of those policemen who smoked were 'medium' and 'heavy' smokers compared to the control population. Consequently, as with those Northern Territories police who drank alcohol, those who smoke like those who drink, tend to do so to excess compared to the average Australian male drinker and smoker — findings which are probably indicative of increased stressor influences in police careers (Davidson, 1979).

Job dissatisfaction and health

Research by Margolis *et al.* (1974) considers job dissatisfaction as an important factor contributing to psychological and physiological strain. These findings have been replicated by Kroes (1975) in an extensive study in which he looked at 23 occupations and found high job satisfaction equated with job security, social support from one's superior, a high level of education, high social support, and low role conflict. In another study of job dissatisfaction among blue- and white-collar workers, Sales and House (1971) interpreted their results as indicating that there was a possible association between low job satisfaction and risk of CHD.

After reviewing the research regarding job satisfaction in the police, it becomes evident that few differences in the causes and degrees of job dissatisfaction are related to cultural variance. Certainly, organizational stressors resulting in low morale and high job dissatisfaction have been attributed to such factors as manpower shortages, role conflict, alienation, and frustration resulting from the administrative and organizational hierarchies of police forces (Chappell and Wilson, 1969; Davidson, 1979; Hurrell, 1977; Kroes, 1976; Wilson and Western, 1972).

Both Davidson (1979) and Hurrell (1977) were unable to compare the degree of job satisfaction in their Australian and US police samples with suitable control group occupations; however both studies reported that approximately 42% of their respective police population samples reported low job satisfaction. Even so, both authors were able to compare the levels of reported illnesses in their police samples with levels in Quinn and Shepard's (1974) US occupational surveys and recent Australian census statistics of incidences of illnesses (Davidson, 1979; Hurrell, 1977). These two separate studies both found the number of illnesses and somatic complaints to be greater in the police populations compared to other US and Australian sample populations (Davidson, 1979). In addition, the illnesses which the police officers most frequently associated with their job *per se,* were injury related maladies such as whiplash, and stress related illnesses such as hypertension, ulcers, and mental ill health (Davidson, 1979; Hurrell, 1977).

The stress resulting from low job satisfaction and low morale has also been correlated with job performance. Robinson (1970) maintained that once a policeman becomes dissatisfied, his standard of work falls along with his morale. Additionally, low morale has been equated with low work-related self-esteem (Kasl, 1978). Both Hurrell (1977) and Davidson (1979) when comparing their respective US and Australian police samples with the US workers sampled by Quinn and Shepard (1974) in terms of their responses to items of the 'Work-Related Self-Esteem Scale', found that police indicated a lower level of work-related self-esteem.

We support Hurrell's (1977) proposal that the explanation for these results requires further investigation. They would appear to be important in relation to the central issue of stress in the police, as low self-esteem has been associated with such job related factors as qualitative work overload (Kasl, 1978), and inadequate support from supervisors and co-workers (McMichael, 1978). In addition to stress-related job variables, self-esteem appears to be of significant importance at the individual interface. According to research by Garrity *et al.* (1977) for instance, strong self-esteem is a factor associated with individuals who are successful at coping with stressors.

While the measurements of job satisfaction may relate to mental and physical health, the relationship cannot be taken as being absolute as concomitant psychophysiological indices are needed before definitive statements can be made. Kasl (1973), for instance, notes that most studies of job satisfaction and mental health are correlational in nature, and often causal interpretations of the data are far from self-evident. He cites two large surveys carried out by Gunn (1960) and Langer (1963), both of which found respondents in higher status occupations reported more job satisfaction and more stress-related work worries than those reporting lower job satisfaction. Consequently, Kasl (1973) concludes that what may be more closely related to job level is job involvement rather than various indices of wellbeing. Finally, in reference to future research, we suggest the administration of the 'Person-Environment Fit Scales' as an additional useful measure of police job satisfaction (Caplan *et al.,* 1975).

Occupational stressors and coronary heart disease (CHD)

The literature regarding the relationship between job stress and the incidence of CHD is conflicting. Hinkle *et al.* (1968) in their 5-year statistical study on the relation between occupation, education, and CHD, among 270,000 male employees of the Bell Telephone and Telegraph Company in the US, found no evidence that men in high level responsibility jobs, or men having been promoted rapidly, frequently, or transferred, had any added risk of CHD. They concluded that rather than job stress, CHD was more closely related to such factors as eating habits, cigarette smoking, and general life style. An Australian study carried out by Ferguson (1973) found no significant association between stress indices, e.g. neurosis, incidences of hypertension, CHD, or other purported stress-related illnesses.

However, other authors (e.g. Byrne and Henderson, 1976; Hurrell and Kroes, 1975) are convinced that the incidence of CHD is stress related and that subsequently, stress within one's job can be an important causal factor in facilitating some of the psychophysical changes which may cause CHD. Certainly, whatever the reasons, CHD appears to be higher in the police population compared to many others (Hurrell, 1977; Kroes, 1976). Recently, Davidson (1979) isolated higher incidences of heart disease or heart trouble in her Northern Territories police sample compared to Australian male population samples. Nevertheless, one should keep in mind that this police sample did have an overall poor history of family health in relation to heart disease (Davidson, 1979). Clearly, the issue regarding the relationship between CHD and occupational stressors is by no means resolved and more research regarding police duties and CHD is needed.

Occupational stressors and minor ailments

Besides mental disorders (including suicide) and CHD, other ailments said to be exacerbated by psychological job stress include asthma, hayfever, thyroid disorders, repeated skin trouble, arthritis, obesity, hypertension, tuberculosis, migraine, ulcers (including ulcerative colitis) and diabetes (Cooper and Marshall, 1976, 1978; Kroes, 1976; Selye, 1976). Kroes (1976) maintains that due to the highly stressed nature of police work, police as a population are particularly prone to these stress-induced ailments. In particular, Kroes refers to diabetes and gastrointestinal malfunctions as being highly related to periods of high job stress or emotional upset.

Certainly, gastrointestinal malfunctions such as ulcers of the stomach and duodenum have been found to be common in certain occupations undergoing severe stress situations (Selye, 1976). However, while anxiety stimulates gastric hydrochloric acid and enzyme secretion, ulceration appears to develop only in predisposed individuals (for many, indigestion may be the only outcome) and not always in high executive occupations as often assumed (Dunn and Cobb, 1962). Stern (1973) proposed that there was a high rate of ulcers in the US police and this has recently been verified empirically by Hurrell (1977).

In addtion to heart disease, Davidson's (1979) isolated stress induced health maladies in the Northern Territories police consisted of higher incidences of hypertension, asthma, hayfever, repeated skin trouble, ulcers, trouble with gastrointestinal tract, migraine and headaches, mental illness or nervous breakdown, and gout, compared to same age and sex Australian male population samples. As in the work arena, Hurrell's (1977) US police sample shared some isolated stress manifestation outcomes with Davidson's Australian police sample. Incidences of hayfever, stomach ulcers, trouble with gastrointestinal tract, hypertension, and migraine or severe headaches, appeared to be higher in both police samples compared to other Australian and US male sample populations (Davidson, 1979). However, the incidence of hypertension and migraine or severe headaches in the Northern Territories police sample was significantly greater than in Hurrell's (1977) US police officers (Davidson, 1979).

As well as adversive job effects on general health, it is important to note that neurosis as well as Type A personality influences (a high incidence of which were both isolated in police populations by Hurrell, 1977; and Davidson, 1979) have been associated with high occurrence of cigarette smoking, heart disease or heart trouble, hypertension, and mental illness or nervous breakdown (Frankenhaeuser, 1976; Hurrell and Kroes, 1975; Ikard and Tomkins, 1973; Rosenman *et al.,* 1976; Selye, 1976). Therefore, there appears to be strong evidence supporting the contention that the police have high incidences of stress-induced illnesses. Hence, we recommend that future research investigating stress in the police service should not only note all incidences of stress-related ailments but also include physiological and medical indices.

SUMMARY

Throughout this review we have emphasized the integration of the existing literature on stress in police toward the end of generating a wholistic view of the stressor-stress paradigm. We have drawn upon research from a number of disciplines and suggested concrete research projects, as well as utilizing a crosscultural approach to cover all the salient issues to demonstrate that basically we are involved in a field that has a vast array of approaches and 'solutions'.

The final point which we would like to emphasize is that priority should be given to the implementation of prospective, empirically based research in the area of police stress and the subsequent implementation of appropriate 'in service' stress awareness programmes. The data show clearly that an adjusted, healthy, satisfied policeman is a much better asset to the community then an unadjusted and dissatisfied officer. Considering the very special role played by police in society, this is a matter which should receive the highest priority by police departments, governmental funding agencies and social scientists.

NOTE

1.   Some of the research literature reviewed here was drawn from an article (Part I and II) published by the authors in *Abstracts on Police Science,* 1978, **6**, 4, 187-199; 1978, **6**, 5, 257-268; and from the 1977 monograph, *Multifaceted Aspects of Stress in the Police Service.* We would like to thank the Criminologica Foundation and the Australian Institute of Criminology for permission to use some of this material.

REFERENCES

Aldridge, J.F.L. (1970). Emotional illness and the working environment. *Ergonomics,* **13**, 5, 613-621.

Allen, R., Pilnick, S., and Silverzweig, S. (1969). Conflict resolution-team building for police and ghetto residents. *Journal of Criminal Law, Criminology and Police Science,* **60**, 251-255.

Appley, M.H., and Trumbell, R. (Eds.) (1967). *Psychological Stress.* New York. Appleton.

Averill, J.R., Opton, E.M., and Lazarus, R.S. (1971). Cross cultural studies of psycho-physiological responses during stress and emotion. In L. Levi (Ed.), *Society Stress and Disease* (Vol. 1). London, New York, Toronto. Oxford University Press, pp. 110-124.

Balch, R.W. (1972). The police personality: Fact or fiction? *Journal of Criminal Law, Criminology and Police Science,* **63**, 1, 106-119.

Banton, M.P. (1964). *The Policeman in the Community.* London. Tavistock.

Bard, M. (1969). Family intervention police teams as a community mental health resource, *Journal of Criminal Law, Criminology and Police Science,* **60**, 2, 247-250.

Bard, M. (1971). The role of law enforcement in the helping system. *Community Mental Health Journal,* **7**, 151-160.

Beehr, T.A., and Newman, J.E. (1978). Job stress, employee health, and organizational effectiveness: A facet analysis, model and literature review. *Personnel Psychology,* **31**, 4, 665-699.

Beehr, T.A., Walsh, J.T., and Taber, T.D. (1976). Relationship of stress to individually and organisationally valued states: Higher order needs as a moderator. *Journal of Applied Psychology,* **61**, 1, 41-47.

Bell, R., Cleveland, S., Hanson, P., and O'Connell, W. (1969). Small group dialogue and discussion: An approach to police-community relationships. *Journal of Criminal Law, Criminology and Police Science,* **60**, 2, 242-246.

Belson, W.A. (1975). *The Public and the Police.* London. Harper and Row.

Brook, A. (1973). Mental stress at work, *The Practitioner,* **210**, (Jan-Jun), 500-506.

Byrne, D.G., and Henderson, A.S. (1976). Behavioural epidemiology and coronary heart disease. Some sources of error and an alternative conceptual model, *Australian and New Zealand Journal of Medicine,* **6**, 425-429.

Cain, M. (1973). *Society and the Policeman's Role.* London. Routledge and Kegan Paul.

Caplan, R.D., Cobb, S., and French, J.R.P. (1975). Relationships of cessation of smoking with job stress, personality and social support, *Journal of Applied Psychology,* **60,** 2, 211-219.

Caplan, R.D., Cobb, S., French, J.R.P., Van Harrison, S.R., and Pinneau, S.R. (1975). *Job Demands and Workers Health.* Washington, D.C. U.S. Department of Health, Education and Welfare. Publication No. (N1OSH) 75-160. U.S. Government Printing Office.

Chappell, D., and Meyer, J.C. (1975). Cross-cultural differences in police attitudes: An exploration in comparative research, *Australian and New Zealand Journal of Criminology,* **8,** 1, (March), 5-13.

Chappell, D., and Wilson, P.R. (1969). *The Police and the Public in Australia and New Zealand.* Brisbane. University of Queensland Press.

Chappell, D., and Wilson, P.R. (1972). *The Australian Criminal Justice System.* Sydney. Butterworths.

Chposky, J. (1975). Cover story, *The Law Officer,* **8,** 4 (Sept.-Oct.), 9-11.

Clark, J.P. (1965). Isolation of the police: A comparison of the British and American situations, *Journal of Criminal Law, Criminology and Police Science,* **56,** 3, 307-319.

Cobb, S., and Rose, R.M. (1973). Hypertension, peptic ulcer, and diabetes in air traffic controllers, *Journal of the Australian Medical Association,* **224,** 4, (23 April), 489-492.

Coburn, D. (1975). Job-worker incongruence: Consequences for health, *Journal of Health and Social Behaviour,* **16,** 2, 198-212.

Colquhoun, W.P. (1970). Circadian Rhythms, mental efficiency, and shift work. In P.R. Davis (Ed.), *Proceedings of the Symposium in Performance Under Sub Optimal Conditions.* London. Taylor and Francis Ltd., pp. 28-30.

Cooper, C.L., and Marshall, J. (1976). Occupational sources of stress: A review of the literature relating to coronary heart disease and mental ill health, *Journal of Occupational Psychology,* **49,** 11-28.

Cooper, C.L., and Marshall, J. (1978). Sources of managerial and white collar stress. In C.L. Cooper and R. Payne (Eds.), *Stress at Work.* Chichester, New York, Brisbane, Toronto. John Wiley and Sons, pp. 81-105.

Critchley, T. (1967). *A History of Police in England and Wales.* London. Constable.

Critchley, T. (1971). The developing role of the police in a changing society. The Police Federation Seminar, *The Police in Society.* London. Constable.

Danto, B.L. (1978). Police suicide, *Police Stress,* **1,** 1, 32-36, 38, 40.

Dash, J., and Reiser, M. (1978). Suicide among police in urban law enforcement agencies, *Journal of Police Science and Administration,* **6,** 1, 18-21.

Davidson, M.J. (1979). *Stress in the Police Service: A Multifaceted Model, Research Proposal and Pilot Study.* Unpublished dissertation, the University of Queensland, Australia.

Davidson, M.J., and Veno, A. (1977). *Multifaceted Aspects of Stress in the Police Service.* A.C.T. Australian Institute of Criminology Press (Monograph, 187p).

Davidson, M.J., and Veno, A. (1978). Police stress: A multicultural interdisciplinary review and perspective (I and II), *Abstracts on Police Science (Leading Article),* **6,** 4, 187-199. **6,** 5, 257-268.

Dembroski, T.M., and MacDougall, J.M. (1978). Stress effects on affiliation preferences among subjects possessing the type A coronary-prone behaviour pattern, *Journal of Personality and Social Psychology,* **36,** 1, 23-33.

Dodge, D.L., and Martin, W.T. (1970). *Social Stress and Chronic Illness-Mortality Patterns in Industrial Society.* Notre Dame. University of Notre Dame Press.

Dohrenwend, B.S., and Dohrenwend, B.P. (Eds.) (1973). *Stressful Life Events: Their Nature and Effects.* New York, London, Sydney, Toronto. Wiley.

Dunn, J.P., and Cobb, S. (1962). Frequency of peptic ulcer among executives, craftsmen, and foremen. *Journal of Occupational Medicine,* 4, 343-348.

Durkheim, E. (1951). *Suicide.* Illinois. Free Press of Glencoe.

Eisenberg, T. (1975). Labor-management relations and psychological stress — View from the bottom, *The Police Chief,* 42 (Nov.), 54-58.

Erickson, J.M., Pugh, W.M., and Gunderson, K.E. (1972). Status congruency as a prediction of job satisfaction and life stress, *Journal of Applied Psychology,* 56, 523-525.

Eysenck, H.J. (1958). A short questionnaire for the measurement of two dimensions of personality, *Journal of Applied Psychology,* 42, 14-17.

Eysenck, H.J., and Eysenck, S.B.J. (1964). *Manual of the Eysenck Personality Inventory.* London. University of London Press.

Fabricatore, J., Azen, S., Schoentgen, S., and Snibble, H. (1978). Predicting performance of police officers using the sixteen Personality Factor Questionnaire, *American Journal of Community Psychology,* 6, 1, 63-70.

Felton, J.J., and Cole, R. (1963). The high cost of heart disease, *Circulation,* 27, 957-962.

Ferguson, D. (1973). A study of occupational stress and health, *Ergonomics,* 16, 5, 649-663.

Finn, F., Hickey, N., and Doherty, E.F. (1969). The psychological profiles of male and female patients with CHD, *Irish Journal of Medical Science,* 2, 339-341.

Frankenhaeuser, M. (1974). *Man in Technological Society: Stress, Adaptation and Tolerance Limits.* Reports from the Psychological Laboratories, The University of Stockholm. Supplement 26 (December).

Frankenhaeuser, M. (1976). *Quality of Life: Criteria for Behavioural Adjustment.* Report from the Department of Psychology, University of Stockholm (No. 475).

Frankenhaeuser, M., Nordheden, B., Myrsten, A.L., and Post, B. (1971). Psychophysiological reactions to understimulation, *Acta Psychologia* (Amst.), 35, 298-308.

French, J., and Caplan, R. (1972). Organizational stress and individual strain. In A.J. Marrow (Ed.), *The Failure of Success.* New York. Amacon, pp. 31-66.

Friedman, M., Rosenman, R.H., and Carroll, V. (1958). Changes in serum cholesterol and blood clotting time in men subjected to cyclic variations of occupational stress, *Circulation,* 17, 852-861.

Gardner, J., and Veno, A. (1976). A community psychology approach to police training, *Professional Psychology,* 8, 4, (Nov.), 437-444.

Garrity, T.F., Somes, G.W., and Marx, M.B. (1977). Personality factors in resistance to illness after recent life changes, *Journal of Psychosomatic Research,* 21, 23-32.

Harrison, R.V. (1975). *Job Stress and Worker Health: Person-environment Misfit.* Paper presented to the American Public Health Association. Convention. Chicago, Illinois.

Hayton, T.H. (1975). Stress syndrome and the police service, *Police Association Victoria,* 44, 13, (Jan-Feb), 55-57.

Heiman, M.F. (1975). The police suicide, *Journal of Police Science and Administration,* 3 (September), 267-273.

Hilton, J. (1973). Psychology and police work. In J.C. Anderson and P.J. Stead (Eds.), *The Police We Deserve.* London. Wolfe Publishers Ltd., pp. 93-105.

Hinkle, L.E., Whitney, L.H., Lehman, E.W., Dunn, J., Benjamin, B., King, R., Plakun, A., and Flehinger, B. (1968). Occupational, education and coronary heart disease risk is influenced more by education and background than by occupational experience. In the Bell System, *Science,* 161, 238-246.

Hurrell, J.J. (1977). *Job Stress Among Police Officers — A Preliminary Analysis.* U.S. Department of Health, Education and Welfare. Publication No. (N1OSH) 7604228. Cincinnati, Ohio. U.S. Government Printing Office.

Hurrell, J.J., and Kroes, W.H. (1975). *Stress Awareness.* Cincinnati, Ohio. National Institute for Occupational Safety and Health.

Hurst, M.W., Jenkins, C.D., and Rose, R.M. (1978). The assessment of life change stress: A comparative and methodological inquiry, *Psychosomatic Medicine,* **40,** 2, 126-141.

Ikard, P.F., and Tomkins, S. (1973). The experience of affect as a determinant of smoking behaviour, *Journal of Abnormal Psychology,* **81,** 172-181.

Jenkins, C.D. (1971) Psychologic and social precursors of coronary disease, *New England Journal of Medicine,* **284,** 6, 307-317.

Jirak, M. (1975). Alienation among members of the New York City Police Department on Straten Island, *Journal of Police Science and Administration,* **3,** 2, (June), 149-161.

Kasl, S.V. (1973). Mental health and work environment: An examination of the evidence, *Journal of Occupational Medicine,* **15,** 6, 509-517.

Kasl, S.V. (1978). Epidemiological contributions to the study of work stress. In C.L. Cooper and R. Payne (Eds.), *Stress at Work.* Chichester, New York, Brisbane, Toronto. John Wiley and Sons, pp. 3-48.

Knowles, L., and Jones, R. (1974). Police altercations and the ups and downs of life cycles, *The Police Chief,* **41** (November), 51-54.

Krocker, C., Forsyth, D., and Haase, R. (1974). Evaluation of a police-youth human relations program, *Professional Psychology,* **5,** 140-154.

Kroes, W.H. (1975). Psychological job stress and worker health — A programme effort. In J.J. Hurrell and W.H. Kroes (Eds.), *Stress Awareness.* Cincinnati, Ohio. National Institute for Occupational Safety and Health, pp. 1-24.

Kroes, W.H. (1976). *Society's Victim — the Policeman — an Analysis of Job Stress in Policing.* New York. Charles C. Thomas.

Kroes, W., Margolis, B., and Hurrell, J. (1974). Job stress in policemen, *Journal of Police Science and Administration,* **2,** 2, 145-155.

Kunzel, R. (1974). The connection between the family cycle and divorce rates: An analysis based on European data, *Journal of Marriage and the Family,* **36** (May), 379-388.

Lazarus, R.S., Tomita, M., Opton, E., and Kodama, M. (1966). A cross-cultural study of stress reaction patterns in Japan, *Journal of Personality and Social Psychology,* **4,** 622-633.

Levine, S., and Scotch, N.A. (1970). *Social Stress.* Illinois. Aldine Publishing Company.

Lewis, R.W. (1973). Toward an understanding of police anomie, *Journal of Police Science and Administration,* **1,** 4, (December), 484-490.

Lotz, R., and Regoli, R.M. (1977). Police cynicism and professionalism, *Human Relations,* **30,** 2, 175-186.

Margolis, B.L. (1973). Stress is a work hazard too, *Industrial Medicine, Occupational Health and Surgery,* **42,** (October), 20-23.

Margolis, B., Kroes, W., and Quinn, R. (1974). Job stress an unlisted occupational hazard, *Journal of Occupational Medicine,* **I,** 16, 659-661.

Martin, J.P., and Wilson, G. (1969). *The Police: A Study in Manpower.* London. Heinemann.

Matsumoto, Y.S. (1970). Social stress and coronary heart disease in Japan, *Milbank Men. Fed. Q.,* **48,** 9-36.

McCrae, R.R., Costa, P.T., and Bosse, R. (1978). Anxiety, extraversion, and smoking, *British Journal of Social and Clinical Psychology,* **17,** 269-273.

McMichael, A.J. (1978). Personality, behavioural, and situational modifiers of work stressors. In C.L. Cooper and R. Payne (Eds.), *Stress at Work.* Chichester, New York, Brisbane, Toronto. John Wiley and Sons, pp. 127-147.

Miller, G., Presley, R., and Sniderman, M. (1973). Multi job holding by firemen and policemen compared, *Public Personnel Management,* **2,** 283-289.

Munro, J.L. (1975). A study of the personality perception of South Australian police officers, *Australian and New Zealand Journal of Criminology,* **8,** 1, (March), 15-24.

Murrell, M.E., Lester, D., and Arcur, A.F. (1978). Is the 'Police Personality' unique to police officers?, *Psychological Reports,* **43,** 298.

Nelson, A., and Smith, W. (1970). The law enforcement profession: An incidence of high suicide, *Omega,* **1,** (November), 293-299.

Niederhoffer, A. (1967). *Behind the Shield.* New York. Doubleday.

Niederhoffer, A. (1974). *Behind the Shield.* New York. Doubleday.

Niederhoffer, A., and Niederhoffer, E. (1978). *Police Family — From Station House to Ranch House.* Massachusetts. Heath/Lexington.

O'Connor, D. (1974). The modern approach to police function, *Australian and New Zealand Journal of Criminology,* **7,** 69-86.

Paulson, S.L. (1974). Orientation programs for the police family, *The Police Chief,* **41,** (March), 63-64.

The policeman's lot is far too much (1978). *The Guardian Weekly,* 30 July, P.1.

Punch, M., and Naylor, T. (1973). The police: A social service, *New Society,* 17 May, 358-361.

Quinn, R.P., and Shepard, L.J. (1974). *The 1972-73 Quality of Employment Survey.* Surrey Research Centre, Institute for Social Research, Ann Arbor, Michigan.

Radelet, L.A. (1973). *The Police in the Community.* Beverly Hills, Calif. Glencoe Press.

Rafky, D. (1974). My husband the cop, *Police Chief,* **41,** (August), 63-65.

Rahe, R.H. (1978) Life change measurement clarification (Editorial). *Psychosomatic Medicine,* **40,** 2, (March), 1-2.

Regoli, R.M., and Poole, E.D. (1978). Specifying police cynicism, *Journal of Police Science and Administration,* **6,** 1, 98-104.

Reiser, M. (1974). Some organisational stresses on policemen, *Journal of Police Science and Administration,* **2,** 156-159.

Reiser, M. (1976). Stress, distress, and adaptation in police work, *The Police Chief,* (January), 14-27.

Reiser, M. (1978). The problem of police officer wives, *Police Chief,* **45,** 4, 38-40.

Rios, B., Parisher, D., and Reilley, R.R. (1978). Need for psychological services as perceived by urban police departments, *Psychological Reports,* **43,** 126.

Robinson, D. (1970). Predicting police effectiveness from self reports of relative time spent in task performance, *Personnel Psychology,* **23,** 1-7.

Rollins, B.C., and Cannon, K.L. (1974). Marital satisfaction over the family life cycle: A re-evaluation, *Journal of Marriage and the Family,* **36,** (May), 271-283.

Rollins, B.C., and Feldman, H. (1970). Marital satisfaction over the family life cycle, *Journal of Marriage and the Family,* **32,** (February), 20-28.

Rosenman, R.H., Brand, R.J., Scholtz, R.I., and Friedman, M. (1976). Multivariate prediction of coronary heart disease during 8.5 follow up on the western collaborative group study, *American Journal of Cardiology,* **37** (May), 903-908.

Rosenman, R.H., and Friedman, M. (1974). Neurogenic factors in pathogenesis of coronary heart disease, *Medical Clinics of North America,* **58,** 269-277.

Rubinstein, J. (1973). *City Police.* New York. Farrar, Staus, and Giroux.

Russek, H.I. (1965). Stress, tobacco and coronary heart disease in North American professional groups survey of 12,000 men in 14 occupational groups, *Journal of the American Medical Association,* **192,** 189-194.

Sales, S.M., and House, J. (1971). Job dissatisfaction as a possible risk factor in coronary heart disease, *Journal of Chronic Disease,* **23,** 861-873.

Schalling, D.S. (1975). Types of anxiety and types of stressors as related to personality. In C.D. Spielberger and I.G. Sarason (Eds.), *Stress and Anxiety.* Washington, D.C. Hemispheric Pub. Corp., pp. 279-283.

Sells, S.B. (1970). On the nature of stress. In J.E. McGrath (Ed.), *Social and Psychological Factors in Stress.* New York. Holt, Rinehart and Winston, pp. 134-139.

Selye, H. (1976). *Stress in Health and Disease.* Boston, London. Butterworths.

Selye, H. (1978). The stress of police work. *Police Stress,* **1,** 1, 7-8.

Sheppard, C., Bates, C., Fracchia, J., and Merlis, S. (1974). Psychological need structure of law enforcement officers, *Psychological Reports,* **1,** 35, 583-586.

Shirom, A., Eden, D., Silberwasser, S., and Kellerman, J.J. (1973). Job stresses and risk factors in coronary heart disease among five occupational categories in kibbutzim, *Social Science and Medicine,* **7,** 875-892.

Sikes, M., and Cleveland, S. (1968). Human relations training for police and community, *American Psychologist,* **23,** 766-769.

Skolnick, J. (1973). A sketch of the policemen's working personality. In A. Niederhoffer and A.S. Blumberg (Eds.), *The Ambivalent Force.* San Francisco. Rinehart Press, pp. 132-143.

Srole, L. (1977). *Mental Health in the Metropolis.* New York. Harper and Row.

Stern, N. (1973). What makes a policeman go wrong? In A. Niederhoffer and A.S. Blumberg (Eds.), *The Ambivalent Force.* San Francisco. Rinehart Press, pp. 125-129.

Stratton, J. (1976). The law enforcement programs for spouses, *FBI Law Enforcement Bulletin,* (March), 16-22.

Stratton, J. (1978). Police stress: considerations and suggestions (Part II), *Police Chief,* **45,** 5, 58-62.

Suicide thoughts plague police-psychiatrist. (1979). *The Australian,* Feb. 16, p. 3.

Swanton, B. (1974). *Protecting the Protectors. A Sociological Description of a Police Association.* Unpublished B.A. Honours dissertation, The University of Queensland, Australia.

Van Harrison, R. (1978). Person-environment fit and job stress. In C.L. Cooper and R. Payne (Eds.), *Stress at Work.* Chichester, New York, Brisbane, Toronto. John Wiley and Sons, pp. 175-205.

Vastola, A. (1978). The police personality: An alternative explanatory model, *Police Chief,* **45,** 4, 50-52.

Veno, A., and Davidson, M.J. (1978). A relational model of stress and adaptation, *Man-Environment Systems,* **8,** 2, 75-89.

Veno, A., and Gardner, J. (1979). An empirical evaluation of a community psychology police training course, *Journal of Community Psychology,* **7,** 210-119.

Ward, R.H. (1971). The police role: A case of diversity, *Journal of Criminal Law, Criminology and Police Science,* **61,** 4, 580-586.

Welford, A.T. (Ed.) (1974). *Man Under Stress.* London. Taylor and Francis Ltd.

Wenz, V.F. (1975). Anomie and level of suicidality in individuals, *Psychological Reports,* **36,** 817-818.

Wilson, J.Q. (1968). *City Politics and Public Policy.* New York. Wiley.

Wilson, P.R., and Western, J.S. (1972). *The Policeman's Position Today and Tomorrow: An Examination of the Victorian Police Force.* St. Lucia. University of Queensland Press.

Chapter 7

Stress in social work practice

Joseph W. Eaton
University of Pittsburgh, USA

THE PSYCHOLOGY OF STRESS

Social workers get paid to deal with stress — other people's problems. But this function also generates stress in their work situation and in them. What is experienced as stressful will vary considerably between persons and organizations. What can be generalized are attributes of the profession and its sub-culture that are often associated with stress or which provide norms for their management. Such generalization may also be useful for those charged with responsibility to educate future professionals. Stress management should be covered systematically in the curriculum.

Stress, like many scientific terms that find their way into the dictionary, has taken on a variety of meanings. 'The word is getting beaten to death,' bemoans Dr. Sidney Lecker, Director of the Stress Control Center ... 'Everybody is using it in so many different ways that stress has totally lost its meaning. It is not simply a synonym of affliction, worry or disturbance. Physiologists use the concept as a specific biological term to relate biological, psychological and social tensions to disease and disease prevention (Goldberg, 1978). Hans Selye (1956; 1974) defines stress as a state, manifested by a specific syndrome of biological events. But he claims:

Stress is not nervous tension.
Stress is not the discharge of hormones from the adrenal glands.
Stress is not simply the influence of some negative occurrence.
Stress is not an entirely bad event.

Selye believes that stress is the spice of life, and that the absence of stress is death. He sums up his view point as follows:

Man is a working animal whose mental and physical qualities must be employed sufficiently for him to remain healthy and prevent emotional and physical atrophy. But

167

he must learn to recognize that sometimes his work is so consuming that it robs him of the ability to develop in other areas of living (Seyle, 1974).

Little data seem to be available about the particularistic manifestations of stress in social work, compared to other professions. An analysis of English (crude) mortality rates does not reveal social work as a profession in which stress reaches abnormally high life-threatening proportions. On the whole, for example, English social workers seem slightly healthier than teachers and medical practitioners, and markedly more so than nurses. Table 1 compares mortality rates for circulatory and respiratory diseases, accidents and all neoplasms with these and other groups. On life expectancy, they compare slightly less favourably with teachers (a closely similar group according to these statistics), but are not one of the occupations with a noteably low chance of surviving to age 55. Table 2 positions social work relative to several similar occupational groupings. These findings run contrary to the mythology of many social workers, a mythology, however, which this field shares with other professions. In much of our world of work there is a commonplace perception that 'our assignments' are stressful. This belief may be related to the fact that within each field, professionals know much more about the tensions of their own work life than those of other fields.

A SOCIAL-PSYCHOLOGICAL APPROACH

The psychological concept of stress is not often relevant in social work situations. Only in extreme situations will workers become conscious of their psychological reactions when they experience stress in social-psychological terms. Hence, stress needs also be defined in appropriate social psychological terms, as *incidents and issues where individuals must deal with conflicting expectations in themselves or their place of work*. Commonplace among such social psychological stresses are discrepancies of the following four types:

(a) *Resources* available and conflict with those perceived to be required.
(b) *Norms* internalized by a professional and others supported by a co-worker, the supervisor, a client or by organizational policy.
(c) *Role expectation* of the professional are not matched by his status in the organization or the role he is expected to perform by a client, co-worker or others.
(d) *Social conflict* is experienced as disturbing by an individual affected by the situation.

Sociological indicators and personal insight can be used to identify social stress situations. They include nervous sensations of 'having too little time', identification with conflicting values, wearing several hats that involve people

Table 1. Mortality by occupation for selected causes of death. Men aged 15-64 given standardized mortality ratios per annum and per 100,000 persons[a]

Occupations	Circulatory diseases	Respiratory diseases	Accidents	All neoplasms
Social Workers	79	32	89	62
Teachers-Primary and Secondary Schools	81	38	54	57
Medical Practitioners	85	34	180	61
Nurses	122	76	147	94
Deck and Engine Room Ratings, Barge and Boatmen	180	250	488	221
Ministers of the Crown, Members of Parliament, Senior Government Officials	66	29	35	70

[a] 'Occupational Mortality' tables, Office of Population Censuses and Surveys, Series DS, No.1, *The Registrar General's Decennial Census Supplement for England and Wales,* 1970-1972, London, Her Majesty's Stationery Office, Table 5N.

Table 2. Number Surviving at Age 55 per 100,000 Persons at Age 15[a] Selected Occupation in England and Wales, 1970-1972

Occupations	Number of survivors at age 55
Electrical Engineers	96,001
Teachers	93,240
Social Welfare and Related Workers	92,715
Armed Forces of the United Kingdom	86,964
Nurses	86,245
Electronic Engineers	82,340

[a] 'Occupational Mortality' tables, Office of Population Censuses and Surveys, Series DS, N.L., *The Registrar General's Decennial Census Supplement for England and Wales,* 1970-1972, Her Majesty's Stationery Office, Table 8A.

in uncertainties about which of their alternate roles are relevant, or statements of open conflicts between individuals and groups. On occasions, it is also possible to measure the psychological and physiological manifestations of such stress experiences. People may blush, sweat profusely, experience a heightened heart-beat or faint. In other words, the social manifestations of stress interact with the following psycho-physical manifestations:

(a) *Psychological conflict* experienced by a professional that may be experienced as guilt, anxiety, fatigue, depression or even exhilaration and or euphoria.

(b) *Physiological stress* in which one or several bio-systems are seriously overloaded, resulting in high blood pressure or abnormal physiological responses such as a stroke, fainting or an injury.

Physiologically, there is no neat boundary between stress and the normal 'wear and tear' of ordinary living. Ultimately both will contribute to death, although stress often accelerates the breakdown process of the cardio-vascular system, ulcers, mental breakdown, and other pathological conditions.

The stress generative elements are not yet well mapped for any profession, social work included. But there has been considerable reflection and occasional empirical research, indicating that certain social-psychological conditions in the social work profession are likely to contribute to stress. Such situations are perceived to be unhealthy, anxiety producing and characterized by ambiguity. There is also much concern with stress overload — too much tension. Stress underload — because of boredom, insufficient challenge or inadequate recognition can also become a problem. Both stress overload and underload are related to work morale, resignation, or firing, and other indices of work satisfaction. They probably affect the professional's health and psychic state as well, but there is as yet little systematic data on how particular types of ambiguities in the work place of social workers affect various types of individuals, although we know that social work students experience role conflict and ambiguity stress when they first begin work.

Stress is not inherently negative. Many of the sociological stress factors are unavoidable elements of the work environment. Few people can escape having to make difficult choices in priority on how to spend their budget or time. In general, social conflict is part of group life. For those who try to avoid stress there are others who seek it as a 'challenge' or an 'adventure'. Stress is a principal feature of our entertainment, on the screen or in novels. Many a professional social worker seeks out 'tough cases'. There is a level of social stress without which life would be perceived as lacking in satisfaction; but it also can become elevated to a point where a professional will feel threatened, exhausted, depressed and may react too in ways regarded as pathological.

Stress has, then, many potentially negative as well as potentially positive consequences. Educators already devote some part of their efforts to teach stress management. Often, however, this is done without a systematic framework for presenting what is known. Social workers need to be alerted to the many unanswered questions about stress as a natural event in their practice.

THE SOCIAL PATHOLOGY QUOTIENT OF SOCIAL WORK

There is scientific evidence to support the validity of the aphorism of some executives: 'I don't get ulcers I give them.' The Metropolitan Life Insurance Company kept track of the three top executives of Fortune's 500 biggest US Companies over a sixty year period. The mortality rate of these men at the top was only 63% of that of the rate of the country's white male population. In 1968, a study of 270 male employees of a major US Corporation showed that the rate of coronary disease was lower with each step *up* the occupational ladder (Goldberg, 1978). The same explanation would be consistent with the finding in Table 1 showing British Ministers of the Crown, Members of Parliament, and Senior Government Officials to be healthier than the other listed occupations.

If stress is inversely correlated with authority, social work would be among the more stressful occupations. Few of its practitioners reach the top of their organization's hierarchy. They function largely as middle-echelon officials, responsible for direct services to people and communities with complex problems. The satisfactions that often accompany top level policy making power eludes them. Much like physicians, social workers are asked to shoulder personal responsibility for other people's 'significant life problems', but they often lack the power and or the means of doing much about them.

Unfortunately, there are no studies to confirm these hypotheses. The pathological quotient may be balanced in many workers by their sense of satisfaction with their work plus a profession-wide system to facilitate coping with stress.

Social workers rarely have to face what Goldberg calls *decision stress,* the need to weigh much information at considerable speed. Overloading the system can lead to a serious breakdown in performance. The closest approximation found in social work is in jobs with large caseloads — as in the field of public welfare and probation. Such jobs rank low in the hierarchy of alternate career outlets. They often are filled by professionally untrained or marginally prepared personnel. They also have a high turn-over rate. Persons employed in such overloaded agencies are protected by a low level of expectation that professional norms be adhered to. It is not then common for social workers to show symptoms of extreme decision stress, when the brain is pushed to its limits to receive, process and remember information.

Normal stresses and their management are an inherent part of living. Like all men, social workers must show up in their office when they might prefer to be at home, to sleep a little longer, to be with a young child, or when they have a headache. There also are particularistic sources of stress inherent in their work-role. They are as much part of their professional role as are the skills for which people seek them out.

INSTRUMENT QUALITY

Social workers have a highly personal relationship with the principal instrument of practice — themselves. Garage mechanics or dentists rely, in large measure, on tools. They can enhance the effectiveness in applying their skill by using the most modern equipment. And they can replace it, whenever the instrument is found wanting or a new model comes on the market.

Social workers are their own instrument of practice. Questions about diagnostic skill become a personal challenge. It is a significant part of their identity. Much of their work is on problems where the probability of dramatic achievements is small. There are few quick restorations of alcoholics or drug addicts. In surgery, patients who survive are available to praise the skill of their doctors. Those who were beyond the doctor's curative power generally die. But in social work, the tough cases continue to challenge the practitioner. They return as recidivists to prisons and mental hospitals; others threaten to commit suicide or are chronic wife-beaters and child abusers.

Even when social workers have promising ideas of what might be done to deal with difficult situations they do not often have the power to apply their knowledge. They must first motivate their client. And they must get permission from their organization. While there are fields, like adoption — where workers get positive feedback from their clients, there are many others where achievement must be measured in modest doses. Some clients have insoluble problems. They can be studied and diagnosed, but no known remedy exists. Evaluative research of social work methods has failed to come up with confidence — inspiring evidence (Fischer, 1978). Workers must therefore learn to live with uncertainty about the outcome of what often is a great deal of dedicated effort and commitment.

Social workers must develop modest and realistic expectations of themselves. Many find this difficult without acquiring a sense of balance about their own alleged 'ineptitude'. Some seek personal therapy as part of their professional training. 'I must understand myself, before I can do much to help others' is a common explanation. But such a professional calibration is quite expensive, beyond the economic resources of most social workers. In addition, there is today widespread scepticism that such an intensive process of self-analysis is necessary. Student training often includes joint analysis by the novitiate and the supervisor of how the personal values, family roles and personal experiences can be kept from interfering in the helping relationship, which is a social worker's principal tool.

STEREOTYPING

Diagnosis is an often useful step of practice. The decision to label stomach cramps as appendicitis can prevent the possible occurrence of a ruptured appendix. In much of social work, a different condition prevails. The ascription of a diagnostic label to a social deviate, and his acceptance of the label, often lock him into the 'sick role' rather than extricate him from it. This negative outcome is common in social work, as in psychiatry and geriatric medicine.

Social work uses many labels that also carry a social stigma. A broken arm leads to its being set for rapid healing; a broken mind can lead to involuntary institutionalization and the loss of certain patient rights for self-management. Well-qualified practitioners therefore confront a complex issue in their practice; a choice between effective communication with fellow practitioners and the avoidance of harming the person they try to help. How should they answer a client who wonders, 'Am I normal', 'Am I crazy'. Should they encourage an optimistic mood in the client that his symptoms are transitory? Or should they tell him he is sick and then have him react to the sick role that leads him to question whether he can ever fully recover (Becker, 1964).

There is no simple line to be drawn between diagnostic realism and the ability to help clients utilize their residual assets in a sick and decrepit role, to maximize their chances of a favourable treatment outcome. This introduces uncertainty and ambivalence with which social workers must cope.

NORMATIVITY

Values and beliefs affect what is done in all professions. But in most, their activities are relatively non-controversial. Few lawyers feel conflicted about the viewpoint that it is their resonsibility to defend a client, even if he is guilty of a serious crime. In medicine, strong normative pressures affect the outlook on abortion and euthanasia. In most other aspects of practice, political and ideological issues play a small role.

There is much questioning today of some of the new social work 'practice fads' of the late 1960s. Those who express a different policy may be attacked as conservative and reactionary. As Specht (1972) points out, social work action involves taking normative positions of considerable controversy. Specht suggests that the majority of social workers would agree with politically controversial programs such as:

1. Redistribution of income by some combination of devices — tax reforms, children's allowances, negative income tax, social security and so forth;
2. Higher degrees of control over utilization of land in the city, ultimately treating it as a public utility to meet needs in housing, open space, recreation and transportation.
3. Social services offered as a public utility;
4. Government as an employer of last resort to guarantee a job to everyone able and willing to work.

Some social workers think they should organize to become political activists; yet their pay often comes from the establishment. How far can they go in attacking their own political base?

Rein (1970) points out that American reformers often repudiate social work, but then embrace the very ideals which they have rejected. Social workers are readily used as a political scapegoat, by those who think the Government is doing too much for the poor, for the deviants and others unable to help themselves — which includes the aged, the infirmed and the handicapped.

But they have not organized well in their struggle against these attacks. The National Association of Social Workers has a one-person lobby in Washington, D.C., but she is in no position, as is the American Medical Association, to lobby powerfully in pursuit of their interest. She can — at best — persuade quietly, by indicating that there is a parallel between the profession's needs and public interest.

Social workers are directly involved in political 'hot potato' issues without much power. They depend for their sustenance on public funds, the good will of legislators or on contributions from the affluent elements of society. It is common, as Knickmeyer (1972) points out, that social workers in low-income communities must make a choice: 'Either they risk losing their professional sanction and rewards, and identify with the interests of the poor, or others will step in to fill the role they have rejected'.

The bulk of the profession often finds itself being attacked by both the right and left. The 'rightists' question its 'do gooder' bias; the Marxists accuse that 'behind all the rhetoric of concern for human dignity, even the more progressive forces in the profession maintain the belief that with a little advocacy here and a few adjustments there, conditions for both the recipient (of service) and the social workers will be improved.' 'After some thirty five years of liberal strategy, the burden now rests on the liberals to demonstrate that conditions for low- and moderate income people will get better' (Cloward and Pines, 1977).

These are harsh charges. Each new cohort of young social work recruits, includes a significant number who were attracted to the field by social reform ideals. Is this field only an 'opiate of people'? Or has the professional endorsement of social security legislation, prepaid medical insurance, federally subsidized welfare programs and many others brought about improvements that may exceed those attained under Marxist rule?

Many social workers enter the field with no intention of becoming involved in political controversy. They want 'to do good', and have a safe and well paying job, as do other employees. Instead, they find themselves in the midst of a bitter political controversy, not out of choice, but because of the nature of the issues with which they must deal professionally.

STATUS AMBIGUITY

Social workers offer help or take responsibility for the management of social, interpersonal, or personal problems of people, who seem to be unable to deal with them unaided. They act without a legally supported or publicly accepted status of having the facility to solve problems. Lawyers, doctors, plumbers and others can require that the public use their services to meet conditions of 'adequacy of service', re-enforced by licensing laws and other administrative regulations.

Social workers are viewed as experts in areas which most people think are 'common sense'. Few lay persons would wish to advise a friend on how to deal with severe pains in the stomach. It might be a sign of appendicitis, which they would prefer to have diagnosed by someone legally licensed for such a task. But lay persons have little or no hesitation in suggesting how to handle a recalcitrant child or on the best way to organize a pre-paid medical care scheme. Social work is everybody's concern. What professionals have to offer, in addition to technical training, is an explicit concern with client-oriented, ethical values. Social work involves *fiduciary* (trust) *relationship* (Levy, 1976). While social workers get paid (a fee or a salary), the service to be provided is not expected to be a function of this monetary exchange, but should depend on professional assessments of client needs.

The status ambiguity of social work in the United States was enhanced by a decision of the National Association of Social Workers to open the ranks of its professional association to persons who merely have pre-professional educational training, i.e. a bachelor's degree. There is a pronounced preference in public agencies to hire the less expensive Bachelor's level persons, rather than staff who have a more advanced professional qualification. Client groups are generally passive about the level of qualification of persons who serve them. While there might be an outcry if a hospital were staffed by novices, the poor, the blue collar, and most white collar groups in the country are rarely defenders of what Lubove (Specht, 1972) has called 'Professional Altruists'.

The status ambiguity of social workers affects their capacity to raise rather than lower minimal technical qualifications. It affects level of pay, and limits their power to influence the formation of policy in areas directly related to their work. Unlike many other professions, where those with policy making power are drawn from within its ranks, a social worker in an influential policy post is the exception, not the rule. What is less known, however, is how this status ambiguity affects the emotional well being of the individual worker. Many of them learn to accept it, as part of the reality within which they must function. Those who find this difficult, often leave the profession.

Social workers function in an *elective* profession (Eaton, 1956). They are likely to be called upon only after people define themselves as having 'failed in handling a problem' which — at other times — they could conceivably deal with unaided. The widespread belief that most problems with which social workers deal can also be handled by non-social workers, results in a loss of status. Social work interaction is not likely to proceed very far until clients understand that they are incapable of functioning without the help of a professional, and the professionals belief that they can step into the breach.

All experts, doctors and lawyers included, work under conditions where their expertise is on trial. Those whom they serve usually can dismiss them. But in the field of social work, the expert status of the professional is unusually tenuous. Research studies, even in agencies staffed with well-trained social work practitioners often produce negative findings regarding program effectiveness (Grey and Dermody, 1972; Fischer, 1972; Rosenberg and Brody, 1974).

There are no enforceable laws restricting social work practice to those who have been qualified by social work's professionally accepted routines. Paraprofessional child welfare workers can do the same work as do Ph.D. level social workers, with years of supervised clinical experience. There is no similar degree of overlap between nurses and doctors, although it occurs to a degree in all fields.

The professional literature is filled with references to role ambiguity (Kahn *et al.* 1964). It contributes to a high turnover of personnel in organizations, where professional and those with less training perform similar work, as is the case in most public welfare and many child care agencies.

The work to be done often involves the physical and psychic well being of a client. In Child Welfare, for instance, children may have to be taken out of their home because of mental illness of a parent or child abuse. Others are unmanageable at home or their parents want to get rid of them. The child welfare worker is almost constantly confronted with bewildering and awesome human situations, in which he must make serious decisions that will affect the fate of the children, as well as the parents and siblings.

Yet, as one report points out, the professional works from a desk — one of many on an open floor. There is little or no privacy. 'He is surrounded by other workers, welfare assistants, clerks, and supervisors, all crowded together. Telephones are constantly ringing, and there is a steady hum of conversation, typewriting, and people moving from place to place.' (Wasserman, 1973)

While working conditions in other agencies may be better, excessive caseloads are commonplace. More often than not, professionally trained workers are required to function more like clerks, handling folders, than to use the professional skills of individualized attention for which they were trained. Many workers report that they can never 'catch up'. Physical fatigue and emotional upsets are commonplace, in part because workers have little or no control over what cases are assigned to them or how many they are expected to handle.

Ambiguity is becoming increasingly pronounced in all areas of modern life. Social workers certainly have no monopoly over this condition. Alvin Toffler's (1970) 'Future Shock' documents well how the rapid change of expectations and facilitating conditions of problem solving require individuals to develop a high level of adaptive skills. The old traditional guidelines often have lost their validity for those who used to accept them. This alarming view must be contrasted with evidence that stress is not inherently damaging. Stress is a necessary part of life, to keep it exciting and stimulating.

MALPRACTICE

Social workers are involved in issues that vitally affect the welfare of individuals, groups and communities. They also help plan social action that may bring about change. So far, however, the field has been immune from legal action charging them with malpractice. No case has yet been reported in the legal literature (Green and Cox, 1978).

Legal actions led to the necessity of malpractice insurance in medicine and psychiatry. In California, physicians went on a partial strike when the Argonaut Insurance Company decided to increase its fees by 196% (Makofsky, 1977). But social work is — in theory — just as liable to malpractice charges as any profession, in terms of the simple rules that guide this form of negligence: Prosser (1971) summarizes them as follows:

1. A duty, or obligation, recognized by the law, requiring the action to conform to a certain standard of conduct . . .
2. A failure on his part to conform to the standard required . . .
3. A reasonably close causal connection between the conduct and the resulting injury . . .
4. Actual loss or damage resulting to the interests (health, finances and emotional or psychological stability) of another.

Social work does not at present have experience of court verdicts and out-of-court settlements against sub-standard practitioners so commonplace in other fields, where people handle difficult cases which provide a tempting target for lawyers in the malpractice business. In 1972, a federal commission studying medical malpractice found that the average patient was paying from 2 to 5% of his fees to reimburse physicians and hospitals for malpractice insurance. This sum may increase ten fold by 1980 (Rubsamen, 1979). Some states have enacted cost — containment laws.

Malpractice concerns have become active in clinical psychology. More and more social welfare agencies in the mental health field are now insuring their staff and the Board of Directors. The National Association of Social Worker's 'Academy of Certified Social Workers' (ACSW) offers its members insurance in case they might he held legally responsible for 'some alleged malpractice, error, or mistake arising out of the performance of professional services as a social worker.' (Green and Cox, 1978) In social work as in the field of psychiatry, where malpractice units are more common, clients could bring charges for treatment without consent (in hospitals), failure to advise clients of the danger of social work treatment, or failure to consult with or refer the client to a specialist as needed. There also could be charges of sexual abuse, inadequate treatment, beating and physical restraint, misuse of psychotherapy, and failure to inform potential victims of threat of bodily harm.

An increasing number of 'social disease' lawyers are being trained all over the USA. This will make more and more of them responsive to exploring as yet untried legal channels to claim compensation for alleged or real complaints which clients often harbour against those whom they have engaged to help them.

At the time of this writing in 1979, the stress of malpractice in social work is more potential than real. But it already is affecting more and more social agencies, as well as private practitioners of social work. More and more of them are insuring themselves against malpractice; their workers are also being made increasingly conscious of their legal liabilities.

This potential risk is enhanced by the fact that in many public agencies, actual practice standards are below those that are professionally normative. The staff do not have the time or other resources to carefully study each case diagnostically and to provide optimal services. It is simply a matter of time before disgruntled clients file malpractice suits in social work.

SUPERVISION

Every worker has a supervisor. Even the President of the United States has his actions monitored by Congress, the Supreme Court, and Press and by Public Opinion. In clinical social work, supervision often assumes an intensely personal quality. It involves more than administrative considerations. The supervisor enters into the personality and detailed treatment process of the individual worker. Personal interactions with clients are being reviewed. Often the supervisor is a respected professional from whom the affected worker can learn much. He (she) provides welcome consultation. In only a minority of cases do social workers perceive their immediate Supervisor as a source of stress. This inference is supported by the findings of Kadushin (1974), who made a comprehensive nationwide survey. He contacted a sample of 750

Table 3. Sources of supervisory power as perceived by supervisors and supervisees

Supervisor's Source of Influence with Respect To Supervisee	As Perceived by Supervisors % ($n = 469$)	As Perceived by Supervisee % ($n = 384$)
Expert power	95.3	65.5
Positional power	2.6	21.1
Coercive power	0.6	5.5
Reward power	0.2	3.1
Referent (Relationship power)	0.6	2.1

Source: Kadushin, Alfred (1974). 'Supervisor-Supervisee: A Survey', *Social Work,* May issue, p.290.

Supervisors and Supervisees in the United States. The overall response rate was 61%, probably optimistically biased in favour of persons satisfied with their supervision.

Table 3 shows that supervisors believe overwhelmingly (95%) that their power is or should be derived from their allegedly superior expertise. Almost two thirds of the Supervisees share this professional norm. Only about one third view their administrative superiors in more conventional industrial terms, as people with organizational power over them.

A minority, 15.4%, reported themselves to be 'fairly' or 'extremely' dissatisfied with their current supervisor. This rate of dissatisfaction is probably higher in public social agencies, where many workers are employed in administrative roles, certifying people for eligibility and providing routine services to large numbers of clients, too numerous to allow workers to practice intensive casework. In such agencies unionization is increasing, thus providing workers with the machinery to protect them from unreasonable coercion, as well as some more justifiable administrative prerogatives.

The norms of the field do not favour the use of arbitrary power by superiors over those for whom they are responsible. Nevertheless, dissatisfaction with administration arrangements probably accounts for much of the prevailing turnover of personnel.

JOB DISSATISFACTION

In all professions, a proportion of those involved don't like their work. They report for work each day, disliking themselves for doing it. The negative stressful consequences will vary with each worker and with the sources of his/her dissatisfaction.

Miller and Podell (1971) studied the attitudes of 970 employees of the New York City Department of Social Services. They work in an organization frequently criticized by clients, politicians and the news media. They suffer from high case-loads and low public prestige.

Many perceived a conflict between their professional responsibilities and the administrative demands that were being made upon them by their organization. Only 29% reported themselves to be 'minimally upset', 43% were 'moderately upset' and 28% felt they were 'severely upset'. Public Assistance workers expressed more dissatisfaction than did child welfare workers; caseworkers reported themselves to be more dissatisfied than their professional supervisors.

The self-reported level of professional-bureaucratic conflict was directly related to plans to leave the City Welfare Department. But there were also 33% who planned to remain, although they felt severely disturbed by role conflicts between their professional and administrative responsibilities! Sixty one per cent of those who were moderately distressed and 79% of those who experienced minimal conflict were planning to continue on their present job.

People spend from about 24 to 30% of their work-week as employees. Those who experience a conflict between their professional and organizational expectations are exposed to a heavy dose of negative stress. Its implications for their performance have not been investigated, but they probably account for many of the disgruntled public servants whom clients meet from time to time, as they bring their problems to a social work agency in order to obtain sympathetic and effective help.

THE STRESS COPING SYSTEM

An individual who experiences uncomfortable stress has many ways of dealing with it, including psychotherapy, drugs, encounter groups, jogging, meditation, or sex. There also are institutionalized defence mechanisms in social work, including the following:

1. The ideology of client autonomy
2. The doctrine of agency responsibility
3. Responsibility sharing, through supervision staff conferences and bureaucratic channels of authority.
4. Unionization

1. The ideology of client autonomy

A neighbourhood worker may work hard to arouse support for a controversial campaign to oppose the building of a highway that would disrupt the existing community structure. But he need not be alone in facing the opposition. He can get policy coverage in the form of a resolution from his Board 'instructing' him to organize such a campaign. When meeting the Press, the spokesperson is likely to be the Association's President, not the social workers. Many social workers accept the theory that they are 'enablers' rather than actors. The professional literature abounds with cautions against allowing clients to become 'overdependent' on the worker. Clients should take final responsibility for decisions that involve them.

An unwed mother has personally to sign papers authorizing an adoption, although an adoption social worker may be working with her intensively to help her come to a decision. It is an exceptional case, when case workers will allow themselves to make decisions for their clients. This may occur in work with neglected and abused children, the mentally ill or the aged no longer capable of making decisions. Even in such situations, the social worker often gets sanctioning for his/her recommendations from a judge, speaking in the name of law, or from close relatives of the clients. Social workers often go some way in focusing the client to specific issues, but for both legal and ideological reasons, the client or a guardian is usually required to assume formal and 'ultimate' responsibility for what is finally done.

2. The doctrine of agency responsibility

Social work is practiced mostly under organizational auspices. Except in the field of private practice, policies and rules, laws and standards are imposed on the professional judgement of each worker. When a social worker's personal preferences make him/her inclined to favour deviations from these norms a stressful decision has to be made. But these agency issues also provide a measure of support.

Adoption agencies have been under great pressure from 'adult adopted persons' to disclose the identity of their natural parents. An individual worker may be torn between the equity of protecting the privacy of the natural parents and the needs of the child to know more about his/her identity. This conflict of norms can be resolved simply: 'Sorry — agency policy (or the law) prohibits violation of confidentiality.'

Impoverished clients have seemingly endless needs. If public welfare workers had to make individual decisions in each case on how much cash supplementation was to be provided, and for what purposes, the decision-making process would be even more stressful than it already is. Many potential conflicts are avoided by the fact that agencies have standards that govern many 'cash and kind' allocation decisions. Social workers do not have to take the onus to say 'no' to a request for special clothing assistance which a client may be pursuing with great emotional intensity. They just have to find a rule and then can solve the problem by saying 'yes', helping a client to demonstrate his/her eligibility or to say 'no', explaining 'I know you feel you need this, but our rules do not authorize the special budget — sorry'.

The doctrine of agency responsibility also protects social workers from a lot of personal liability from negatively perceived outcomes. Only those engaged in private practice are more on the direct firing line. They must carry malpractice insurance, for they can be held personally accountable for what they do or advise. Social workers employed by agency are protected, except in rare instances where personal negligence can be proven.

3. Responsibility sharing

In surgery, an individual physician makes an incision. He alone must decide what organ, or part of it, is to be removed. Such focused personal responsibility is uncommon in social work. Difficult cases or community issues tend to be discussed with a supervisor, with a consultant and may be brought to a staff conference. In mental health settings, clients are generally diagnosed by a team of specialists. Major treatment recommendations are reviewed in staff conferences ranging from a psychiatrist to a staff nurse. If a social worker's patient commits suicide while undergoing treatment, he or she is not likely to be consumed by feelings of guilt. Risks inherent in such situations were assessed by a group.

The bureaucratic process facilitates decision making on normatively controversial issues on the basis of organizationally sanctioned procedures. Individual workers will often be perceived by clients as showing personal interest and concern, when the helping process is viewed positively by them. When negative actions have to be taken, the adoption worker can inform the disappointed couple of their ineligibility by referring to the anonymity of 'the Committee had a long meeting and made some hard choices — you were not among those selected'.

The bureaucratic structure of most social work practice can frustrate the worker, but as Kadushin's study previously referred of supervision suggests, the majority of social workers feel comfortable with it. They always have the option of finding another job if the agency process frustrates them too much.

There are many occasions when social workers are involved in decisions that affect vital life options of persons, groups, and communities. They lack the attributed charisma of the knowledge and insight of God. But they can be involved in such weighty issues because they can face the complexities of their work with the support of a professional and administrative reference group.

4. Unionization

Social work has become organized, in part to protect its membership. The National Association of Social Workers (NASW) of the United States established in 1956 through a merger of more specialized professional organizations. The NASW will hear complaints from members against violations of professional standards by their employers. When the evidence warrants it, the organization will try to mediate controversy. In an extreme case, the organization will publicly condemn the profesional standing of the agency and those who represent it.

There also are an increasing number of social work labour unions, especially in public welfare and public child care agencies. Like any other labour unions, members are to be protected through negotiated contract and the readiness of the union staff to champion their part in almost any bureaucratic controversy. The social worker is not likely to be alone in a stress-potential bureaucratic controversy.

Social work is well organized to cushion negative stresses on its practitioners in the work place. Direct service workers and their immediate administrative supervisors tend to work more closely than is common in other professions, like nursing and teaching. It is uncommon for clients to hold them accountable. Few clients have the capacity to organize or to use legal counsel. Practice generally succeeds in forcing the client or the community group to take ultimate responsibility even when the process involves the professional quite actively in the problem solving effort.

CONCLUSION

Responsibility is endemic in social work. Most issues which are brought to its attention professionally involve people in severely stressful circumstances. They want more than mere 'help'. They often ask for it in situations where no profession-wide standard prescription can be applied. There are many gaps in knowledge in the fields of practice. Practice involves frequent confrontation of uncertainty, guesstimation, and 'trial and error' type experimentation. The profession often lacks some of the budgetary resources and political powers required so that social workers can apply what they know.

Social workers as individuals and as a profession are cushioned ideologically and organizationally. As students in professional schools their initial cases are handled under close supervision. Supervision and consultation also become generally available, once workers take on full time and paid professional jobs. Close monitoring can continue over the entire lifetime of clinicians, who work in settings where consultation is a well established practice of supervision, and this can become a source of negative stress for a minority of workers.

Social work ranks low among occupations whose practitioners become ill with premature circulatory diseases or who suffer fatal accidents. Many learn to live with the uncertainty about their techniques. Social work is not one of those 'killer' occupations, where so many tensions have to be internalized that it becomes difficult to take full responsibility for the remainder of one's life. Unions and agency auspices provide commonplace buffers against negative stress.

The social structural emphasis of this chapter does not exclude concern with individual variations in how workers internalize the inherent stresses of their careers. Most social workers learn to protect themselves professionally even those who work with human tragedies and chronic problems. They function every work day with a high level of empathy with their clients who may endure tragedy or chronic adversity — be it a rape, child abuse, abortion or a terminal illness. Most social workers learn to insulate these professional exposures from affecting their personal life. They can go home at night to enjoy their family, see a play or plan a vacation.

There always are individual cases, with excessive feelings of guilt, who worry to the point of extreme anxiety or who feel so personally involved in the social ills of their community that they will devote their life to an up-hill struggle for change — be it orderly or revolutionary.

In no field of work is there a shortage of stressful challenges. What varies is how each individual deals with these situations. There are social workers who commit suicide. Some will neglect their children or marriage because of their professional involvement. Others will leave the profession or seek psychotherapy to deal with tensions and uncertainties that affect them very personally. But the field as a whole has developed a professional sub-culture within which well trained persons are able to spend a life time in helping others with problems beyond the client's coping capacity.

REFERENCES

Becker, H.S. (1964). *The Other Side: Perspectives on Deviance,* Free Press, New York.

Butler, H.F. (1972). Student role stress. *American Journal of Occupational Therapy,* Vol.26, No.8, 399-405.

Cloward, R.A. and Piven, F.F. (1977). The acquiescence of social work. *Society,* January/February, 55-63.

Eaton, J.W. (1956). Whence and whither social work. *Social Work,* Vol.1, No.1.

Fischer, J. (1973). Is casework effective. *Social Work,* Vol.18, January.

Fischer, J. (1978). Does anything work. *Journal of Social Service Review,* Vol.1, No.3, 215-244.

Green, R.K. and Cox, G. (1978). Social work and malpractice: a converging course. *Social Work,* March, 100.

Grey, A.L. and Dermody, H.E. (1972). Reports of casework failure. *Social Casework,* November, 534-543.

Goldberg, P. (1978). *Executive Health,* McGraw Hill, New York.

Kahn, R. *et al.* (1964). *Organizational Stress: Studies in Role Conflict and Ambiguity,* John Wiley, New York.

Knickmeyer, R. (1972). A Marxist approach to social work. *Social Work,* July, 58-59.

Levy, C.S. (1976). *Social Work Ethics.* The Human Sciences Press, New York.

Makofsky, D. (1977). Malpractice and medicine. *Society,* January/February, 25.

Miller, R. and Podell, L. (1971). *Role Conflict in Public Social Services,* State Office for Community Affairs, New York, N.Y.

Presser, W.L. (1971). *Handbook of the Law and Torts.* West Publishing Company, St. Paul, Minnesota.

Rein, M. (1970). Social work in search of a radical profession. *Social Work,* Vol.15, No.2, 13-28.

Rosenberg, M.L. and Brody, R. (1974). The threat or challenge of accountability. *Social Work,* May, 344-350.

Rubsamen, D.S. (1979). 'Medical malpractice'. In Albrecht, C.L. and Higgins, P.C. (Eds.) *Health, Illness and Medicine: A Reader in Medical Sociology,* Rand McNally, Chicago.

Selye, H. (1956). *The Stress of Life,* McGraw Hill, New York.

Selye, H. (1974). *Stress Without Distress,* Lippincott, Philadelphia.

Selye, H. (1978). 'Introduction' to Goldberg, P., *Executive Health,* McGraw Hill, New York.

Specht, H. (1972). The de-professionalization of social work, *Social Work,* March, 3-15.

Specht, H. (1972). Harry Specht replies. *Social Work,* September, 3.

Toffler, A. (1970). *Future Shock,* Random House, New York.

Wasserman, H. (1973). Early careers of professional social workers in a public welfare agency. *Social Work,* July, 93-101.

PART IV

Stress Experienced by Technologists

White Collar and Professional Stress
Edited by C.L. Cooper and J. Marshall
© 1980 John Wiley & Sons Ltd.

Chapter 8

Stress and the Professional Engineer

Tony Keenan
Heriot-Watt University Edinburgh Scotland

In recent years speculation about the reasons for the continuing economic demise of Britain has almost reached the level of a national pastime. Much of this speculation has naturally focused on the productive sector of the economy, and on the possible reasons for its apparent lack of efficiency. One area of particular concern has been the quantity and quality of the supply of technical expertise in the form of professional engineers and other technologists to industry and the use which is made of their skills.

As is so often the case in matters of this sort, forceful, but unsubstantiated, opinions are easier to come by than factual material. Nevertheless, some potentially worrying statistics are available, relating both to the recruitment of technologists to industry in the UK, and to the ability of such recruits to meet the needs of industry. There is some suggestion that manufacturing industry attracts fewer graduates in mechanical engineering in the UK than in some other European countries. In 1971, 55% of UK graduates in mechanical engineering entered manufacturing industry, whereas in 1970, 76% of German mechanical engineering graduates entered manufacturing industry. (*Department of Employment Gazette,* 1979). In May 1976 the Confederation of British Industry (CBI) carried out an enquiry among its members on graduates in industry and concluded that the quality of scientific and technological graduates has declined in recent years with an increasing amount of poor to mediocre talent being recruited into industry. The report complains of 'poor personal motivation', 'lack of flexibility', and 'deficiencies of communicative skills' among technology graduates. Similarly, a report of the British Association for the Advancement of Science pointed out that only a small proportion of good students were attracted by engineering. It seems therefore, that the available evidence, while inadequate in many ways, does at least suggest that the frequently expressed concern over the role of technologists in the UK economy may well have some foundation.

The present chapter is not directly concerned with broad issues such as the contribution engineers and technologists make to the economy as a whole, but rather it is concerned with the psychological difficulties and strains encountered by individuals who occupy these work roles. Although the primary focus of the chapter is therefore on work stress and its impact on professional engineers and other technologists, many of the issues raised undoubtedly have implications for the efficient use of engineering manpower, as well as for the well-being of the individuals themselves. In reviewing research on professional engineers and scientists in industry, it is immediately apparent that very little empirical work has been done which specifically focuses on the stresses and attendant psychological strains experienced by these groups of professional workers. Consequently, this chapter will be exploratory and somewhat speculative in nature and will in no way attempt to give a definitive account of the work pressures experienced by technologists.

METHODOLOGICAL CONSIDERATIONS

Before proceeding to the research findings themselves, it is worth pointing out some of the methodological limitations of much of the work done in this area. First of all, many writers have tended to assume that engineers and scientists are so similar to each other that they can be automatically equated without any need to make an empirical comparison between them. However, as Ritti (1968) points out, there may be important differences between engineers and scientists which render such assumptions invalid. Indeed, it is possible to go further and suggest that there may even be important variations in the experiences of engineers working in different branches of engineering. Also, there have been very few attempts to study technologists in relation to non-technical white-collar occupations in order to isolate work pressures and strains which are unique to technologists and which are not common to white-collar occupations in general. Many of the studies only look at individuals at a single stage in their career, often after they have been in employment for several years. Thus we know little about how work pressures vary at different career stages, or about how individuals attempt to adjust to work pressures over time. Some investigations have compared groups of respondents who are at different stages in their careers with each other, but often the findings have been difficult to interpret. The problem is that groups of individuals at different stages of their careers may also differ from each other in many unknown ways which are quite unrelated to the work they do. Finally, it should be borne in mind that many of the studies quoted in this chapter are based on self-report data where the investigator relies on the respondent's ability and willingness to describe himself and his work experience accurately and without bias. It is well known that self-report data of this sort is frequently prone to error and inaccuracy.

THE HERIOT-WATT STUDY OF GRADUATES IN INDUSTRY

This chapter also draws on some of the findings of a study carried out by the author along with Peter Hadden and Freda Todd into the work pressures and adjustment problems experienced by graduates of Heriot-Watt University during their first year of full-time employment in industry following graduation. The sample consisted of 77 engineers, 66 scientists, and a group of 61 graduates from the Faculty of Economic and Social Studies. By including this last group it was possible to compare the work experiences of the engineers and scientists directly with those of non-technical graduates.

Heriot-Watt is fundamentally a technological university and as a consequence the Faculty of Economic and Social Studies at Heriot-Watt University is very different from traditional arts faculties. The degree courses offered tend to be vocationally oriented (e.g. Business Organization; Economics) and to be geared towards careers in industry and commerce. Thus, because of this, and because of the way in which the sample was selected, the majority of respondents in the sample were working in industry or commerce.

Respondents were approached one year after graduation by postal questionnaire and their replies sought to a series of questions about their jobs and the problems, difficulties, and dissatisfactions they were currently experiencing. The data from this study will be referred to from time to time where they are of relevance to the work which has been done elsewhere, most of which is concerned with individuals who have had more work experience than those in the Heriot-Watt sample.

THE STATUS OF ENGINEERS IN SOCIETY

In order to take a comprehensive view of the problems encountered by professional engineers in their work roles, it is necessary to give some consideration to the position of the profession in society as a whole rather than simply to look at individuals within the context of particular employing organizations. After all, the individual's feelings of satisfaction or dissatisfaction with his occupational role will surely be partly determined by his perception of his occupation and its place in the broader scheme of things.

It has often been suggested that professional engineers are accorded an inordinately low status in society, given the level of their academic qualifications and the importance of the contribution they make to society. Peter Herriot (1978), in a succinct analysis of this problem, has argued that it is part of a general syndrome in our society, where the ability or inclination to carry out practical tasks is regarded as a low level activity. According to Herriot 'Doing and making has continued to have a lower status than disputing and arguing in English society. Our contempt for the source of so much of our wealth, our manufacturing industry, is written large in our national institutions.' He has argued that there is a general view that engineers are incapable of holding highly responsible positions, and points to the fact that the proportions of top executive who are engineers is much lower in the UK than in Germany or France.

Is there any evidence to support the view that professional engineers are accorded low status in society? Herriot (1978) quotes one study carried out by Palmer, Bignell, and Levy on sixth form school children's perceptions of mechanical engineers in relation to other professions. The sixth formers thought that mechanical engineers required less intelligence than vets, solicitors, pharmacists, and members of several other professions. Taylor (1977) concluded from a study of the attitudes of final engineering students that they believed that the public accorded engineers low status. Gerstl and Cohen (1964) asked over 1,000 members of the general public and roughly the same number of engineers to rank ten white collar occupations, including that of professional engineer, for social prestige. The public accorded the professional engineer low status, with only the occupations of primary school teacher and works manager receiving lower prestige rankings. Not surprisingly, the engineers ranked themselves more highly. However, when asked to rank the occupations as they thought the public would, their rankings were even lower than those of the general public.

Given that the professional engineer seems to have a low status in society, one can only speculate as to the many possible adverse effects this could have on the morale and motivation of technologists. However, there is evidence that the question of status is a source of dissatisfaction and frustration for many engineers. For example, Gerstl and Hutton (1966), in their study of 977 professional mechanical engineers report findings supporting this view. Less than a third of their sample were satisfied with the status they were accorded in Britain and over half expressed specific dissatisfactions and frustrations. A sizeable number felt that their non-engineering work colleagues had an unfavourable view of engineers. In fact only one third of the sample felt that their colleagues had a favourable view of engineers.

PROFESSIONAL OR ORGANIZATIONAL GOALS?

A number of writers have argued that scientists and engineers who work in industrial organizations are likely to experience strains arising from the conflict between their professional values and the goals of the organizations for which they work (Blau and Scott, 1962; Cotgrove and Box, 1970; Kornhauser, 1962). It is suggested that professional values are incompatible with organizational values in a number of respects. According to Kornhauser (1962), the basic dilemma is one of autonomy vs. integration. The professional engineer or scientist must be given sufficient autonomy to enable him to fulfil his professional needs, yet at the same time his activities must be seen to contribute to the overall goal of the organization. Thus, for example, the technologist may desire to involve himself in projects because of their fundamental technical or scientific merit, whereas the primary concern of the organization is with product marketability. Even where scientists are allowed to pursue more basic research, problems arise, because the low priority given to such work by the organization means that it is always vulnerable to termination when times are hard or business needs more pressing. Thus conflicts can arise over which projects are to be tackled, how they are to be tackled, and how much time is to be spent on them.

Because of his 'cosmopolitan' orientation, the loyalty of the scientist or engineer is primarily to his profession or field of speciality, rather than to his organization. Thus he wishes to be judged by his professional contribution. This often involves making his knowledge public, which leads to further tensions since the economic aims of the organization often dictate that information be withheld from possible competitors. If technologists wish to be judged by their fellow professionals on the basis of their scientific or technical achievements, it seems reasonable to assume that they would also feel that their career progression should also be on this basis. However, in terms of the goals of the organization, career progression is more likely to be based on the contribution made to commercial success than to technical accomplishments *per se*.

If these theoretical speculations are accurate, then there seems little doubt that conflicts between professional and organizational goals constitute a stressful situation for many technologists. What available evidence is there to support or refute these views? Cotgrove and Box (1970) studied research chemists working in industrial laboratories and found evidence of strains arising out of conflicts between the professional values of the scientists and the goals of the organization. For example, respondents felt that their autonomy was threatened in their jobs. They also complained of having insufficient opportunity to utilize their research skills and a number felt that their creativity was hampered in their jobs.

There is some controversy about how far the professional *vs*. organizational values conflict can be applied to engineers, as opposed to scientists. Ritti (1968) compared the work values of engineers and scientists and found that the former group had primarily business goals, rather than scientific or professional ones. On the other hand, some studies of young scientists and engineers found that their work values were very similar (Davies, 1974; Underhill, 1966). The Gerstl and Hutton (1966) study referred to earlier is of relevance in this context. They found that, while a majority of younger engineers expressed a preference for strictly technical work, only a minority of older engineers did so. They argued that this was because the older engineers had learned that in industry the greater rewards go to managers rather than to those who remain strictly engineers. Perhaps the mechanical engineers in Gerstl and Hutton's study started out with strong professional values but were later seduced into abandoning these for organizational goals.

Quite apart from possible differences between scientists and engineers at a group level, there are also likely to be differences at the individual level in commitment to professional values. Cotgrove and Box (1970) classified the scientists in their sample into three types. Public Scientists were particularly interested in establishing their status in the wider scientific community, especially through scientific achievement and publication. This was the group which experienced most strain as a result of conflict with organizational goals. Private scientists also sought recognition of their technical ability but were content with the esteem of their immediate work colleagues. This group experienced less strain than the public scientists. Organizational scientists had little interest in science for its own sake and valued their scientific expertise only insofar as it was a means of advancement in their organizations. The values of these individuals seemed to be generally well integrated with organizational goals.

Cotgrove and Box showed that some scientists had values more in accord with the goals of manufacturing industry than others, and it seems reasonable to suppose that an element of self-selection probably occurs so that technologists make career choices in accordance with their personal values. For example, public scientists might be expected to be more heavily represented in pure research than in manufacturing industry. With regard to engineering, there is evidence that some self-selection of this type does occur. Taylor (1979) found that final-year engineering students who took jobs in either research and development or design had work values indicating a strong 'technical' orientation, whereas students with a strong 'managerial' orientation tended to select jobs outwith engineering. Those who entered the 'operations' field also tended to have a 'managerial orientation'.

Self-selection is unlikely to be such as to ensure that all individuals will end up in jobs commensurate with their work values, and inevitably situations will occur where there is a lack of fit between the individual's values and the goals of the organization. It is in these situations that stress-related problems are most likely to occur. For example, in the Heriot-Watt study of young graduates no less than 32% of respondents claimed that they 'had to do things which conflicted with their personal values' in their jobs 'sometimes', or more often. In addition, those were often in this position also reported that they frequently experienced feelings of anxiety and tension in relation to their work.

Miller (1967) found that organizational variables could modify the extent to which scientists and engineers experienced dissatisfaction as a result of the professional *vs.* organizational values dilemma. Respondents reported less dissatisfaction when given professional incentives. These included freedom and facilities to do research; promotion based on technical competence; and the availability of opportunities to improve professional knowledge and skills by attendance at scientific meetings and the like. Dissatisfaction was also less when perceived organizational control over activities was low.

THE WORK EXPECTATIONS OF TECHNOLOGISTS

What immediate and ultimate rewards do technologists expect to obtain from their jobs? This is an important issue in the context of the present chapter, since any serious disparity between expectation and subsequent reality is likely to constitute a stressful situation for the individual.

The Heriot-Watt sample of engineers, scientists, and social studies graduates were asked to recollect what they had expected from their jobs when they first took up employment one year earlier. They were then asked how far each expectation had been realized in terms of their level of satisfaction with that aspect of their current job. In this way it was possible to investigate discrepancies between initial expectations and reality one year later. In general, it was the intrinsic features of the job, rather than the pay or other extrinsic features, which respondents most frequently valued when starting their first job. Thus, 95% of respondents thought it important that 'the work itself would be interesting', and 87% said that it was important that the job would offer a challenge. Approximately two thirds of respondents reported being satisfied with the intrinsic content of their work one year later. Although all three types of graduate were similar in placing high value on the intrinsic features of the job, there were significant differences in the extent to which these aspirations were realized. Thus, the scientists were most satisfied with the intrinsic content of their work, while the social studies graduates were least satisfied. The engineers occupied an intermediate position in this respect.

Earnings, job security and promotion prospects were also quite highly valued. The proportions of respondents who rated each of these as at least 'quite important' where 48%, 69%, and 60% respectively. Approximately half of the respondents were currently happy with these aspects of their jobs. There were few differences among the three types of graduate in responses to these items. However scientists were more satisfied with the promotion opportunities in their organizations than either of the other two groups.

Although 68% of respondents had thought it important to have a job which would afford them 'the opportunity to make full use of their academic qualifications', only 49% were currently satisfied with their jobs in this respect. Indeed the engineers, despite being the group whose degrees were most obviously vocationally oriented, were, if anything, slightly less satisfied with this aspect of their jobs.

While a proportion of the Heriot-Watt graduates were dissatisfied with the way in which their first job had matched up to their expectations, a number of others were in general happy with their jobs in relation to their initial aspirations. However, both people and jobs probably change as careers develop and it would be of interest to know what changes occur in the expectations and satisfactions of technologists over a longer time period. However, little hard evidence is available on this issue. Kelsall, Poole, and Kuhn (1972) studied work satisfactions in graduates who had been qualified for six years. Individuals doing research, development, and production work (presumably these were mainly technologists) reported favourably on their colleagues, their working conditions and their opportunities for intellectual development. However, at the same time, they seemed to suffer from 'the lack of participation in high level decision making and from limitations placed on opportunities for promotion to the key posts in industrial organizations' (p.108).

There is evidence that, in one respect at least, engineers lower their aspirations as their career progresses. Taylor (1978) asked professional engineers of varying ages how they rated their chances of eventually becoming a partner or director in a company. Undergraduates and qualified engineers under the age of 30 were quite optimistic in this respect. However, after the age of 30 only about 10% of the engineers in the sample agreed that there was a good chance of this happening. One wonders to what extent a watershed occurs in the engineer's career around this age.

ROLE CONFLICT AND AMBIGUITY

Probably more has been written about the psychological consequences of role conflict and ambiguity than about any other organizational source of stress. Authors vary in their definitions of these two concepts but for the present purposes it is assumed that, to a considerable extent, role ambiguity and conflict arise because of the nature of the social network of relationships at work. Thus role ambiguity exists where there is uncertainty over the meaning of the communications the focal person received from others, whereas role conflict occurs where role senders make mutually incompatible or contradictory demands on the focal person. In other words, both ambiguity and conflict are people-oriented problems.

Are technologists more or less likely to experience role ambiguity and conflict than other white collar workers because of the nature of their occupational role? French and Caplan (1973) studied role stress in a sample of 205 scientists, engineers, and administrators at Goddard Space Flight Centre, one of NASA's bases. They found that all three groups experienced role ambiguity and attendant psychological strain. However, they also found that engineers reported less role conflict than either scientists or administrators.

The Heriot-Watt study of young graduates in industry indicated that role ambiguity was a problem for a number of respondents, even at this early stage in their careers. Thus, 57% stated that they had to carry out tasks where they were not sure what other people expected of them 'sometimes' or 'often'. In addition 22% worried about this aspect of their job 'very much' and another 29% worried about it to some extent. Although the engineers reported slightly less role ambiguity than the scientists and social studies graduates, the difference was small and not statistically reliable. Role conflict seemed to be less of a problem for the young graduates, although 13% of them said that they worried about the fact that they had to carry out tasks in which there was more than one person telling them what to do.

It will be apparent to the reader that we cannot draw hard and fast conclusions about the extent to which engineers and scientists have to cope with role ambiguity and conflict in their jobs, although the NASA finding that engineers suffer less from role conflict is intriguing and needs to be followed up. However, it should be borne in mind that the jobs engineers and scientists do are very varied, as are the environments in which they work. Consequently, we would expect levels of ambiguity and conflict to vary considerably from one job to another. As mentioned above, ambiguity and conflict are essentially people-oriented problems and we might therefore predict that those technologists whose jobs are primarily managerial (and therefore people-oriented) would experience greater ambiguity and conflict than those whose jobs are primarily on the technical side. This is an issue to which we will return later in the chapter.

ROLE OVERLOAD

The concept of role overload refers to those situations in which the individual is faced with excessive work demands. It is possible to distinguish between quantitative overload and qualitative overload. When there is more work to be done than there is time available, the individual experiences quantitative overload. It is not the difficulty of the tasks the individual is faced with that create the problem here, but rather the time which is allowed for their completion. Qualitative role overload occurs when the tasks to be accomplished are too difficult, given the individual's abilities, skills, and experience. Thus it is not the number of tasks, but their difficulty level which is a source of stress for the individual. While quantitative and qualitative overload are conceptually distinct, in practice they are often interrelated.

QUANTITATIVE ROLE OVERLOAD

In recent years quantitative role overload has been extensively studied and there is little doubt that prolonged overload can have adverse psychological, and perhaps even physiological, consequences (Sales, 1969).

There seems no particular reason for assuming that technologists *per se* should be subjected to particularly high levels of quantitative overload when compared with other white collar occupations. One objective measure of quantitative overload is the number of hours an individual works in his normal week. Gerstl and Hutton (1966) asked their sample of professional mechanical engineers about the length of their working week and found that the modal period was 38 to 39 hours per week. More interesting, was the finding that extra work outwith this time was not extensive. For example, the average working week, including take-home work, was 42 hours. In addition, only 10% found themselves with 12 hours or more of additional work. Finally, those who worked longer hours were in managerial positions, often with small firms.

The findings of the Goddard study would seem to be broadly in line with Gerstl and Hutton's results. Engineers and scientists were in fact found to be low on quantitative overload compared with administrators (French and Caplan, 1973). This would seem to imply that the administrators in this study faced greater environmental pressures in terms of work demands than engineers and scientists. While this may have been the case, at least one other explanation of the finding is plausible. Quantitative role overload may not just be a function of the environment but may also come from within the individual as a consequence of his own attitude to work. Some individuals deliberately take on excessive work loads and adopt a highly committed and perfectionist attitude to their work. In other words, their work involvement and striving for achievement leads them to create situations of role overload for themselves. Friedman and Rosenman (1974) have called this type of behaviour at work Type A behaviour. Type A individuals are characterized by being hard driving, competitive, and possessed of an enhanced sense of time urgency. Returning to the Goddard study, the administrators were indeed found to be higher on Type A behaviour than the scientists and engineers. So we are left with the possibility that the administrators experienced more role overload than the engineers or scientists either because of their achievement orientation, or because they faced greater environmental work pressures, or because of some combination of the two.

Turning to the young engineers and scientists who took part in the Heriot-Watt study, it will come as no real surprise to the reader that quantitative overload was little in evidence among the majority of these respondents at such an early stage in their careers.

Before leaving this section it is worth reiterating once again the fact that both engineers and scientists working as technologists do a wide variety of different types of work, some of which no doubt lead to considerable quantitative overload. Identifying these jobs is an important, but as yet largely untackled, research problem.

QUALITATIVE ROLE OVERLOAD

In contrast to the amount of research effort into the effects of quantitative overload, relatively few attempts have been made to look specifically at qualitative overload and its possible effects on well-being. This is unfortunate, since there are good reasons for expecting qualitative overload and its problems to be of particular relevance to technologists. Given the phenomenal rate at which scientific and technological knowledge is increasing, the task of keeping abreast with technical development must be a daunting one. In many areas of engineering increasingly complex technical problems have to be faced, often with considerable urgency. The exploitation of natural resources from inaccessible places such as the North Sea; the revolutionary developments in micro-electronics; and rapidly advancing space technology are but three examples of this.

However, while it seems reasonable to suggest that, at least in some work situations, qualitative overload may create psychological strains in technologists, unfortunately there is, as yet, little hard evidence to substantiate this point of view, although some of the Goddard study findings are relevant here. French and Caplan (1973) reported that the engineers and scientists experienced higher levels of qualitative overload than the administrators. In addition, an interesting difference was found between the scientists and engineers. Those scientists who were high on qualitative overload also reported feelings of lowered self-esteem, whereas in engineers qualitative overload and self-esteem were unrelated. In this respect, the engineers were similar to the administrators. To speculate a little, this may conceivably be an example where the engineer is less professionally oriented than the scientists and is thus similar to the administrator. It would be very interesting to know how far these scientists' and engineers' perceptions of qualitative overload referred to problems associated with the scientific or technical problems in their work, as opposed to managerial or administrative ones.

There was some evidence in the Heriot-Watt study that a number of the young graduates were experiencing problems associated with qualitative role overload. A number of respondents agreed that they sometimes had to 'make technical decisions without having the necessary know-how', and indeed 19% of respondents were worried about how they were handling this aspect of their job. The scientists worried most about this problem, followed by the engineers, then by the social studies graduates. Of course only a few individuals in this last group made technical decisions anyway, so that it is only the comparison between the scientists and engineers which is of any real interest. Perhaps the scientists worried more about technical decision making because their university training was less vocationally relevant than that of the engineers. In fact many of the respondents admitted that there were aspects of their job for which they had received insufficient training, and indeed 25% of people said that this was a source of worry for them. However, there was no evidence that lack of adequate previous training was any less of a problem for the engineers than for the scientists, judging from the fact that the proportion of engineers who were worried about having had insufficient training was about the same as the proportion of scientists who had similar worries.

ROLE UNDERLOAD

It has been argued above that excessive work demands, whether they be of a quantitative or of a qualitative nature, are stressful for the individual. This is not to say that the complete asbence of work pressures of any sort would create a psychologically comfortable state. Indeed many psychologists, among whom Herzberg (1966) is probably the most vocal, have argued that individuals need an element of challenge in their jobs in order to maintain an interest in the job and to give them job satisfaction. Thus, while it is true that excessive or impossible job demands are stressful for the individual, nevertheless most people probably respond positively to demands which, while they may be difficult to meet, can still be coped with given the skills and resources the individual has available. Indeed, as we have seen earlier, interesting and varied work and a job which provided a challenge were highly valued by the young graduates.

Many individuals in fact find themselves in a position where the demands of their job are insufficient to make full use of their skills and abilities. This state of affairs has been termed role underload and, for the kinds of reason outlined above, it is also believed to be stressful for the individual. Theoretically role underload can be either quantitative (where the individual has insufficient work to do), or qualitative, in which case the level of the tasks are so low as to be inappropriate for the individual's skills and abilities. Qualitative role underload is of more relevance in the present context and it is now pertinent to ask to what extent it is prevalent in the work of technologists.

Evidence comes from a number of sources that role underload is quite common among engineers and other technologists. For example, in Gerstl and Hutton's (1966) study of mechanical engineers, over half of the sample agreed that aspects of their work could be handled by someone with less training than themselves. Many of them complained of having to do routine clerical work (cited by over a third of all respondents) or simple technical tasks. According to Gerstl and Hutton, 'not having opportunity to exercise skill in the work being done' (p.120) was a source of frustration among the engineers in their sample.

Taylor (1978), in his examination of the work attitudes of professional engineers, asked respondents if they felt their skills were well utilized at work. No less than 38% replied that their skills were under-utilized. In addition, under-utilization of skills was related to job dissatisfaction. Only 36% of those who felt their skills were under-utilized were satisfied with their jobs, compared with 88% of those whose skills were not under-utilized. Not surprisingly, Taylor found that those who had higher responsibility levels in their jobs were less likely to feel that their skills were under-utilized.

There is some evidence that the prevalence of routine work varies from one branch of engineering to another. A 1964 Gallup poll found that electrical engineers came top of the list for feeling that their work had a large routine component, followed by mechanical and production engineers. Chemical and electronic engineers were least likely to feel burdened with routine tasks.

To what extent is under-utilization of skills also a problem for scientists working in industrial organizations? The Cotgrove and Box (1970) investigation referred to earlier provides valuable evidence that the position may well be no better for scientists. They found, for example, that over one third of their respondents were dissatisfied with the use of their skills and capacities. Also, over one third were dissatisfied with the quantity and quality of supporting personnel available to them. This presumably meant that they themselves would be forced to spend time on relatively routine and undemanding work. According to Cotgrove and Box, there may be a difference between British Industry and their American counterparts in the level of work they require from highly qualified scientists. They argue that in Britain compared with the USA, there is less willingness on the part of industry to carry out fundamental research projects whose practical application may be some time away in the future. Finally, it is worth pointing out that Cotgrove and Box found marked differences between organizations in the extent to which they utilized the research skills of their scientists, suggesting that strains arising from role underload were by no means an inevitable consequence for scientists working in an industrial research setting.

Turning to the young graduates in the Heriot-Watt study, there was evidence that a number of respondents experienced strain arising from role underload even at this early stage of their careers. For example, 45% of respondents claimed that they 'often' had to carry out tasks which could be done by someone less qualified than themselves. However, there was no indication that this was any more of a problem for the engineers or scientists than for the non-technical social studies graduates, since the proportions of respondents who reported this experience was similar for all three types of graduate. 16% of respondents claimed that they 'often' had to carry out tasks which were routine and boring. A further 41% of respondents stated that they were 'sometimes' required to do routine or boring work. When responses to this question were broken down according to type of qualifications, it was the social studies group who were most often faced with routine work. In fact the physical scientists came off best in this respect, with the engineers occupying an intermediate position. There were indications that role underload was a source of strain, insofar as those who did work for which they were overqualified or who had to carry out routine tasks also had high levels of job dissatisfaction.

At first sight, the differences in frequency of role underload reported by the three types of graduate in the Heriot-Watt study seem to contradict the findings of the other investigations which were described above. In these studies it appeared that role underload, particularly in the form of under-utilization of skills, was an especially prevalent problem among technologists. Of course, an important limitation of the majority of these studies in the present context was the failure to include an equivalent group of non-technologists in the sample against which the engineers' and scientists' responses could be evaluated. However, perhaps more important is the fact that the Heriot-Watt graduates were all at a very early stage in their careers, and it is possible that the social studies graduates would not continue to be in jobs with a high proportion of routine work as their careers developed. It may simply be that, because their degrees are less vocationally relevant, employers are less able or willing to use them immediately on non-routine tasks. On the other hand, perhaps the difference arises at the recruitment stage. Greater educational opportunities in recent years have resulted in an increase in the number of individuals taking degree courses and subsequently entering the job market. As a consequence, it is quite possible that a proportion of graduates are being forced to take jobs which were previously done by less qualified individuals. Given the current shortage of professional engineers, and to a lesser extent, applied scientists, it would not be surprising to find that it is the social studies graduates who are likely to find themselves in this situation. Whatever the underlying reasons for these variations in the responses of the young engineers, scientists, and social studies graduates in the Heriot-Watt investigation, the findings illustrate once again the need for longitudinal studies in this area, so that changes in job demands and attendant strains at different career stages can be properly monitored.

The investigations of Gerstl and Hutton (1966), Taylor (1978), Cotgrove and Box (1970) as well as those of others (Kornhauser, 1962) all support the view that role underload, especially expressed in terms of under-utilization of skills, is frequently a source of strain for the engineer and scientist working in industry. In large measure, the blame for this state of affairs can be laid at the door of the organizations themselves. As Drucker (1952) has pointed out, industry is particularly prone to under-employ professional capacities, either because management are not fully aware of the potential contribution they can make or because they employ scientists mainly for window display purposes. Many organizations fail to provide adequate career ladders based on technical or professional competence, but rather advancement often means abandoning technical work for management. Therefore, the engineer who wishes to remain in engineering as such finds few avenues for personal development through technical achievement.

Earlier in this chapter, it was suggested that engineers and scientists may also suffer from qualitative overload. This apparently poses a contradiction. How can technologists on the one hand experience strain because the work they do makes insufficient demands on their skills, while on the other hand they report feelings of strain because the work makes excessive demands on their skills and abilities? In fact there is no real contradiction here. The work done by engineers and scientists in industry is so varied as to encompass a wide spectrum of difficulty level, responsibility, and so on, depending on the individual job in question. The point is that, because of the nature of their personal values, their education and training, and the nature of the jobs engineers have to do, the successful accomplishment of meaningful technical work is at the centre of their perception of themselves in their jobs. Thus, work which is failing to utilize technical skills and work which is so demanding that the individual feels unable to complete it successfully are likely to both be unsatisfactory from the technologist's point of view.

It would be useful if it were possible to specify the circumstances under which qualitative overload or underload would be most prevalent. Unfortunately, clear-cut answers to this question are simply unavailable in the present state of research knowledge, and any comments in this regard must be tentative ones. Most of the data on qualitative overload come from the Goddard study. The engineers and scientists in this study were engaged in the American Space research programme at a time of feverish activity in this field. Thus they were working in the forefront of technological innovation on a programme with a huge financial and human resource investment. Generalizing from this, it could be argued that qualitative overload is likely to be higher for those working in areas which are at the forefront of knowledge and where technological advances are rapid. Conversely, underload probably occurs more readily in old-established branches of engineering or science, where technically challenging problems are less common. Of course, as has already been pointed out, the conditions for role underload and under-utilization of the skills of professionals are often firmly entrenched in the structure and philosophy of many organizations.

BOUNDARY ROLES

Most large organizations are formally divided into sub-units corresponding to functional specializations, each making its own contribution to the overall operation of the organization. Sub-units may be departments, sub-sections of departments, geographically separate divisions of the organizations, and so on. Individuals who, by the nature of their role, have substantial contacts across such sub-units are said to occupy boundary roles. The term boundary role has also been used to describe the situation where the individual's contacts are between the organization and the wider environment. Finally, in the present context, the term boundary role will also be applied where a person is in a work environment where his occupational background is different from that of the majority of his colleagues.

There is evidence that boundary roles are associated with high levels of stress and strain (French and Caplan, 1973). Presumably, this is largely because it is the person at the interface who is so often in the firing line when conflicts of interest between departments and the like arise. It seems likely that many engineers and other technologists occupy boundary roles. Such roles are many and varied, ranging from the consultant civil engineer at the interface between his own organization and those of his clients, to the quality control engineer who has to interact with production departments (whose priorities might well be very different from those of his own department.)

Although empirical data about the stresses encountered by engineers operating in boundary roles is very sparse, there are reasons for believing that technologists who are in this position may well experience problems. In the Goddard study, engineers who worked mainly in an engineering environment were compared with a separate group of engineers who worked in an administrative environment (boundary role occupants). The latter group showed several signs of stress and strain compared with the former, including: greater deadline pressures from their own branch, less opportunities to do the sort of work they preferred, poorer opportunities for advancement, and lower self-actualization (French and Caplan, 1973).

Earlier in this chapter the low status of the professional engineer in Britain was discussed, and it was pointed out that many engineers themselves felt that they were poorly regarded by their colleagues. If this is indeed the case, then it is easy to see how those in boundary roles involving contact with non-engineers would find the status issue particularly salient and a source of dissatisfaction.

It was suggested above that engineers and scientists working in industrial organizations frequently experience conflict between their professional values and the goals of the organizations which employ them. Once again this is a problem which is likely to be exacerbated for many individuals who occupy boundary roles, especially when they involve interaction with more managerially oriented individuals or departments. For the individual working in an isolated research laboratory, conflicts over priorities, business *vs.* scientific objectives, and so on, are probably much more remote than for the boundary role occupant for whom such conflicts are likely to be much more to the fore in his everyday interactions with non-technical colleagues.

TECHNOLOGISTS IN MANAGERIAL ROLES

On several occasions in this chapter reference has been made to managerial functions in relation to engineers and scientists occupying technological roles. Any discussion of stresses and attendant strains in white collar employees must inevitably include a discussion of managerial roles, if only because so many of the strains arising in organizations are centred around people and their interactions with each other. After all, an essential feature of most managerial roles is responsibility for other people in one form or another. Indeed, French and Caplan (1973), and others since then, have shown that having responsibility for persons is more closely associated with work strain than is responsibility for things. They defined responsibility for persons as including responsibility for their work, for their careers and professional development, and for their job security. Responsibility for things included responsibility for budgets, projects, and equipment. They found that those who spent more time carrying out responsibility for the work of others spent more time under deadline pressure, smoked more and had higher diastolic blood pressure.

Having suggested that certain aspects of the managerial role, (namely those relating to responsibility for others), are likely to lead to strain, it is important to establish how many professional engineers ultimately become managers, or at least have to carry out substantial managerial duties. It is difficult to arrive at precise estimates of the number of engineers in managerial roles, especially since the term, 'manager' is itself rather vague and is applied to a multitude of activities. However, Gerstl and Hutton (1966) have produced some useful statistics for mechanical engineers. They subdivided their sample into those working in management; in operations; in research and development; and in a residual category which included education and consultancy. There were more engineers in management than in any other category (almost 40%). The proportion of 'managers' increased with age and by age 55 over half the profession were in this category. According to Gerstl and Hutton 'the "typical" engineer not only has administrative responsibilities, but *is* a manager' (p.89, their italics).

But what of other types of engineer? Taylor (1978), surveyed 194 professional engineers from six British companies. The sample included respondents from each of the main branches of engineering. Respondents were asked to make a forced choice between describing themselves either as 'managers' or as 'engineers'. Beyond the age of 30 or so, the proportion calling themselves managers remained constant at just under half of the sample. Bearing in mind the fact that the subjects were asked to choose one category to the exclusion of the other, it seems likely that a number of those who described themselves as 'engineers' nevertheless spent a good proportion of their time on managerial activities.

The evidence indicates that managerial roles are often stressful and that a high percentage of engineers ultimately find themselves doing primarily managerial, rather than strictly technical, work. The question which now needs to be asked is: how many of these engineers were willing, rather than reluctant, recruits into the managerial ranks? It seems reasonable to suppose that those who are reluctant managers and who are pushed into a managerial role because of inadequate career opportunities on the technical side or for some similar reason will be more adversely affected by the stresses inherent in the role than those who are pulled into management because of the perceived positive attractions of the managerial work itself, irrespective of career opportunities.

One way of approaching this question is to consider how engineers feel about managerial vs. strictly technical roles at the outset of their careers. Jahoda (1963) in her study of technology students, found that only 29% wished ultimately to go into 'administration', whereas 57% wanted to stay in technology. If the managerial role is conceptualized in terms of responsibility for other people and their work, there is some indirect evidence from a large scale American study that engineering students as a group are less likely than other types of student to have an intrinsic interest in managerial work. Davies (1964), in a study of undergraduate career decisions, found that engineering and the physical sciences tended *not* to be chosen by those who were oriented towards working with people. However, while a proportion of engineering students do have managerial orientations according to a study carried out by Taylor (1979), these individuals tend to go into non-engineering jobs at the outset of their careers. Those with a technical orientation tend to choose R and D or design work. In summary, it would seem from Jahoda's study and that of Davies that engineering students do not have a strong leaning towards managerial, as opposed to technical work, and in fact those who do have a managerial orientation tend to choose non-engineering work. Does this mean that the large numbers of engineers who change from technical to managerial work do so reluctantly?

Evidence from Gerstl and Hutton's (1966) investigation lends some support to this view. For example, they found that almost half of those in their sample who were in operations and almost two thirds of those in R and D and design would prefer to stay in technical posts if the pay were the same. Despite this fact, they found that many engineers changed from R and D and design into management in mid-career. Quite simply their data indicated that the pay and material rewards were not the same in technical posts and management and that greater rewards were offered to those in managerial posts. Thus, according to Gerstl and Hutton, 'there would appear to be a considerable amount of reluctant entry into the administrative side attributable to the absence of upper rungs on technical career ladders' (p.92). They found that 70% of those holding top positions were in management, compared with 6% in R and D and design. Even among those currently working as managers, many expressed a preference for technical work even though their work was mostly non-technical. It seems then, that many of those engineers who enter management do so reluctantly because of the rewards associated with such work rather than for its intrinsic interest. This view is supported by another of Gerstl and Hutton's findings. When asked whom they respected more, someone in top management or someone who had made a technological contribution, 50% were more impressed by the technological contribution, whereas only 20% were impressed by someone having reached top management (The remainder were undecided).

All of this suggests, at least tentatively, that the managerial roles in which many professional engineers find themselves are often a source of psychological strain. In the first place, to a large extent, they seem to be reluctant recruits to management whose real interests in technical work are frustrated. Particularly difficult problems are likely to be found in those individuals who hold strong professional values with their inherent conflict with the goals of the manager who is expected to be very much an organization man. Indeed, it may well be that engineers and technologists are not particularly good at many aspects of the managerial role, given that it appears from the work of Davies (1964) that one reason people take up engineering in the first place is their preference for working with things, rather than people. Furthermore, while few would argue with the quality of the technologists' technical training, it is doubtful if many universities or other institutes of higher education provide their engineers with an adequate grounding in managerial skills. When Gerstl and Hutton's respondents were asked what should be included in an ideal course in engineering, the largest difference between what was thought to be ideal and the reality of current university courses was in the area of non-technical subjects, where there was felt to be a need for a greater emphasis on industrial administration, economics, and social sciences, among others. Of special interest is the fact that it was the older engineers with managerial experience who placed greatest emphasis on the need for an increased emphasis on non-technical subjects.

Although there seem to be good reasons for expecting that many engineers would find the managerial role a stressful one, unfortunately direct evidence that this is the case is lacking. The Heriot-Watt study, although it was concerned with professional engineers, is of limited relevance here, given the lack of managerial experience of the respondents. However, it did provide a few preliminary indications that the respondents in the study might well experience difficulties if and when they became heavily involved in managerial roles. For example, respondents were asked how often they had to supervise manual workers or white collar workers. They were also asked how frequently they had to make decisions which had implications for the lives of others, or might make them unhappy. Only a minority of respondents were required to carry out any of these activities 'often', although many indicated that they had to do them 'occasionally'. For example, 20% of the sample said that they often had to supervise manual workers and 23% said that they often had to make decisions that had consequences for other people at work. In addition, each respondent was asked how much he worried about how he was handling each of these aspects of his job. Of particular interest was the close correspondence that occurred between how frequently the individual carried out these tasks and how much he worried about this aspect of his work performance. In other words, those individuals who had to carry out these activities frequently worried considerably about them. It was the engineers who were especially likely to experience strain over the supervision of manual workers, followed by the scientists. Only a few social studies graduates had direct responsibility for supervising manual workers. Of course the managerial role covers a wide range of activities which could not be meaningfully investigated in graduates with one year's work experience. Nevertheless the findings support the view that more extensive study of the strains encountered by technologists who are in managerial roles might well prove to be very worthwhile.

CONCLUDING REMARKS

This chapter has not attempted to provide a definitive or exhaustive list of the work pressures and attendant psychological strains encountered by professional engineers and applied scientists working in the field of technology. Rather it has been an exploratory and at times speculative account of some possible sources of work stress which seem to be particularly applicable to individuals with high level technical qualifications working in industrial organizations. This speculative approach was inevitable, given the paucity of information of a psychological nature on this occupational group. The terms 'engineer' and 'technologist' both encompass a variety of work roles and are applicable to individuals employed in a wide diversity of organizational settings. This fact must qualify any generalizations that can be made about stress in relation to engineers and other technologists.

At a macro level, the question of the status of the professional engineer both in society as a whole, and among his work colleagues, is a central issue with many implications for the engineer's job satisfaction and motivation. A closely related issue concerns the career prospects available to engineers in Britain, particularly their access to the top positions in industry.

Several writers have alluded to the existence of a conflict between the professional values of engineers and scientists which emphasize autonomy, technical accomplishment, and the public availability of knowledge, and the typical organizational goals of profitability, marketability of products, and the safeguarding of knowledge which might have commercial value. The issue of whether or not engineers are less likely to hold strong professional values than scientists working in industry remains largely unresolved.

Strains arising from qualitative underload and overload appear to be a particularly important problem for technologists. This is partly because organizations under-utilize the skills of their technical specialists, leading to role underload. On the other hand, some technologists complain of qualitative overload and experience strain associated with the demanding nature of the work. This probably occurs most frequently where the technology is new and complex (and decisions have to be made in an atmosphere of uncertainty) or where the technology is advancing at a rapid rate (so that it is difficult to keep up to date). It is not simply the objective conditions of qualitative overload or underload which result in strain, it is the fact that the whole philosophy of the technologist's training has encouraged him to evaluate himself in terms of his ability to successfully complete qualitatively demanding technical tasks. Thus, when the work environment either fails to provide the demanding tasks, or makes the challenge too difficult, strain results.

Many engineers begin their careers working in a technical capacity, but poor career prospects apparently push many of them reluctantly into management. In many cases, neither their training nor their basic work interests and values are particularly suited to primarily managerial roles. Thus, there is much potential for conflict, dissatisfaction, and strain. This is an area which is in particular need of further investigation. Once research has clarified the nature and extent of this and other problems faced by engineers and scientists in industry, the way will be open for action aimed at improving the technologist's lot. No doubt this would ideally involve a change in the value organizations place on technical expertise and how they use it, as well as a wider appreciation by those who train technologists that the nature of their work is such that inevitably they will require a number of non-technical skills to add to their technical armoury. There may even be a case for more adequate vocational guidance for those thinking of entering these professions. Surely these changes would be worth the effort that would have to be invested in carrying them out successfully. After all, technologists get things done and make things work and what society can afford to undervalue such obviously essential skills?

REFERENCES

Blau, P.M., and Scott, W.R. (1962). *Formal Organizations,* Chandler, San Francisco.
Cotgrove, S. and Box, S. (1970). *Science, Industry, and Society,* Allen and Unwin, London.
Davies, J.A. (1964). *Undergraduate Career Decisions,* Aldine, Chicago.
Department of Employment Gazette (1979). *Going into Industry,* January, 1979.
Drucker, P.F. (1952). Management and the professional employee. *Harvard Business Review,* **XLI,** 103-114.
French, J.R.P., and Caplan, R.D. (1973). Organizational stress and individual strain. In *The Failure of Success* (Ed. A.J. Marrow), pp.30-66, Amacom, New York.
Friedman, M, and Rosenman, R.H. (1974). *Type A Behavior and Your Heart.* Knopf, New York.
Gerstl, J.E., and Cohen, L.K. (1964). Dissensus, situs and egocentrism in occupational ranking. *Brit. J. Sociol.,* **15,** 254-261.

Gerstl, J.E., and Hutton, S.P. (1966). *Engineers: The Anatomy of a Profession.* Tavistock, London.

Herriot, P. (1978). *Engineering and the Great Debate: Doing and Making or Just Making Do.* Unpublished Paper.

Herzberg, F. (1966). *Work and the Nature of Man.* World Publishing, Cleveland.

Jahoda, M. (1963). *The Education of Technologists: An Exploratory Case Study at Brunel College,* Tavistock, London.

Kelsall, R.K., Poole, A, and Kahn, A. (1972). *Graduates: The Sociology of an Elite.* Methuen, London.

Kornhauser, W. (1962). *Scientists in Industry: Conflict and Accommodation.* University of California Press, Berkley.

Miller, G.A. (1967). Professionals in bureaucracy: alienation among industrial scientists and engineers. *Am. Sociol. Rev.,* **32,** 755-768.

Ritti, R. (1968). Work goals of scientists and engineers. *Industrial Relations, 7,* 118-131.

Sales, S.M. (1969). Organizational role as a risk factor in coronary disease, *Admin. Sci. Quart.,* **14,** 325-336.

Social Surveys (Gallup Poll), (1963). *Technical Staff Recruitment Survey,* London.

Taylor, R. (1977). *Survey of Imperial College Engineers.* Unpublished Paper.

Taylor, R. (1978). *The Careers and Work Attitudes of Professional Engineers,* Unpublished Paper.

Taylor, R. (1979). Career orientations and intra-occupational choice: A survey of engineering students, *J. Occ. Psychol., 53,* 41-52.

Underhill, R. (1966). Values and post-college career change, *Am. J. Sociol., 72,* 163-172.

White Collar and Professional Stress
Edited by C.L. Cooper and J. Marshall
© 1980 John Wiley & Sons Ltd.

Chapter 9

Stress Among Technical Support Staff in Research and Development

Stephen Fineman
University of Bath, England

It is common to encounter discussions about the key role of research and development activities in advanced technology organizations. In many instances it is the output of research and development departments which provides the very life force of the organiztion; the essential knowledge, expertise and ideas upon which products and new technologies are created.

The 'front liners' in research and development are the researchers themselves — often professionals with skills in particular scientific disciplines. But these people rarely work unaided. For many there is a crucial back-up staff who provide essential technical resources for the research. This chapter is addressed to a specific group of such support staff, and to the sources of some of their work stresses.

THE RESEARCH SITE AND SAMPLE

The study findings reported here are based upon the writer's research involvement with a sample of industrial technical support staff. They work in physical science laboratories which are housed on a single site in a rural setting. One's first impression on visiting the site is of a spacious, clean, modern complex of purpose-built accommodation. Security and safety procedures seem to have been meticulously planned; various zones of potential hazard are clearly delimited, and access is carefully restricted in places. To the uninitiated the equipment and language appear weird and sometimes wonderful. The pace of life seems unhurried, even casual — yet one gains the feeling that one is entering a rather special elite scientific community.

About half of the laboratory's 750 staff are graduate scientists and engineers, many of whom (in particular the researchers) are Ph.D.'s. The support function is made up of a range of specialisms which would usually be

211

outside the researcher's immediate experience. These include computing, health and safety, engineering, photography, draughtsmanship, design, and specific crafts involved in laboratory activities. In addition, the laboratories employ professional administrators to undertake the more standard organizational back-up activities — such as personnel, accounting, and planning.

Some support staff are organized as separate specialist departments (for example, Computing and Design) where they can be consulted by the researcher. Others are linked-in more intimately with the day-to-day activities of the researchers by working within particular research sections. Each researcher himself reports to a Section Leader, who in turn is subordinate to a Division Head.

The company's senior occupational health physician was personally interested in an exploratory study on stress and its cause at the laboratories, so he facilitated the researcher's entry into the organization. Several meetings with senior management and relevant union representatives took place, the outcome being an agreement to go ahead with a research study. Notices were displayed stating that the writer, a research psychologist, would be conducting interviews with people who wished to participate in an independently sponsored* study on organizational factors which may influence physical and psychological well-being at work.

THE DESIGN OF THE STUDY

The study was a comparative one between stressed 'cases' and non-stressed 'controls' — all of them technical support staff. The control procedure was adopted in an attempt to match the two groups on some of the grosser variables which may account for observed stress differences. Thus cases and controls were all paired for similarity in age (plus-or-minus 5 years), sex and division within the company. Also, wherever possible, a control had the same job, and was of the same marital status as the case with whom he was matched. The sample reported here comprises twenty cases and twenty matched controls, drawn from the complete range of technical support functions mentioned previously. All but two of the sample were male.

All participants were selected from people who voluntarily presented themselves to the company's medical unit ostensibly for the purposes of medical care. The occupational health nurse in attendance invited individuals to participate in the study if they met specifications for case identification, or control.

A case would need to present two or more of the following symptoms: overt anxiety signs, changes in sleep pattern, irritability, dizziness, awareness of heartbeat, hypertension, anterior chest pain, changes in smoking or drinking,

*The study was supported by funds from the (U.K.) Medical Research Council.

digestive problems, weight change, tremor or sweating. This list was drawn up for the study by an independent panel of occupational health physicians and the nurse was given extensive notes on the symptoms to help her in her diagnosis. Data on all of the criteria were gathered for each case. Control subjects displayed none of the stress symptoms, but reported usually for reasons of minor physical illness — such as a cut finger, or a sprain.

INTERVIEWING PARTICIPANTS

The writer conducted interviews of about one hour with each person. He had no prior knowledge of that person's designation as a stress case or control. The interviews were tape recorded in full with the permission of each subject. Anonymity and confidentiality were preserved as far as possible by the use of Christian names only and by keeping all raw data with the researcher.

Each interviewee was allowed considerable freedom to generate and discuss his own perceptions of his problems, job satisfactions, and dissatisfactions, feelings about himself and his working relationships. Furthermore, participants were encouraged to talk about non-work issues if they wished. The important point here was to avoid straight-jacketing respondents with the researcher's *a priori* views about their sources of stress, and to permit each person to generate what he or she saw was important. This inductive method is a rather different approach to more traditional deductive social research where one would attempt to precisely predefine what was to be answered by research subjects, and in what exact form (usually quantitative) they should respond. Thus the main type of data gathered in this study are very 'broad-banded' and qualitative.

The researcher did not ask direct questions concerning stress, the focus being more on job and self perceptions. Nevertheless, some participants would spontaneously talk about their health or stresses while others revealed little in this way. Inevitably this left the writer making guesses as to whether or not a particular individual was indeed a pre-designated case. In fact subsequent analysis suggested that these hunches based upon overt statements, or signs, were *not* a very reliable indicator of stress.

Typically the atmosphere during the discussions was concentrated and sometimes intense. For some participants the experience was cathartic; they would remark that they felt that it was good to talk freely about things, and that the time had passed more quickly than they had expected. Very few people appeared reserved, or less-than-frank, in their discussions.

THE THEORETICAL FRAMEWORK FOR ANALYSIS

The interviews generated considerable data about the world of work as perceived by the technical support staff. In order to make sense of this information from the point of view of stress we need some theoretical guidelines and categorization procedure. In the present setting, three broad features were focused upon:

1. The type of problems and their background as perceived by the participants.
2. The extent to which these problems were experienced as threatening to the interviewees
3. What they did about the threats and the effectiveness of their actions.

These factors are used as a framework for the analysis which will follow and they represent central features of a particular view about the nature of the stress process (Fineman, 1978, 1979). This view states that stress is an *individual psychological and/or physical response state of a person who fails to successfully master threatening problems.*

Let us consider this proposition in a little more detail, as it lies at the heart of the analytic procedure. One can envisage a range of demands which a person may perceive. At work there may be production demands from a boss, demands for sympathy and understanding from an overworked secretary, deadlines and quality control pressures, and so on. There are also non-work demands, such as doing repairs to the house, meeting mortgage repayments, coping with growing children, and handling some of the ups-and-downs of married life. Or leisure activities such as the demands arising out of positions of responsibility in sporting or club activities. Yet a further source of demand is the individual himself. Many people make strong demands on themselves which reflect personality needs, such as, for achievement, security, recognition, or self-actualization.

Most people handle such demands in a fairly routine way; it becomes a familiar, habitual process which tends not to overly disturb the balance of life. But some demands may be less easy to regulate and they can be experienced as specific *problems* to be addressed and solved. This can be a disquieting process, but again can fall within the coping capacities and resources of most people. Some of these problems may arise because of the change in the balance of demands in the various spheres of life. For example, an increase in family demands because of sickness may sap energy which was previously devoted to work issues, so precipitating problems of overload at work which were not previously experienced as such. It should be emphasized the definition of a 'problem' here is 'phenomenological' — it is the individual's *personal* way of construing his or her demands.

While we may all face many problems to solve, only some of these problems will be *potential stressors* — those problems which *could* bring about stress depending upon how they are ultimately handled. In the present view, a potential stressor arises from a problem which is *highly threatening* to a person; it is a problem which a person may feel will expose particular weaknesses in his or her competence or ability if a satisfactory solution cannot be found. The personal costs then may be very high — perhaps loss of face, loss of prestige, or loss of security.

Feeling threatened in this way is likely to be a very uncomfortable process; anxiety and tension will rise as the person mobilizes energy to do something about the predicament — an effort to ward off the threat. It is the effectiveness of this action which will determine the level of experienced stress. Three broad *interdependent* actions are possible — confrontation, avoidance and withdrawal. In confrontation the threatening problem is met head-on and a deliberate course of action taken to control or master it. If success soon follows this action, or success is confidently anticipated, then the threat is effectively managed or removed, anxiety falls, and there is no stress. If, however, there is failure in this respect, then we have the unfortunate state of affairs of having to cope with the still persisting anxiety in face of the threat, *plus* the anxiety from the failure experience itself. This is a condition of stress.

Yet confrontation of this sort is very difficult for some people; it becomes too painful to face up to the problem. In such cases natural psychological defence processes may emerge which help cope with the anxiety provoked by the threat. Avoidance is one of these; the threatening problem is denied or ignored. Yet such defence mechanisms demand considerable energy to maintain. In the short term they may operate very effectively and a low anxiety, more normal state appears. However, over time, energy resources will be severely taxed, the defences become less and less effective, and the threat re-emerges. The person can be partly exhausted by this time and experiencing stress from failing to cope with his or her difficulties.

A more extreme defence process against threat is to withdraw psychologically, to shut off from much of the world's demands. Again, it is unlikely that such a response can be maintained for long without severe consequences for effective coping in many spheres of life, besides those concerned with the initial threat. A short term withdrawal from the world may indeed be beneficial, especially if the threat happens to 'go away' in the meantime. But, perhaps more likely, the personal costs of inaction will increase and simply serve to exacerbate the perceived threat, so leading to stress.

This conceptualization of the stress process suggests that we need to focus our initial analysis of stress at a strictly individual level. We cannot assume that, for example, particular jobs, or aspects of jobs, are intrinsically stressful. It depends on how a particular job holder perceives the demands of that job, whether or not they emerge as threatening problems, and then how they are coped with. Clearly, such perceptions and actions will be strongly influenced by personality factors. Hence, one might expect people who are habitually predisposed to anxiety or who are of low self esteem, to be more likely to view certain aspects of their work as threatening. Also past experience in coping with threats will be very important in determining how a particular threatening situation is handled; successful confrontation in the past can provide valuable learning for the present and future.

This background provides us with a foundation and rationale for data analysis. Let us now examine our findings from the research population in terms of their problems, their threats, and their coping styles.

PROBLEMS PERCEIVED BY THE TECHNICAL SUPPORT STAFF

The problems expressed by all of the support staff can be grouped in terms of six major areas of concern — inferior status, lack of intrinsic rewards, poor use of skills and abilities, difficult working relationships, powerlessness and anonymity, and scientists as poor man-managers.

Inferior status

Forty three per cent of the sample made statements concerning their status in the organization, in particular feeling undervalued with respect to the better academically qualified research officers:

'There's a big dividing line here between graduates and non-graduates. In a research establishment like this you're just a small fish in a very big pond if you're not a graduate.'

'I know where I am in the family tree here ... underneath it.'

'There is a view here among the top echelons that all research officers are worthy because they went to university; a technician can't be very good because he hasn't got a degree. So even a lesser research officer is worth more than a good technician.'

'A lot of people come straight from university so they are very narrow in the way they look at things. They often see us in the way they may see a painter, carpenter or plumber ... *we* provide a service for *them*.'

'People here seem to have gone qualification mad. I literally haven't got any qualifications at all and I'm treated a bit like a leper.'

Some people were rather more bitter than others:

'The Ph.D.'s — I don't know whether they think we're a bit thick or what, but they will come and seek our advice and then totally ignore it! It's probably because they've got Ph.D.'s that they think they're better than anyone else.'

'Some chaps come from universities and expect us to just run around mopping up benches. In fact, many of us have come from very responsible jobs in outside industry.'

'You feel that you are just part of the furniture here. For example, you get nice and settled in your job and along comes management to tell you that you have to work with someone else. The decision's been made and we're the last to know!'

For some, their organization labels and titles were seen as indicative of inferior status:

'Being an *assistant* technician in this place they say you needn't think at all. The label itself is derogatory. "Assistants" work in shoe shops, don't they?'

'The technician's role is fairly downgraded in status — we are sometimes seen as similar to tyre technicians or garage technicians. Surely a technician should be a person who thinks for himself — an independent individual.'

The status issue was also viewed in terms of the way it limited their advancement in the organizations:

'People with much higher qualifications than me are coming in to get the better jobs — the company's resources go to them, not us.'

'I feel that the system can't accommodate the idea that maybe support people and research staff should be graded equally; they prefer us *not* to have expectations of career advancement.'

'You are soon earmarked here for getting on or not getting on ... and it's the better qualified people, not us, who get on!'

Lack of intrinsic rewards

There has been much discussion in the area of 'job enrichment' about the desirable effects on people's work motivation when they can see some tangible end-products connected with their own efforts, or at least understand and value their place in the bigger scheme of things at work. This point was forcefully illustrated by the lack of intrinsic rewards experienced by many (60%) of the support staff:

'The end products of this place are bits of paper — usually reports in a language I find difficult to understand which are filed away somewhere. This job lacks glamour and a feeling of involvement; at least in my previous job, aircraft manufacture, I could finally sit in a shiny aeroplane and get the feel and smell of the product.'

'When the job's over, you've nothing to show for it; it becomes routine.'

'It's difficult to feel you're doing anything but just a measurement job for someone else, and saying "Here's the result". I get no follow-up so I've no idea how important things are.'

'I feel I'm working in a blind alley. Although I'm making things they are only a tiny part of the end product of what's going on; I never see a whole end result.'

'I guess many of us are sort of odd job boys . . . we never see the complete end of a job or task.'

The influence of other people in the feedback and reward process was also significant:

'I do feel very satisfied when a research officer thanks me for my help, but more often they just take my work for granted.'

'I think the bad thing about the job is that you don't get any reward — nobody gives you any praise. I once mentioned this to one of our management chaps and he said "Well, I don't get any praise either".'

'It's rather routine and there's a certain amount of resentment about the fact that you can work like a beaver all day and get no more recognition than sitting around doing the Times crossword.'

'I've been involved in lots of projects and I have a wealth of experience here — but I get no recognition for this; no-one seems to notice or care. This kills my enthusiasm.'

'You neither get praised or torn apart in this job — you're left in a sort of limbo.'

Inadequate *extrinsic* incentives — salary level and promotion — were also perceived as issues by some staff:

'There seems to be a feeling that it's fine if we retire on exactly the same salary band as we started on.'

'It doesn't matter how much effort I put into my job — it's still one increment at the end of the year.'

'My design work has led to dramatic savings in time in my section, but there has been no formal recognition of this — no financial reward.'

'Soon I'll be at the top of my salary scale. I've been here long enough to do the job blindfolded, so where's the "carrot" going to come from?'

Poor use of skills and abilities

Fifty eight per cent of the sample were concerned about how well their potential was being used in their jobs. Many skilled tradesmen and qualified craftspeople felt bitter, or despondent, about their under-utilization while, in contrast, others felt that they were being pushed beyond their capacities in a fairly rarefied research environment. Let us firstly illustrate some of the former views:

'Theres so much I'd like to do to re-design and create new elements in the job — but I'm allowed little scope for such imagination.'

'All the detailing work I have to do is so boring and mundane. My skills are wasted. I really come into my own laying out the initial schemes — the creative bit; but that's just a minority part of the job now.'

'Most of us have lost our skills because they haven't been made use of. The research staff have had lots of encouragement, but not the technical staff.'

'They're not getting their engineering value out of me. They might be getting what they want, but from my point of view I'm a bit under-run.'

'There's so little creativity and development in my job — this is one of the big disappointments to me. It's just not demanding enough decision making from me.'

'I feel understretched. So much of the work is rough and ready. When I try to do a professional job, many people sneer at it.'

'I feel a gradual erosion of ability as rules and demarcation have increased. Although I'm a skilled tradesman with five years' apprenticeship. I can't even use the machines which I know like the back of my hand.'

Looking at the other side of the coin, problems for a minority of the staff stemmed from their inability to keep up with technical changes and skill requirements.

'Technical changes occur which push my skills into unknown territories.'

'Some of the mathematical concepts are beyond my knowledge. I get nervous if I cannot understand them.'

'Once your inventiveness has gone, there's no power on earth can help you — there's nothing left to draw upon.'

'I sometimes lose track of what the research people are saying. There are, for example, long equations which are way beyond my own training and education.'

'Work on calculations and formulae really confuse me at times.'

Difficult working relationships

Relationship problems featured with thirty five per cent of the sample. Problems concerning the difficulties in relating to, or working with, research officers, section leaders, or colleagues:

'The relationship between me and the researcher are critical to the job. I find them too genteel — they have a university attitude and don't understand my way of working.'

'There is a barrier between research officers and ourselves. The research officers seem to be trying to defend themselves all the time — you can't get any information from them. This has caused a lot of bad feeling.'

'I've mixed feelings about the research officers. I find that a number of them seem to be looking for ways to put me down.'

'Although I've been working with my section leader for years, I can't agree with him on many work issues. At a personal level he's hopeless — just jokes about my personal problems.'

'Sometimes I feel very much on my own in this place. I took this work problem of mine to my superior the other day and he left me feeling empty — no support or help.'

'If my chief would recognise me as a *person* rather than as an automaton — maybe just talk about the holidays or weather sometimes — I'd be much happier.'

'My superior wants me to work like a machine and I'm not like that. We seem to have little common ground between us and the less we communicate, the further the gap is.'

'One person in my section really rubs me up the wrong way. It's a small group, so working in complete silence with this person makes things very tense.'

Thus, it seems a mixture of issues underlies these difficulties — perceived communication barriers because of status and style differences, feelings of a supervisor's lack of support and understanding about personal needs, and ongoing conflict problems.

Powerlessness and anonymity

Forty per cent of the sample expressed some of their problems in terms of the way that they experienced the atmosphere of the organization. Two dimensions were prevalent: powerlessness and anonymity.

Comments typically illustrating their powerlessness were:

'As you can't ever hope to understand the full technical details of the research, you are always powerless ... most things are above your head.'

'People like us at the lower end are usually reluctant to stir things up as it's like putting your head on the block. We are pretty well paid so few would want to jeopardize that security.'

'In a ponderous, gigantic machine like this, it's very difficult to advance oneself or change things.'

'I still feel strange working in this place — I can't get *decisions* from anyone; no one is *really* your boss.'

And expressions about the anonymity of the organization:

'It's impersonal. There's no doubt that at times I get the impression that my section leader doesn't know who I am — and my Divisional Head certainly doesn't.'

'It's a place with good working conditions, a good canteen, and masses of excellent equipment — but there's little attempt to think of you as a *person*.'

'You're a very anonymous person in a big organization — most people get trampled on, unless you can shout loud enough.'

'No one really cares about us, you're a tiny cog in a big wheel.'

Scientists as poor man-managers

Thirty three per cent of the sample viewed their management as creating problems for them. Broken promises, restrictive rules and regulations, ignorance about the job, and even deviousness appeared amongst the lengthy catalogue of less-than-complimentary statements. But the most predominant concern focussed on the competence of the research scientist in managing people and their problems:

'My God! Scientists are one minute trying to write a paper on Thermodynamic Theory, and the next minute trying to sort out some labour dispute. It's pathetic; no wonder they make a total mess of it.'

'Our section leaders get promoted for doing good research, not good man-management. They are predominantly scientists, they're not trained in management.'

'There are no *real* managers here, like in industry. Researchers *can't* be managers as well.'

'One major problem here is that a lot of researchers come straight from university with no experience of getting on with people. They then move up the ranks to be managers; but unfortunately having a Ph.D. doesn't make a manager.'

We can now see a range of problems which face support staff in this setting. With the exception of powerlessness and anonymity, which are sentiments often expressed by more junior personnel in large bureaucratic organizations, the problems do appear to reflect certain peculiarities or idiosyncracies about the role of technical support. But if we now examine Table 1, where these problems have been classified according to their occurrence amongst the separate groups of stress cases and non-stressed controls, it is clear that they spread fairly evenly across both groups. In other words, the problems themselves are in no way *uniquely* associated with stress although they do give rise to concern or disquiet in those who face them. What we do expect, from the theoretical viewpoint outlined previously, is that stress will occur only amongst those people who have (a) experienced their problems as *threatening*, and (b) have thus failed to adequately cope with the threat. Therefore, we must further analyse the data in Table 1.

Table 1. Types of problems experienced by stress cases and matched controls.

No.	Stress Case	No.	Control
1*	Skills, Relationships	21	Power
2*	Skills, Relationships, Power	22	Power
3*	Relationships	23	Status, Rewards, Management
4*	Rewards	24	Relationships
5	Status, Rewards, Skills, Relationships	25	Status, Rewards, Management
6*	Rewards, Power	26	Rewards, Relationships, Management
7*	Status, Skills	27*	Status, Skills, Relationships, Power
8*	Rewards, Power	28	Skills
9	Rewards, Skills	29*	Status, Rewards, Skills
10*	Status, Rewards, Skills, Management	30*	Rewards, Skills, Power, Management
11*	Rewards, Skills, Relationships	31*	Status, Rewards, Skills, Power, Management
12*	Status, Rewards, Skills, Management	32*	Status, Rewards, Skills, Relationships
13*	Skills, Relationships, Management	33*	Rewards, Skills, Management
14*	Status, Skills, Relationships, Power, Management	34	Rewards, Skills
15	Status, Skills	35*	Skills
16*	Status, Rewards, Skills	36*	Rewards, Power, Management
17*	Rewards, Skills, Power	37	Rewards, Power
18	Skills	38	Status, Relationships, Power
19*	Status, Rewards, Relationships, Power, Management	39	Status, Relationships, Power
20	Status, Relationships, Power	40	Status, Rewards, Power, Management

Status	= Inferior status	Power	= Powerlessness and anonymity
Rewards	= Lack of intrinsic rewards	Management	= Scientists as poor man-managers
Skills	= Poor use of skills and abilities		
Relationships	= Difficult working relationships	*	= threat experienced

THREAT AND STRESS

Each person's problems were examined for overt indications of threat to self image or esteem. The sort of statements identified varied considerably, for example:

'I feel I *have* to win the battle to keep my self respect.'

'The work used to be challenging and prestigious, but now I feel an enormous vacuum as I don't fully understand what I am supposed to do.'

'I see no way for promotion I want so much, while these young chaps go past me and off into the distance — *they* get all the attention.'

'I've got to face up to the problem ... it's most unbearable when I just don't feel in control of things.'

'It would be *my* section that would get the rap if I don't take some action to prevent it happening again.'

The analysis resulted in the picture presented in Table 1 — an asterisk marks the evidence of threat. Of the stress cases, seventeen out of the twenty indicated that some aspects of their problem(s) were felt to be threatening, while only eight controls felt threatened.

Our expectation now is that the stress cases are experiencing stress because of their failure to cope with the problems which threaten them. The failures to cope may be characterized in terms of the three major activities already mentioned: *confrontation* attempts whereby a person may directly face up to his difficulties and attempt to change the situation, or perceptions of the problem, to eliminate the threat; *avoidance* and *withdrawal* are the psychological defence processes aimed primarily at managing the anxiety associated with the threat. Various combinations of these were evident amongst the stressed group:

Confrontation attempts

Case 1 Deep rifts between him and researchers — feels totally misunderstood. Still hits back forcefully and aggressively, but it doesn't help. Exhausted and frustrated.

Case 4 Feels guilty about vegetating in a job with no further prospects. In a rut, channelled, life passing by. Tries to adjust by accepting it, but can't.

Case 6 Tried again and again to rectify believed unjust treatment in a pay claim. Gets strangled by the bureaucracy — feels like he's hitting his head against a wall.

Case 10 Bitter about failing the promotion panels. Feels injured and hurt as he's given so much to the job. Has fought and complained, but no success.

Case 11 A good colleague blocked his promotion. Amazed and injured at such behaviour — thought he deserved promotion. Tried to change jobs to help, so far failed.

Case 16 Resents lack of value placed on his services. Bitter that researchers load him with work at the last minute. How can he achieve the quality he so desires? Tried to educate them, but unsuccessful. Feels alone, unsupported by superior.

Confrontation, followed by avoidance or withdrawal

Case 8 Sees the work as a fruitless activity — just filling in forms. Life is slipping by with no high points at work. Tried to improve job, but severely limited. Now stopped trying — no energy, not worth the effort.

Case 12 Been demoted, despite recognition for excellence in more responsible job. Tried confronting boss, but he's not sympathetic. Given up; unsolveable problem. Great sense of failure and frustration.

Case 14 Feels enormously underutilized and undervalued. Tried and tried to improve things by complaining to management, but has failed to get anywhere. Massive energy devoted to protecting himself from uncomfortable interactions. Doesn't really work, though. Now exhausted.

Case 17 Last year much praised for good performance, this year completely opposite. Strong self doubts and resentment. Tried to save face by obtaining promotion, but failed several applications. Nothing more to be done — feels in hopeless position, and feels victimized.

Avoidance and/or withdrawal

Case 2 Great difficulty adapting to new assignments and frequent changes in boss; also long personal conflict with colleague. Tries to avoid most engagements with researchers, but self doubt haunts him.

Case 3 Works in silence with a colleague — they are totally incompatible. All direct interaction avoided, but immensely tense atmosphere prevails.

Case 5 Convinced he's doing his job well, but superior has castigated him for his work and style. Pride severely injured; self doubts have set in. Can't face up to boss with the problem, so it continually nags him. Feels burned out.

Case 7 Trapped in job which provides him little satisfaction or scope. Forlorn and depressed. Convinced there's nothing he can do as expects any action will be blocked — so does nothing. Also coping with recent deaths in family.

Case 13 Feels his superior totally lacks understanding of his work and personal problems. Marriage just broken up. Dreads confrontations with boss so tries to avoid contact. But an impossible stance to maintain. Anxious and lacks concentration.

Case 19 Recently moved from working with a researcher who caused him much anguish and conflict. Fears that he will be moved again into such a position. Feels like a pawn — undervalued. Powerless to influence the issues so doesn't try.

The above stress cases had manifestly failed to effectively cope with the problems which threatened them. For some, failure occurred after eventually confronting their difficulties, for others failure emerged when anxiety defences no longer afforded sufficient protection. Some of the brief vignettes presented do illustrate the influence of non-work demands in the stress process. Moreover, the influence of personality characteristics are often implied — such as aggressiveness, needs for achievement, recognition, and security. Several people stated that they were 'fairly anxious' people, or usually a 'bit nervous'. Thus we cannot divorce the nature of the perceived threat, and the type of coping process, from the individual's personality.

In four cases there was no detectable work threat, but in one of them domestic issues seemed to dominate. This person was exceedingly worried about his wife's health following a serious operation she had had and he was also trying to cope with the needs of his children. This left him little spare energy to meet his work demands, which he used to take in his stride. It is possible that the other three cases were facing non-work difficulties which they did not reveal in their interviews.

Successful coping with threats

If we now turn to the controls, twelve do not perceive any threats, so according to our theory, would not experience stress. Eight, however, do mention problems which have threatened them. Have these people avoided stress because they have effectively coped with the threats? Let us look at this issue for each of the relevant individuals:

Control 27 Had been very upset that the organization would not permit him to improve his qualifications, despite commendations of his work by outside academic bodies. Felt victimized by immediate boss, but didn't know what to do about it, so avoided confrontation. Finally aired the problem with the Personnel Department. Fully accepts their reassurances and now feels very much happier — can re-start with a clean slate.
Control 29 Recently suddenly struck by 'male menopause'. Felt confused and frightened by the lack of intrinsic satisfaction in his job and rest of his life. Thought very hard about it, confronting its implications for him. Decided that he still has the best job he could find, so he accepts the limitations. Will pursue his need to achieve in outside business ventures and sport; the job allows him such freedom.

Control 30 Lack of praise for his effort frustrates him and can get him down. But he's adapted by confrontation and acceptance. 'It's like water off a duck's back for me now, you have to see it for what it is and take the rough with the smooth. If you don't try to fit in you get nowhere.'

Control 31 Feels he is being transferred to a job where he will have nothing to do — results from management politicking and he's the victim. This worries and upsets him especially as he's already had many job moves. Nevertheless he fights hard, throwing the problem back to management and unions. This energizes him, reducing the threat. Restricting work activities to his own choice further enhances the feeling of control over the source of threat.

Control 32 Gets fearful with each new assignment — an awful feeling of panic hits him. 'Can I cope with this whole job?' Over time he has learned to cope by reviewing carefully what he needs to manage the job. Makes generous deadlines for himself, so that it allows him 'safe time to flounder a bit'.

Control 33 Feels a complete failure in some ways for not finding work which gives him the interest and rewards that he needs. Initially resentful and irritable, but has now adjusted his expectations about the work, shifting his satisfactions to his non-work activities. What used to threaten doesn't any more.

Control 35 His mind used to go blank when researchers talked to him using many concepts he couldn't understand. He would get tense and nervous. Now it doesn't bother him because he has, over time, come to see the problem in terms of the minimum amount of information he needs to do the job effectively. He now doesn't need to understand all they say.

Control 36 He's worked hard to build up a small empire at work, of which he is proud; some of this is to be taken away from him and he's very threatened. He's constantly confronting the problem, and is fighting to protect his job. But the problem may take months to solve. Meanwhile, his non-work life is featuring as more and more important to him as he adjusts to possible failure, and acceptance that his job satisfaction might well be reduced.

This small sub-group does highlight how, over time, some people engage in confronting their difficulties in ways which can result in changes (through learning and experience) in how they see their problems, often accompanied by a reduction in the expected negative consequences of not solving them. Here, stress may not emerge because threat is no longer experienced. This seems an important part of the adaptation process, facilitated for some by attractive out-of-work pursuits. Yet coming to terms with their difficulties in this way did not necessarily mean that work or life suddenly became a fulfilling enterprise — absence of stress does not mean that all concerns and anxieties have disappeared.

AN OVERVIEW AND CONCLUSIONS

As a group of professional workers in a particular research and development organization, the technical support staff who are the focus of this chapter do indeed have their problems. We might *speculate* that many of these problems are a reflection of the type of role that they occupy, with features which are special to that occupational group. Thus, a person entering a research support role may well need to face issues of:

Inferior status Working for better academically qualified people who themselves seek professional advancement by using the support staff more as servants rather than co-workers. Indeed, this may be endemic to the intrinsic nature of research endeavour where the natural focus of attention will be upon the researcher. He is likely to be particularly favoured by the organizational reward system, which may in turn offer the supporting staff a less privileged career and 'inferior' titles.

Lack of intrinsic job rewards The creative work seems mainly the province of the researcher, not the support staff. Support staff can find themselves involved in the less consequential, less meaningful 'bits' of the research endeavour — possibly a thankless task which does not relate clearly to any overall product or end.

Poor use of skills and abilities Technical trade skills and qualifications can be underutilized on the job. At worst one becomes an 'odd job man' with little to do. On the other hand, the demands of a fast changing research environment can overstretch or outdate existing skills, with 'language' problems emerging between researcher and support staff.

Difficult working relationships Status, reward and use-of-skills problems can be reflected in difficult working relationships particularly with research superiors. At the extreme, if the support staff member is viewed merely as an instrument of help in the research process, his specific needs are of little interest to the research hierarchy.

Powerlessness and anonymity If the organization is large and hierarchical, the support staff may soon feel like helpless fish in a big pond. Power and influence tend to emerge at higher levels, unlike many strongly unionized blue collar establishments.

Scientists as poor man-managers A research establishment is likely to recruit and promote its research staff on the basis of their academic excellence, not their general management skills, or sensitivity to people problems. The subordinate support staff will be one group who may feel the consequences of this policy. This is not to suggest that, for example, a researcher will go out of his way to ignore the personal desires and feelings of his support staff. It is more a question of him not being specifically equipped for this task. He has, in effect, fallen into a managerial role by default — what he really wants to do (and indeed is contracted to do) is research, and in the physical sciences this involves dealing with ideas and things, not people.

These features are generalizations which hold true for many of the people in the present study. Yet our analysis has revealed that they are but the start of understanding stress and its causes in the sample; the problems only emerge as stressors amongst *certain* people — those who tend to experience them as threatening *and* who have failed to effectively cope with them. To ignore such facets is to miss the very essence of what the stress process seems to be about and leads to what can seem fairly banal generalizations about the causes of stress. Thus, for example, it would be very convenient to conclude that technical support staff are in a stressful occupation because of their inferior status, lack of intrinsic rewards and so on (a level of generalization frequently made about certain occupational groups in studies of stress). The truth, it would appear, is more subtle and complex. Like any occupational group, technical support staff are not a single homogeneous conglomerate; they are different people with individual needs and concerns. Many of them are, for example, concerned about their status; but only some of them find such concerns threatening in a way in which they cannot cope effectively, and hence stressful.

Alleviating stress

The theoretical framework for analysis in this study offers a number of points of potential intervention to help reduce individual stress. Let us, by way of concluding this chapter, briefly examine some of these.

   If, as was the case in the present study, many commonly shared problems seem to be at the heart of individual stresses, it may be possible to tackle them on a company wide basis. Thus, for example, promotion policies, titles and career prospects would need to be carefully reviewed if the present group's perceived status was to improve. Job enrichment, better matching of support staff to their superiors, and more attention to the scientists' management skills should be a step towards lessening other difficulties. Yet such a broad sweep approach would need to be handled very carefully as the problems were not stressors for everyone, and attempts to remove them wholesale could be resisted by some ('It's better the evil you know . . . '). As some organizational development studies have shown, people sometimes find that they value the continued existence of certain problems because they reinforce a particular *status quo* that they actually enjoy (Warr *et al.*, 1978). Clearly any efforts at such organizational change would be better handled within a negotiated, consultative framework, than one which is unilateral.

Some of the commonly shared problems could provide valuable job data in the selection and subsequent training of new employees. Thus some stress may be ultimately avoided by improving the congruence between the known demands and perceived problems of the job and the expressed needs and aspirations of new job holders. So, for example, it may be more expedient for the organization in the present research to continue the existing recruitment and development policy for its research staff, but to devote extra resources to selecting future support staff who will feel more able, and more comfortable, working with 'academics' or 'poor man-managers'. Clearly any action of this sort, or indeed of any sort which is directed towards stress alleviation or avoidance, must be conducted within the political logic of the organization — a logic which may lead to rather different conclusions from those which naturally emerge from a scientific analysis of stress.

Our theory places much emphasis on the individualistic features of stress and it is here that there is much scope for intervention. If we can identify the stressed population and its features in the way presented in this study, we can then focus on the perceptions of threatening problems, and individual action to cope with threat. At the action level, confrontation behaviour can be encouraged with the help of a third party counsellor/researcher. Ways in which the problem can be tackled can be explored, and relevant support and resources offered. Dependence on withdrawal or avoidance activities can be reduced, if necessary by emotional support in individual or group situations. Individuals can be helped to review and perhaps reconstrue their problems. Are the costs of failing necessarily as high as originally anticipated? Can the problem be shared and tackled with others, and so reduce the threat? Can the interventionist help facilitate an effective problem solving situation, perhaps by bringing together people who apparently contribute to an individual's perceived threat? Such strategies could be potentially pertinent to relationship and reward problems of the type experienced by the technical support staff.

It is likely that any efforts to alleviate individual stress within an organization will be most effective if it is initially built up from the perspectives of those individuals affected, rather than from some normative prescriptions from an outside 'expert'. Our help is then highly contingent and flexible and does not assume that some organizational-wide panacea (e.g. 'more participation', 'clearer roles', 'transcendental meditation') is *the* answer to our stress problems.

REFERENCES

Fineman, S. (1978). The stressless redundancy? *Management Decision,* **16,** 331-337.

Fineman, S. (1979). A psychosocial model of stress and its application to managerial unemployment. *Human Relations,* **32,** 323-345.

Warr, P., Fineman, S., Nicholson, N., and Payne, R. (1978). *Developing Employee Relations,* Saxon House.

PART V

Stress Among Public Servants

White Collar and Professional Stress
Edited by C.L. Cooper and J. Marshall
© 1980 John Wiley & Sons Ltd.

Chapter 10
Occupational Stress among Members of Parliament

Mike Noble
Ex-member of Parliament

In a period when the procedures of industry are becoming increasingly formalized, and employees at all levels are given job descriptions outlining their main responsibilities, no-one has thought of, or dared to give a definition of the work of a Member of Parliament. Nowhere are the duties and responsibilities of a Member of Parliament clearly and comprehensively set out in a form which enables the public — or even an incumbent — to clearly understand what the job entails. When an individual is elected he receives no instructions about what is expected of him other than a minimum of advice on House of Commons procedure, the geography of the Palace of Westminster, and the occasional indication from the Whips of the lobby in which he is expected to vote. The new Member's expectations of his job are probably as much at variance with the truth as are those of the public who have elected him. In the vernacular of industrial training, he will 'learn by Nellie', picking up tips from experienced colleagues, stumbling through the customary forms of address used in the House and occasionally tripping over the procedural requirements of the Mother of Parliaments. As he grows in experience the Member will realize that the parameters of his job are largely those he determines for himself. The extent of his duties in the House of Commons may range from those that are self-imposed (when a Member feels his/her interests are being considered), to those of Government and Opposition Whips who are generally present for every vote. Similarly the extent to which a Member carries out constituency duties are determined by his own sense of commitment, the demands of his constituency Party and the exigencies of the constituency. There are no hard rules.

Members of Parliament are, therefore, a heterogeneous collection in terms of the way in which they do the job. No other occupational group, enjoying a single generic description, can display such variety. And the variety extends beyond the way in which Members fulfil their role to their social origins. They may be stockbrokers, lawyers, doctors, businessmen, lecturers, teachers, engineers, miners, seamen, or farmworkers by occupation, sharing a common ambition. There can be little wonder then that the response from Members to the requirements of the job is so individualistic.

In any attempt to analyse stress among Members of Parliament, it is important to recognize that there is no such being as the average Member. Parliament attracts to it individuals from all walks of life, although certain definable classifications can be found within the variety. Thus a majority of Members had a 'middle class' occupation prior to entering the House and have enjoyed the advantages of University education. In the October 1974 Parliament, 24% of Labour Members were formerly teachers or lecturers, 14% had been barristers or solicitors, 9% had been journalists, and a further 9% had been managers or administrators. Only 9% of Labour Members had formerly been manual workers. More than a quarter of all Conservative Members were Company Directors and a further 21% were from the legal profession. There were no Conservative Members from a manual background.

This middle-class bias is further demonstrated if one examines the educational background of Members in the October 1974 Parliament. 60% of Labour Members and 76% of Tory Members had been to a University, and whilst only 8% of Labour Members were ex-public-school, no less than 63% of Tories had attended such an establishment. At the other extreme, 19% of Labour Members and 1% of Tory Members had terminated their formal education at secondary or elementary level in the state system.

A University education and a professional occupation enable many individuals to acquire the particular skills necessary to fulfil the role of a Member of Parliament. Others acquire those skills by a more difficult and circuitous route. All suffer one common difficulty, however, that there is no specific training for the job as such.

Some occupations in the world outside Westminster provide an excellent training ground for the Member of Parliament, developing communications skills, understanding committee procedures and tactics, and the all important facility to handle public relations. Equally, Parliament is an excellent complementary activity for many 'extra mural' jobs. Membership of the House confers prestige, access to information, material for writing and opportunities for travel and does not tie Members to a 52-week annual commitment. Many businessmen, members of the legal profession and journalists can, therefore, take advantage of this but there are few occupations beyond these accessible to the Member. It is among these categories that the 'part-time' Members are found, and many full-timers complain that the procedures and hours kept by the House are solely to the advantage of this substantial minority. It is from the full-time Members that Committees are filled and the other functions of Parliament carried out, and it is certainly the full-time Members who face the greatest physical and mental stress.

Recently one veteran Member of Parliament remarked that the House of Commons is full of willing members: 'those who are willing to work and those who are willing to let them'. Those who are conscientious about their duties will spend much of their time in gathering information, either informally from journals and newspapers and through discussion with colleagues, or more formally by study in the library or fact-finding visits to Government institutions or factories. A great deal of time, perhaps in some cases over 50%, is spent on constituency affairs, dealing with letters from constituents with grievances, or meeting them in person. Frequently, Members of Parliament are in demand as Speakers at meetings outside the House of Commons, including specialist interest groups and political parties. Members are also required to participate in House of Commons Committees and attend meetings of their respective Parliamentary party. They may speak in the Chamber or simply listen to debates. At weekends they travel to their constituencies to hold 'surgeries' (consultation with local electorate) attend meetings and generally display themselves at public functions.

Those Members of Parliament who regard the job as a full-time occupation may work up to 14 hours per day during the Parliamentary session. This is certainly true for supporters of the Party in Government. During the 1974-79 Parliament, where the Government enjoyed at best an overall majority of 4 and later became a minority, the House seldom rose before 10.00 p.m. and frequently business continued until the early hours of the following morning or even beyond. Because of the procedures of the House a relatively small group of Opposition Members, by threatening to divide the House, can ensure the continuing attendance of a substantial number of Government supporters. The sheer physical pressure this imposes on Members is regarded by the Opposition as a legitimate tactic for wearing down a Government, but there is no doubt that it has led to the breakdown or even death of some individuals, and within months of the commencement of a new Parliament familiar rumblings of discontent emanate from new Members who have difficulty in adjusting to the hours. There is a substantial case for reform but the conservative nature of the House of Commons has always re-asserted itself and the traditional procedures show a remarkable resilience. There is a reason for this. The only weapon readily at the disposal of the Opposition is *time*. By skilful manipulation of procedures controversial legislation can be delayed and even lost, and as the Government of the day always faces pressure from the Parliamentary timetable an Opposition jealously protects those procedures which enable it to use these tactics.

Similarly backbenchers fight a continuous battle to safeguard their rights to scrutinize Government legislation. Any change in procedures will probably be interpreted as a means to diminish those rights. Thus, an Opposition opposed to Government attempts to amend procedures may be joined by backbenchers of the Government party in safeguarding the rights of the House. The price paid for this conservatism is the long hours spent by Members incarcerated in the Palace of Westminster.

Nowhere is the power to delay legislation more apparent than at the Committee stage of Bills. Here the details of Bills are debated line by line, clause by clause, amendment by amendment by Members sitting in political parties as in the main Chamber, on the basis of proportional representation. Crudely described the task of Government is to get its legislation with as little amendment as possible in the shortest time, while the Opposition's main objective will be to delay passage of the Bill. The view expressed in many of the less sophisticated text-books on Government, that it is at this stage when effective scrutiny takes place, is not borne out by the facts. Seldom can Opposition force through its own amendments, and normally the only successful ones are those proposed or accepted by the Government as improvements to the wording of the Bill. The effect of the adversary nature of the Committee stage is, therefore, to prolong the sittings of the Committee.

Committees normally sit on Tuesday and Thursday mornings from 10.30 a.m. to 1.00 p.m. but where the delaying tactics are successful the Government may extend them by introducing additional evening sessions, usually on the same days and commencing at 4.30 p.m. Occasionally for major bills which are an essential part of the legislative programme, sittings may continue well into the night. Finance Bills only sit in the evenings, usually commencing at 4.00 p.m. and all-night sittings are common.

The voting system in Committee usually means that Members are restricted to the Committee room or the corridor outside and even visits to the toilets have to be taken circumspectly. As in the Chamber, the work itself is not arduous but time-consuming.

However, the combination of Committee work with other duties can impose physical hardship. Thus in 1975 one member of the Finance Bill Committee who combined that duty with the work of Parliamentary Private Secretary to the Prime Minister died from a heart attack. Though no medical diagnosis confirmed it, many of his colleagues believed that the physical effect of working round the clock was an important factor in his death.

The greatest strain is undoubtedly borne by Government Ministers responsible for piloting legislation through Committee. In addition to normal departmental duties they have to be briefed on every aspect of the Bill and in Committee debate they have to 'field' criticism and comment from Opposition and their own backbenchers. In a typical sitting of a Finance Bill Committee they may be in almost continuous session up to 12 hours or more. It is not surprising, therefore, when one considers the legislative and administrative load of modern Governments, that they tend to 'run out of steam' towards the end of a Parliamentary session.

Many observers believe, however, that despite these long hours back-benchers are little more than 'lobby fodder' for the Cabinet or Shadow Cabinet and have little real influence, and because they are starved of resources and information they cannot play a fully effective role in policy formation. These observations are not strictly true. Parliament consists of many subtle sounding boards and Members are able to exert pressure to influence, change or even stop legislation. Thus in the 1974-79 Parliament the Labour Government was compelled to handle all EEC matters delicately, because of the large anti-Common-Market lobby within the Parliamentary Labour Party, while many believe that the Labour Government ultimately fell because it was unable to convince its own supporters of the benefits of devolution. It is in the exercising of political pressures where the greatest stresses and tensions lie. Ministers have a commitment to their own legislation, and Members of Parliament of their own Party, as well as outside bodies, will seek to change or halt that legislation, through use of the Chamber, in private meetings or the media. Pressure may include the withholding of a vote on the issue.

At the same time the Government itself exerts considerable pressure on recalcitrant Members. Whips interview 'difficult' colleagues. Ministers also pressurize privately and the use of patronage by the Prime Minister is a sharp means of bring more ambitious Members to heel. On the other hand, those who are threatening rebellion may do so because of pressure from their constituency party. It is in resolving these conflicts that most Members face the greatest stress.

Just as Members of Parliament are a heterogeneous group in terms of social and occupational background, and display a wide variety of interest, commitment, and talent in the House, they are equally diverse when one examines the constituencies they represent. Electorates vary from over one hundred thousand down to about twenty thousand. Constituencies may be rural, covering hundreds of square miles or urban 'pocket handkerchiefs'. Members at constituency level may have to deal with a single Local Authority or several. The seats may be safe with a majority of ten or even twenty thousand or marginal with a majority of hundreds or less. They may contain large areas of social stress or be composed of communities where average incomes and life style are to a considerable extent middle-class.

A Member in a marginal constituency suffering economic decline, perhaps combined with significant social problems, therefore, faces enormous pressures compared with those in safe seats. While many Members in safe seats have the same commitment to constituency work as their colleagues in marginals, they have the luxury of continuity in their profession. For the marginal Member life consists of balancing this pressure against that, counting the votes that a particular course of action may cost, devotedly holding surgeries, attending public functions, and being photographed for the press. An example of this is the way lobbies are built around interests in marginal constituencies. In the 1974-79 Labour Government Members representing the volatile textile towns of the North West formed a vociferous pressure group in the House. In the post-1979 Conservative Government there are already signs that Tory Members who gained marginal seats with large immigrant communities are forming a pressure group to ease proposed restrictions on immigration. These pressure groups are a direct function of the external forces operating on Members. Despite the evidence that the vast majority of seats move with the National trend at election times, marginal Members work assiduously in their constituencies in the hope that, should there be a swing against their Party at election time their efforts will be sufficient for them to retain their seats. Most election results do not bear out their faith!

For many Members constituency work is the most demanding and at the same time the most rewarding part of the job. Because of the procedures of the House of Commons and the overriding power of the Government *vis-à-vis* backbenchers many Members easily become frustrated by the House. In the constituency, however, they have status and influence. They can remove bureaucratic log-jams, at local and National level, securing the rights of constituents. Though many of the cases brought to them will be insoluble they create an image of the conscientious hard-working Member. The work is time consuming and uses civil service resources, more perhaps than its positive results justify but it keeps open a channel of protest which occasionally — and always potentially — is very effective.

The amount of surgery work required of a Member of Parliament is a product of two factors. His own constituency image generates a case load as he is recognized for his energy and activity. Constituents on whose behalf he has acted recommend neighbours or colleagues at work to approach him with their problems, varying from housing cases (the most common) to advice on family problems. Frequently a sympathetic ear is all that is required, but many cases lead to an exchange of letters and sometimes to protracted correspondence, visits to Government or Local Authority Departments, interviews with Ministers and occasionaly raising matters on the floor of the House. Recently a Labour Member revealed in the Press that a one year surgery work involved him in writing no less than 5,000 letters — a work load which would not be regarded as excessive by many Members.

The second factor is the nature of the constituency. Members representing areas where there are significant social problems — slum properties, inner urban blight, decaying industries, substantial shifts in population or large immigrant communities for example, face much higher demands on their time and energy than do those from middle-class constituencies. Moreover, the population of such an area is less articulate than that of middle-class areas, and while this may relieve the Member of some problems it often involves him in more difficult and time consuming interviews at surgeries, as he struggles to establish facts. For many Members therefore, much of the weekend is taken in constituency work of this nature.

Constituency parties also impose demands on the Member. These are the voluntary organizations which have promoted the Member of Parliament in the first place and demand that their representative reports back to them regularly. Few Members of Parliament succeed in pleasing all of their constituency activists and there are constantly shifting pressures and tensions behind the scenes. Sometimes pressure on Members is organized on an unofficial group basis and recent history demonstrates that Party dissatisfaction with a Member of Parliament at local level may unseat him. Many fear that the re-selection procedures now adopted by the Labour Party will lead to further job insecurity.

On the other hand, most local Parties promote their Member of Parliament publicly as much as possible. They are anxious that he is seen frequently in the constituency and many individual members are equally anxious to be seen publicly with their Member of Parliament. They parade him around clubs and pubs, garden fetes and galas, charity occasions, hospitals, factories, and schools. Much of this work takes place in the recess but time for some public relations activity has usually to be found at weekends. Most Members willingly accept this. By nature they are publicity-seeking animals and nothing gratifies them more than reading accounts of their own activities.

Members anxious to meet constituency requirements resent the way in which they are starved of resources necessary for their work. They have rudimentary office accommodation in or near the House of Commons, and reimbursement of part of their secretarial expenses — enough for a part-time secretary, and perhaps a minimum of research. For the rest they do their own secretarial, research, and administrative work. As constituency activity becomes more and more demanding these resources become increasingly inadequate, and cause frustration and resentment among Members.

What are the main causes of stress among Members? Physically for 35 to 40 weeks of the year the job is demanding. If one adds hours spent in the House of Commons to those working in the constituency or travelling they accrue to a total in excess of that spent at work by most of the population. Bearing in mind that the average age of Members of Parliament is relatively high, the physical strain of the job can bear heavily on many individuals.

Secondly, there are the pressures and tensions imposed by the nature of the work itself. The public perceives Members of Parliament as problem-solving animals with power and influence. Members of Parliament undoubtedly contribute to this image, but it is scarcely the truth. They do have influence; their letters secure an early response from bureaucrats in public service; the media are anxious to publish their views. But they have little real power, and may be frustrated in their failure to influence Government on the one hand or satisfy constituents on the other. Despite this they must encourage an image of success, and this dichotomy between the image and the reality is a particular source of stress for many.

Thirdly, by any standard being a Member of Parliament is an insecure profession. Few Members can claim as much as twenty-five years service and many last for only one Parliament. The financial rewards are slight and for those defeated in elections, particularly Labour Members, there are difficulties of securing alternative employment.

Generally, Members of Parliament are ambitious people, but for the majority there will be no Ministerial career. In any decade only a few score of men or women will reach senior Ministerial Office, whilst the chances of electoral success and failure may leave unsatisfied a generation of aspirants. Certainly older Labour Members who were in the House of Commons throughout the fifties and early sixties confirm the boredom and frustration of a long period in Opposition. Furthermore, because Prime Ministers usually seek some balance of interests, attitudes, and ideologies, as well as regional views in their Governments, politicians of ambition and talent may be left on the backbenches. In people of this kind frustration is probably the major single cause of stress.

A particular cause of stress — not only for Members of Parliament — but also for their wives and families is the inevitable separation which occurs for the families of those representing constituencies distant from Westminster, and who choose to make or retain their homes there. These Members normally leave home on Monday, to a full and rewarding professional involvement in the House, and do not return until the following Friday. The busy round of constituency and other engagements which fills the weekend, leaves little time for family activities, and even when the Member is at home there is a constant demand imposed by the telephone, the need to read newspapers and documents and to prepare for the coming week. Little time or energy is left for family activities. But it is during the week that the main difficulties arise. Many couples can endure the physical separation, what may become unendurable and finally create the ultimate marital breakdown is the inevitable divergence of interests and commitments which develop. Wives at home raising children can easily grow to resent what they perceive as the more 'glamorous' or committed life of the husband. Few marriages are contracted with the possibility of one partner entering full time politics; many end, however, when one of them is elected.

The stresses are peculiar and varied. They may extend from the neglect of parental responsibility in bringing up children, more than a few members have suffered the embarrassment of children involved in conflicts with the law, to the gradual separation of interests as each partner is compelled by circumstance to pursue his or her career. The divorce statistics provide an ample demonstration of the reality of this form of stress.

Suggestions have been made that a reform of the procedures of the House of Commons might, among other things, at least ameliorate this problem. But the procedures are only a single cause among many. It is not simply the separation, the long hours which create marital stress, but in the majority of cases it is the total way of life, the commitment, the demands of constituents and the media, and often the ambitions created in the individual. It is a feature of Parliamentary life of which relatively few married Members are aware when entering the House but which becomes for many of them a significant cause of stress during their Parliamentary careers.

The situation for women Members is rather different. Many enter Parliament when families are grown up, or they have no children. Few attempt to combine a political career with the task of bringing up children. Where women Members have young children it is difficult to perceive how they can manage the dual role without a home in London.

Despite all these stresses and tensions few Members display them, at least outwardly. For a relatively elderly occupational group there are surprisingly few deaths and even fewer mental breakdowns, although the electorate might argue with that particular point. Perhaps this is because of the way in which Members of Parliament themselves perceive their work. Despite its insecurity and relatively modest remuneration, it yields, for the majority, enormous job satisfaction, status, and achievement; and the physical and mental demands when Parliament is in session are balanced by the relatively long recesses when Members can fulfil duties at a leisurely pace. And despite all the drawbacks there is always a long queue of aspirants for the job at election time.

White Collar and Professional Stress
Edited by C.L. Cooper and J. Marshall
© 1980 John Wiley & Sons Ltd.

Chapter 11

Only from the Outside: Stress in Trade Union Leaders

Clive Jenkins
General Secretary, Association of Scientific, Technical, and Managerial
Staff

My sister-in-law put her finger on the corner of my mouth and said 'smile'. The Margaret Rutherford-style lady in the American University wanted me to 'unpurse and widen your eyes'. So my lips were tight; I was, on other persons' observations, tense, stressed.

The pressures on a senior trade union officer who is the organization's chief executive officer are more centrifugal than hierarchical. You become engaged on so many fronts, facets. But I have found no stress in conflict — only in frustrations.

My brief was to discuss stress on General Secretaries. I missed the deadline on this chapter twice. This is in spite of having the clear plastic file highly visible on the side table in my room in the Woodrow Wilson Centre for Scholars in Smithsonian Institution in Washington for five weeks for I had promised to write it there whilst quietly immersing myself in Washington politics. But it didn't just sit there: it gathered to itself all sorts of memoranda, memorabilia, and clippings.

It was then I knew it was going to be difficult to write because when I have a block I overresearch and keep on researching.

I also share a reaction with Tennessee Williams who said that he couldn't write until he had read every unread piece of print in the house. It seems to have taken hours of searching on occasion to find something else to read before starting with the menacing blank white page.

So why? Obviously, stress is always self-created — for me anyway. I have been trying to analyse what stresses me — as a compulsive achiever with a need regularly to notch up specific gains and terminate specific and unsatisfactory situations.

I was struck by the front cover of the *San Diego Magazine* in June 1979 which trailed a piece: 'Waiting in line for gas . . . making love . . . competing . . . "How To Handle Stress."'

It was for Richard Louv's feature, describing an interview with a physician dealing in bio-feedback machines and responsible for 'stress management' and reporting her as saying:

'Like most professionals, you're probably catastrophizing: You're thinking that there's no way you'll meet the deadline, that you dread the long hours of typing, that it may be not up to par, please your peers, or win the Pulitzer, right?'

Well, yes, except I don't catastrophize, ever. There are allegedly good financial reasons for having these 'programmes' because he also wrote:

'The US Clearing house for Mental Health Information estimated last year that United States industry has experienced a $17 billion annual decrease in its productive capacity over the last few years due to stress-induced mental dysfunctions. Other studies estimate the losses may be as much or more than $60 billion.'

But all this probably is not much of a guide to what stresses trade union officials and why they never really talk about it.

So I have looked for clues.

I put high on my own list the tyranny of fixed dates for committee meetings. I think, if you are not a professional, committees really can be fun. But if you see committee work as either a tool to use or a mountain to be bulldozed away, you can develop different attitudes.

One of the problems about developing trade union seniority is that you really do want to be on and help to influence key committees, say, in the Trade Union Congress or on public bodies. But there are very substantial tensions in planning around these poles and a common union official's complaint will be that he read the key file in his car on the way to the meeting.

There is a major stress factor there. But I put high on my own list of stress causes the key question of frustration, of finding that the time scale lengthens all the time and while one can show a highly satisfactory (and budgeted list of accomplishments) you are also aware you are getting older and it should all have been done sooner.

For a group of us in the Labour Movement there is another very special conditioning factor and this relates entirely to the puritanical-religious childhoods that we had either in South Wales or, say, in the chapels of Yorkshire or Lancashire.

The Evening News recently asked me to write an article on class attitudes in my youth. I did but it turned out to be about chapels, sermons, and how streets were graded and classified by impressions (and always bench-marked back to the chapels).

This creates a feeling in later life that it is ignoble or, worse, worthless, not to be doing something. There is always a goblin or friendly nagging angel on my left shoulder asking the question 'why aren't you working?'.

This sets up all sorts of tensions.

The American experience is so different from all of this.

One union leader said to me that when he felt strained or worried he had a fairly simple approach.

He picked up two telephones at the same time, held them as weights in his hands, thrust them up and down in the air and screamed 'YEEKE' and he said it gave him some satisfaction.

He had another method as well. He ran up the stairs two at a time because he said he had a feeling that with more adrenalin in his bloodstream it somehow or other took the weight off his mind.

It is pretty obvious that all of these pressures are self-induced but it is also hard to detect when they are becoming intolerable.

The most familiar relief is self-induced physical illness. I have been aware in myself in years past that when overworked I caught (or incubated) a cold. My problem now is that this fail-safe mechanism has failed and I now no longer catch (or incubate) a cold so I seem to have a newish problem.

But there are other symptoms as well which I find strangely common amongst my friends and that is the blurring of the sense of geography when driving a car. I thought this was my problem and that I was really a rather extreme case becoming absolutely absorbed in driving without retaining any sense of the target — and I don't like driving. But it seems, to my surprise, that a number of my peers have the same psychological problem.

So what are the classic causes of stress in the literature?

Mental Health
Overload
Job satisfaction, absenteeism and labour turnover
Work alienation
Working on assembly lines

I then saw that:

'A different approach has developed from the work of Friedman and Rosenman (Rosenman *et al.* 1964, 1966; Friedman, 1969) who found that individuals whom they called type A were a much higher coronary risk than those whom they called type B. Type A personability characterized by being hard-driving, ambitious, engaging in multiple activity, impatient, having a sense of urgency, being aggressive, hostile, upwardly mobile, and showing tenseness of facial musculature with feelings of being under time pressure and the challenges of responsibility.'

When I read this description I didn't like it at all. I seemed to recognize myself.
My sister-in-law (and my wife) had good vision.
The chief officer of a large British trade union is no Cardinal, he has no Pope.
As long as he has the confidence of his executive committee and general approval of his active members the only other indices of success or approval are the opinions of leaders of other unions and in some cases of the other members of public boards to which she/he has been appointed and their managers.
The media doesn't matter in terms of personality or work approval.
The stresses are not there. So where are they?
In the classical list of 'life pressure' i.e.

Community demands — 'keeping up with the Joneses'
Marital status
Family — wife, children, others
Race
Age
Medical and dental treatment, or lack of it
Finance
Inadequate diet
Inadequate housing
Bereavement
Traumatic experience
Being subjected to psychological tests
Flying — driving
Physical danger
Sex

I could only list, as having a personal impact of any kind:

Family — wife, children, others
Religion
Medical and dental treatment, or lack of it
Sex

and of the list of organizational pressures from

Role ambiguity
Role conflict — interpersonal conflict
Excessive role loading
Responsibility for people
Size of enterprise
Abilities inadequate for task
Task making too little demand
Lack of appreciation
Lack of promotion
Too little scope for initiative
Size of work group
Being 'eased out' or 'sacked'
Position in hierarchy

My only reaction was to ring only 'responsibility for people': the others are simply irrelevant to me.

But I know when I'm stressed even if I don't know why. The classic symptoms are surface irritability, boredom, and dryness of the mouth.

So I, like my friends, dilute or anneal it in alcohol (plus lack of exercise) or — and here comes the new rub — in taking on fresh responsibilities as a great relief and often a lot of fun.

Stress in a General Secretary?

Manageable — and often a fuel.

Concluding Remarks

The Editors

This book has given us a new look at several occupations — not the glamorized view of the careers' advisor or the TV producer, but an insight into the serious health, psychological, and social risks of taking up a particular kind of work.

The contributions represent a range of levels of analysis, complementing and overlapping each others' perspectives. Some are generally-based literature reviews; nurses, teachers, police, and engineers particularly fit this format. Whilst each achieves a broad mapping of the relevant area, the authors are swift to point out the conflicts between available research evidence and the subtleties and qualifications necessary in their interpretation. One of the main recurring criticisms is that investigators tend to *assume* that factors are sources of stress without asking job holders themselves about their meaning. Kyriacou illustrates this in relation to the poor ability of pupils. Contrary to expectations, some teachers may prefer such work and see their jobs as more worthwhile because of it. Whether workers see a particular task as a core or a peripheral part of their 'real job' seems to offer an explanation here. Policemen may not object to routine patrols because they see these as 'part of the job'. They do not, however, have the same opinion of excessive paperwork and find this stressful.

Because of these qualifications, the overview chapters cannot achieve an integral picture of stress for their occupational group. To achieve this, we must look to the chapters which deal more specifically with a particular research study or person's experience of the occupation, for example, those about dentists and technical support staff. These take a more narrowly focused starting point and test out a more limited range of variables. The chapters about school administrators also fulfils this role as well as illustrating the behind-the-scenes work on *concepts* and *methods* on which other authors draw.

Viewing this volume as a whole, certain themes are repeated across its chapters and deserve consideration here. This overlap is by no means complete, however, and several authors make the case for the 'distinctive features' of their occupational group. This view is taken, for example, concerning teachers facing discipline problems and student violence, police and physical danger, and the nurse confronted by death and dying.

Several of these common themes are in fact related to the needs of researchers, writers and interventionists to recognize and take account of significant differences within the populations with which they deal. The first major theme we should like to highlight is that of variability and complexity in understanding job stressors. Davidson and Veno, for example, distinguish between the rural and the urban policeman in the factors which cause stress, while Kyriacou reports on several studies in which type of school and sex of the teacher interact in predicting different causes for concern.

A concern that even further discrimination is required is apparent in most authors' attempts, sometimes unsuccessfully, to include an understanding of the impact of individual differences in their profile. Many report the lack of relevant research material. Studies which have addressed this issue are also often sadly lacking in findings. Here, for example, Cooper finds surprisingly little association between personality factors and the occurrence of stress among dentists. There are, however, indications in several chapters that person-related factors (but not those easily measured on standard scales) are relevant. Factors identified as predisposing the individual to suffer stress are becoming attached to a particular patient for the nurse; greater belief in external control amongst teachers, and perceptions of threat and a failure to cope for technical support staff. The issue of the role of individual differences is fascinating but as yet largely untapped apart from interest in the Type A — Type B dichotomy. It is certainly an area for further research.

A further interesting suggestion made by several authors is that causes of stress change over the individual's career sequence and that these changes need to be recognized in both research work and stress-alleviating interventions. This idea of phases appears to be best documented for teachers and school administrators. Phillips and Lee, for example, discuss the possibility that stress does not increase or decrease with experience, but that the relevant pressures follow a developmental sequence from personal competence through task demands to the needs of the student. For both school administrators and engineers, taking on managerial responsibilities plays a major part in determining the pressures of a particular career phase. Keenan also points to the action of 'self-selection' in relation to career and choices within occupations as a mechanism which may accentuate changing attitudes and relationships at work. It appears, for example, that there is a greater disparity between the professional values of newly graduated engineers and their organization's (mainly commercial) goals than is apparent for their older colleagues.

In one recurrent theme there are significantly more common elements of substance than in those 'concerns' and qualifications discussed above, that is, the job holders' relationships with society as a major source of stress. For the teacher, 'accountability' is depicted as a source of conflict. Engineers' low status causes them frustration. Dentists suffer ambiguity about their public image. Moving up the scale of impact, society is reported to be highly critical of social workers' activities and their poor public image is a significant pressure. For police their role in relation to society dominates the stress literature. Davidson and Veno conclude that relationships with the public are generally poor and affect not only work behaviour but also social and family relationships (although here there may be cultural differences). Public image plays a similarly significant but, in substance, very different role for the nurse. The power of people's expectations is felt as a stress because their public image is too idealistic. Striking similarities between occupational groups seem to relate to this general concern. Cohesion within the occupation is particularly marked for the last three groups — social workers, policemen, and nurses — who are the most threatened from this source. Relationships with colleagues and immediate superiors (although not, typically, more distant 'administration') are reported to be particularly good. For the latter two groups social isolation (encouraged by shift work) fosters group ties. For both social workers and nurses the organizational hierarchy and work procedures are depicted as contributing to stress-alleviation, doing so by clarifying and diffusing the attribution of responsibility. Exposure to the possibility of accusations of mal-practice is another common element in the stress profiles of this group of occupations. It is these authors too who see a future of increasing stress for their 'subjects', largely because of developments in this relationship with society.

The above pressures and reactions to them unify particularly the society-serving occupations covered in this book. It is striking how very different the pressures reported for the two technological professions are in comparison. A dominant theme for technical support staff and engineers is the amount and nature of their workload. Keenan explains why this should be most succinctly: 'The successful accomplishment of meaningful technical work is at the centre of their perceptions of themselves in their jobs.' Also relatively 'unusual' in the context of this book is concern about career opportunities and development.

The ultimate aim of identifying causes of stress and understanding how they operate is to manage stress at tolerable levels. Several authors draw implications from their work about how this might be achieved. Most suggestions are appropriately broadly and flexibly worded, given the complexities and individual variabilities in stress experience identified in the text. Taking physical and psychological care of oneself at an individual level are the dominant themes here, and Tung and Koch's results show that for school administrators these are the two approaches most favoured in practice. The third individual-oriented proposal of developing new skills was in fact used by only 10% of their large sample. A few actions the organization can take are also identified. Providing social support in one form or another is advocated, as is more attention to stress as a factor during selection and training. The authors' emphases on variability leads them away, sensibly we feel, from sweeping organization-wide reforms unless across-the-board causes of stress can be identified (e.g. Fineman).

This book has been as much a beginning as an end in itself. The contributors have 'spoken to each other' in their similarities and differences and voicing of concerns about the direction research has taken to date. This provides new avenues of development in addition to those they specifically identify. We hope the material and perspectives this volume contains will interest and stimulate the reader, and at the same time act as an impetus to future, increasingly discriminating development of occupational stress.

Index

abortion, 34-5
absenteeism, 102-3, 124
achievement motivation, 105
age, 11, 78, 193
alcoholism, 156
alienation, 133
anonymity, 221, 228
anxiety, 24-5, 93, 103-4, 122-3
attachment, 38
avoidance, 46, 50-2, 215, 224-5

biographical data, 115
blood pressure, 9, 12-13
boundary roles, 65, 69, 77-9, 82, 203-4
bureaucracy, 182
burnout, 102, 108

career development, 151-2, 195, 202,
    206, 242, 253
change, 100-1
cognitive control, 81
community factors, 97, 99-100, 121, 240-
    241
community relations, 133-5, 151
conflict, 31, 68, 78-9, 192-5
confrontation, 215, 224-7
coping, 21, 126
coping strategies, 46-7, 50-2, 80-1, 215,
    224-7, 253-4
    organizational, 180-3
coronary heart disease, 159
courts, 149

crime, 100
cultural differences, 134-5, 138-9, 201

deadlines, 246
death, anxiety, 40-4, 56-7
    reactions to, 38-40, 43
detachment, 51, 80
discipline, 116-9, 120-1
dissatisfaction, 157-8, 179-80, 200-1
divorce, 137-8
dreams, 39
dying, care of, 29, 37-8

electrocardiograph, stress, 9, 13-14
emergencies, 27
empathy, 31
equipment, 146
exercise, 5
exhaustion, 123
expectations, 195-6
experience, 65, 78, 98, 103-4, 252
external control, 124
extroversion, 142

factor analysis, 67-76
family life, 136-9, 242-3
frustration, 122-3, 246

group cohesion, 46
guilt, 36-40

humour, 46, 51

illness, phases of, 30-1
individual differences, 194, 229-30, 236,
    252
influence, 237-9, 241-2
intensive care nursing, 41-49
interaction, person-environment, 94
introversion, 142
isolation, 133, 139

job function differences, 78-80, 198-9,
    201-3
job security, 195, 239-42

legal factors, 106-7
life events, 140-1

malpractice, 177-8
managerial role, 6, 204-8, 222-3, 228-9
mental health, 155-6
minority groups, 104-5
monotony, 4
mortality rates, 168-9

neuroticism, 142

organizational environment, 64, 97, 99
organizational level, 171
organizational setting, 28, 45, 99
organizational structure, 22, 36, 51-2

paperwork, 148
pay, 6, 14, 116-7, 152, 195, 206
performance criteria, 21
personal variables, 78-80, 98
personality, 8, 12-15, 50, 125, 141-4, 226
    'police', 142-4
personnel selection, 48
physical activity, 80
physical danger, 149-50
physical demands, 241
physical environment, 65
physical health, 77-8, 124, 247
politics, 174
posture, 4
powerlessness, 221, 228
professional competence, 172
professional status, 32
public image, 5, 15, 33-4, 135, 191-2,
    236, 253
pulse rate, 9
pupil ability, 117, 119

rationalization, 51
relationships, 27-33, 43-4, 220-1, 228
relaxation, 80
reorganization, 119
research methodology, 7-9, 40, 66-8,
    115-6, 190, 212-3, 251
resources, 241
responsibility, 26-7, 51, 77, 150-1, 180-1,
    205, 249
rewards, lack of, 217-9, 228
role, ambiguity, 106, 119, 150-1, 196-7,
    235
    conflict, 32, 34-6, 44, 47, 96-7, 119,
        150-1, 196-7
    expectations, 68, 78-9
    requirements, 21
rural living, 135-6, 138

satisfaction, 37, 47, 49, 117, 195-6, 240,
    243
self-esteem, 224
self-selection, 115
sex differences, 101, 132
shiftwork, 26, 146-7
Sixteen Personality Factor Inventory, 8
skills, 81, 108
smoking, 157
social support, 153
staff meetings, 39, 49, 53-6
staff turnover, 103, 117, 124, 180
staffing, 105-6
status ambiguity, 175-7
status, inferior, 216-7, 228
stress, concept of, 63-4, 69, 80, 84-5, 94,
    102, 167-8, 170, 214-6
    prevalence of, 113-5
    prevention, 107-9, 229-30
    questionnaires, Administrative Stress
        Index, 66, 68, 79, 82, 84
        General Health Questionnaire, 124
        General Well-being Questionnaire,
            124
        Job-Related Strain Index, 66, 68, 84
        self report, 114
    remedial action, 107-9, 229-30
    self-created, 245
suicide, 3, 138-40
supervision, 154, 178-9
symptoms, of stress, 122-5

task, 68, 78-9
technological contribution, 194, 207

threat perception, 21, 223-7
thresholds, 46
training, 35-6, 53, 56
Type A behaviour, 15, 123, 144-5, 198

uncertainty, 26-7
unionization, 182-3
unpleasant tasks, 25, 43
urban living, 135-6, 138

values, 173-4, 192-5, 207
violence, of pupils, 100

withdrawal, 215, 224-5
work ethic, 247
work overload, 25, 43, 77, 116, 147-9,
    197-200, 238, 253
work underload, 147-9, 200-3, 219-20,
    228
working conditions, 4, 42, 48, 119
working hours, 6, 237-9